Disability Matters

From the critique of 'the medical model' of disability undertaken during the early and mid-1990s a 'social model' emerged, particularly in the caring professions and those trying to shape policy and practice for people with disability. In education and schooling, it was a period of cementing inclusive practices and the 'integration' and inclusion of disability into 'mainstream'. What was lacking in the debates around the social model, however, were the challenges to abledness that were being grappled with in the routine and pragmatics of self-care by people with disabilities, their families, carers and caseworkers. Outside the academy, new forms of activity and new questions were circulating. Challenges to abledness flourished in the arts and constituted the lived experience of many disability activists.

Disability Matters engages with the cultural politics of the body, exploring critiques of abledness through the arts, teaching, research and varied encounters with 'disability' ranging from the very personal to the professional. Chapters in this collection are drawn from scholars responding in various registers and contexts to questions of disability, pedagogy, affect, sensation and education. Questions of embodiment, affect and disability are woven throughout the contributions, and the diverse ways in which these concepts appear emphasize both the utility of these ideas and the timeliness of their application.

This book was originally published as a special issue of *Discourse: Studies in the Cultural Politics of Education*.

Anna Hickey-Moody is a lecturer in Gender and Cultural Studies at The University of Sydney, Australia. She is the author of *Unimaginable Bodies* (2009) and *Youth, Arts and Education* (forthcoming in 2012), and co-author of *Masculinity Beyond the Metropolis* (2006).

Vicki Crowley is Senior Lecturer at the School of Communication Languages and International Studies, University of South Australia, teaching in gender studies and cultural and communication studies. She has contributed chapters to *Cultural Theory and Everyday Practice (2008)* and *Vibrant (2007)*.

Disability Matters

Pedagogy, media and affect

Edited by
Anna Hickey-Moody and Vicki Crowley

Routledge
Taylor & Francis Group

LONDON AND NEW YORK

First published 2012
by Routledge
2 Park Square, Milton Park, Abingdon, Oxfordshire OX14 4RN

Simultaneously published in the USA and Canada
by Routledge
711 Third Avenue, New York, NY 10017

First issued in paperback 2014

Routledge is an imprint of the Taylor & Francis Group, an informa business

British Library Cataloguing in Publication Data
A catalogue record for this book is available from the British Library

ISBN 13: 978-0-415-69350-9 (hbk)
ISBN 13: 978-1-138-81771-5 (pbk)

Typeset in Times New Roman
by Taylor and Francis

Disclaimer
The publisher would like to make readers aware that the chapters in this book are referred to as articles as they had been in the special issue. The publisher accepts responsibility for any inconsistencies that may have arisen in the course of preparing this volume for print.

For those who will live on in our hearts.

Anna dedicates this book to her much loved grandmothers:
Sarah Elizabeth Nancy Moody and Patricia Hickey.

And Vicki writes:
For my parents, Ursula Crowley and George Crowley.

Contents

CONTENTS

Part III: Art, Affect and Becoming

INTRODUCTION

Disability matters: pedagogy, media and affect

Anna Hickey-Moody[a] and Vicki Crowley[b]

[a]Gender and Cultural Studies, University of Sydney, Sydney, Australia; [b]School of Communication, Languages & International Studies, University of South Australia, Adelaide, Australia

This edition of *Discourse* comes into being after two decades of engagement with the cultural politics of the body – through the arts, teaching, research and varied encounters with 'disability' ranging from the very personal to the professional. From the critique of 'the medical model' of disability undertaken during the early and mid-1990s, a 'social model' emerged, particularly in the caring professions and those trying to shape policy and practice for people with disability. In education and schooling, it was a period of cementing inclusive practices and the 'integration' and inclusion of disability into 'mainstream' (Northway, 2002; Vincent, Evans, Lunt, & Young, 1996; Vislie, 2003). What was lacking in the debates around the social model, however, were the challenges to abledness that were being grappled with in the routine and pragmatics of self-care by people with disabilities, their families, carers and caseworkers. Outside the academy, new forms of activity and new questions were circulating. Challenges to abledness flourished in the arts and constituted the lived experience of many disability activists. In the early 1990s, for instance, performing arts companies such as the London-based CanDoCo and Restless Dance Theatre[1] in Adelaide, Australia, were making dance and redefining its boundaries as physically based performance sourced in bodily capacity (in preference to disciplining the body into extant genres of 'the dancing body').

It was the body, arts, and dance in particular, that provided us with our first touchstone as colleagues, researchers, performers and educators and which constituted our earliest professional precursor to this special edition. CanDoCo Dance Company and Restless Dance Theatre captured, and continue to press into being, expressions of worlds in which bodies and embodiment and the complexities of intellectual actualities can incite curiosity, challenge and redefine how bodies (including the thinking body) foster convivial communities of diversity and complexity. Restless and CanDoCo expressly create performance art through collaborative processes between disabled and non-disabled dancers and performers. Restless frames itself as 'a centre of excellence for disability ethos and practice' (Restless Dance Theatre, 2010). CanDoCo views its work as 'pushing the boundaries of contemporary dance' in ways which 'broaden people's perception of what dance is and who can dance'. As CanDoCo's website states, 'We want to excite by being daring, inspire by being excellent, and question by being diverse' (CanDoCo Dance

Company, 2010). Here we see, in Jean-Luc Nancy's (2000) terms, that there is no existence without co-existence and the necessity of being becomes a necessity of 'being-with', a being-with that is a mutual exposure to one another.

As editors of this special issue, we are drawn to the capacity of art and media as forms of cultural pedagogy that confront, challenge and re-define knowledge and practice, and mediate altered sensibilities. Further, we are inspired by the ways in which encounters with different forms of knowledge (art, philosophy, curriculum) can shift the *techne* of disability from its historically and continuingly oppressive ideation and practice into a *techne* of possibility.

A precursor that brought impetus to this special edition was a two-day seminar titled 'Ordinary Lives: Narratives of Disability' sponsored by the Cultures of the Body Research Group at the University of South Australia. The seminar brought together disability activists, policy makers, artists (performers, writers, film-makers) and academics. Conversations arising from this event bring diverse explorations of the body, education, media, art and a range of theoretical frameworks into this issue. This special issue, therefore, is not a collection of articles on disability read through select philosophers, or cultural theorists, or community arts-based works,[2] or a direct selection of papers from the seminar. It is a collection of articles whose critique arcs toward emergent epistemologies hinged to technologies of disability, their myriad refusals, joys, curiosities, tensions, convergences and re-shapings through digitization, medical interventions and 'advances'. Some of the articles brought together here also gesture towards the role played by the concept of affect and affect theory in education over the past seven years, and as such we would like to offer a contexualization of this concept in relation to the field of education.

Affect in educational theory

Affect, influenced as it is by the work of Deleuze (1988, 1990a, 1990b, 2002) and Deleuze and Guattari (1983, 1986, 1987, 1994), is beginning to be utilized widely as a conceptual resource in educational theory. Across the past seven years, educational theorists have begun to work with this concept. Here, we consider some of the earliest theorists to bring affect into education because the conceptual move that accompanies this turn towards affect creates space for embodied knowledges of disability. Affect validates emergent epistemologies, which all too often remain silenced from theorizations of education. Christa Albrecht-Crane and Jennifer Daryl Slack (2003), Megan Watkins (2006) and Elizabeth Ellsworth (2005) are theoreticians working in and across education who have begun to employ the idea of affect. Other cultural studies theorists who take up the concept of affect in ways that are of use in considering classrooms include Elspeth Probyn (2000) and Anna Gibbs (2002). We would like to point towards their scholarship, as well as that of Brian Massumi (2002), Felicity Colman (2002, 2005), Gregory Seigworth (2003) and Melissa Gregg (2006), as resources of significant importance in the theoretical project of taking up affect to consider the pedagogical nature of culture.[3]

The concept of affect was not specifically introduced into educational practices until 2003 when Albrecht-Crane and Daryl Slack (2003, p. 191) made the argument that '[t]he importance of affect in the classroom is inadequately considered in scholarship on pedagogy'. While the work of the theorists cited above moves to address the current gap in research on affect and education, the potential of affect to reconfigure theories of education in significant ways has not yet been fully realized. Affect maps the micro-political relations that constitute the beginnings of social change. In order to understand the lived politics of disability in education and, indeed to read disability as a kind of cultural pedagogy, we must begin by thinking through affect (Hickey-Moody, 2009). It is our contention that understanding, naming, illustrating and analyzing the beginnings of social change is imperative if we are to recognize and instantiate disability as a valuable cultural resource and create classrooms that are disability friendly.

Albrecht-Crane and Daryl Slack provide a critical structure for thinking pedagogy through affect by establishing a framework well suited to educational policy and discourse analysis. They do this in a discreet chapter in a cultural studies style anthology of applied Deleuzian theory, titled *Animations (of Deleuze and Guattari)* (2003). Taking Deleuze's Spinozist body as a point of departure, Albrecht-Crane and Daryl Slack note:

> In most pedagogical models, individuals are defined or positioned to take up posts or places in terms of who they are; that is, in terms of their social identities: gender, race, class, ethnicity, and so forth, and they are seen as possessing varying degrees of agency – that is, an ability to act – as an attribute of who they are. In contrast, Deleuze and Guattari do not begin with the question 'What is a body?' but 'What can a body do?' and 'Of what affects is a body capable?' (2003, p. 192)

While Albrecht-Crane and Daryl Slack's reading of the body as affective is certainly core to Deleuze and Guattari's work, this model for thinking the body is not at all contra agency. In fact it is quite the opposite. Within Deleuze and Guattari's work, agency changes along with subjective experience and evolves in relation to the affects of which a body is capable. Agency is an inherent part of any body, be it a disabled human body, a body of water, a political party. Following Spinoza, Deleuze takes individual material bodies as a challenge to think through the physical dimensions of agency. Deleuze states:

> Spinoza ... proposes to establish the body as a model: 'We do not know what the body can do' ... We speak of consciousness and its decrees, of the will and of its effects, of the thousand ways of moving the body, of dominating the body and the passions – but *we do not even know what a body can do.* (1988, p. 18)

'What a body can do' is a material act and it is also a degree of agency. After establishing the affective body as the primary site – or origin – with which a pedagogy of affect would be concerned, Albrecht-Crane and Daryl Slack's focus shifts from the body of the subject and the micro-political realm to social machinations, and it is here that their theorization gains particular momentum. Adopting a meta-perspective, they note that:

> Deleuze and Guattari's project of rhizomatics maps three types of lines that are central to understanding the work of the socius: molar lines, molecular lines, and lines of flight. Molar lines 'overcode' dual segmentations that follow 'the great major dualist oppositions: social classes, but also men–women, adults–children, and so on' ... the molecular, distributes 'territorial and lineal segmentations' ... a 'supple fabric without which their [molar lines] rigid segments would not hold' ... The third line, the line of flight, is also a molecular line (as opposed to a molar line), 'one of several lines of flight,

marked by quanta and defined by decoding and deterritorializations'... This third line acts as a line of mutation, of decoding; it is 'the ultimate quantum line' (p. 225). (2003, pp. 194–219)

It is this positioning of Deleuze and Guattari's work as a tool with which to analyze the 'Molar lines [that] "overcode" dual segmentations that follow "the great major dualist oppositions: social classes, but also men–women, adults–children, and so on"' (2003, pp. 194–195), which lends Albrecht-Crane and Daryl Slack's work to analyzing affective movement of social bodies more than of individual bodies. Disability studies in education, as an academic field, or the disability rights movement, might be considered molar discourses that overcode the affective everyday experience of disability education.

In contrast to Albrecht-Crane and Daryl Slack, Watkins (2006) takes a micro-analytic approach. Watkins' research methodology was designed in order to evaluate pedagogy through the concept of affect. As such, Watkins' research is of particular interest because the methodology she employs has been designed specifically to record and 'capture', if you will, the embodied negotiations pertaining to – and arising from – affect in the classroom. Whereas Albrecht-Crane and Daryl Slack offer affect as a tool that will support a meta-analysis of classroom politics and discourses, Watkins takes up affect with a focus on learning and teaching literacy. The ways in which her classroom-based research methodology is oriented towards capturing embodied affect are illustrated in the extended quotation below:

> Merilee … gave particular attention to this textual form in a unit of work about pirates in which she used *Treasure Island* as the focus text. In addition to reading this novel, Merilee set a term assignment that students read another two texts dealing with themes related to pirates or the sea. At the same time the class was working on writing their own narrative. She explained that in this lesson they were going to write a description of one of the characters for their story … Merilee asked students for suggestions for words to describe either the protagonist or antagonist that they would be writing about in their story. Students offered an array of words relating to personality. She recorded students' suggestions on the board and then asked which referred to the protagonist and the antagonist. The class then moved on to list words describing the character's appearance … Throughout this brainstorming session, Merilee did not simply act as a scribe, but encouraged students to use their imagination by offering her own examples. (Watkins, 2006, p. 278)

Students really responded to this performance and added to the image Merilee had created with one student calling out, 'He might have a wart on his face'. Merilee replied jokingly that 'Oh, yes, all antagonists have warts!' At this point the class all laughed, clearly enjoying the discussion and enthused about writing their own description which Merilee then asked them to begin. She allotted the class 20 minutes to do this and insisted they write no more than half a page. During this time Merilee progressed around the room offering advice. After 20 minutes she asked students if they were finished and then had them read out their work. The first student to do so was a boy called Adrian. He had written the following about the pirate:

> A hideous fellow walked through the door.
> Unkempt with black hair, he was staring hard at me.
> His scared face, a scarred and wrinkled face, like a soldier back from battle.
> His clothes ragged and torn. He stank like a dead animal.

After reading this out he was met with spontaneous applause from the class and Adrian beamed. This example is significant in terms of what it suggests about a notion of pedagogic affect demonstrating three different ways in which it can function, that is as discipline, praise and contagion (see Watkins, 2006, pp. 278–279).

As the negotiations between student and teacher in this passage of text illustrate, embodied affects occurring in the classroom constitute a kinesthetic economy of knowledge exchange. Learning is about moving the margins of knowledge from exterior to interior locations and this process of movement, or folding, is an embodied act. The affective image of the pirate prompts this young student to negotiate the margins of their knowledge and technical skills of writing. Watkins' data show this clearly and also unpack the kinesthetic economy of relations between teacher and student that leads the student to 'invent' or arrive at the affective image of the pirate. The teacher deploys affects in her pedagogic practice: 'she took on the character of the pirate she was describing using an exaggerated tone in her voice to heighten the impact of what she was saying' (Watkins, 2006, p. 278). For Watkins, then, affect in the classroom is mediated as three pedagogical forms: discipline, praise and contagion.

Ellsworth (2005) talks about affect as a material entity and also as a mode of cognition. She does not draw on Deleuzian theory, although her arguments pertaining to affect have strong parallels to those advanced by Deleuze. Deploying the word 'affect' to articulate a material state of affairs, Ellsworth says:

> Experience, of course, presupposes bodies – not inert bodies, but living bodies that take up and lay down space by their continuous, unfolding movement and that take up and lay down time as they go on being. When we begin to think of experience as an event in time that also takes place, we can see why a number of contemporary theorists are using media and architecture to help them structure their concepts about experience. While both media and architecture can be said to communicate ideas, sensibilities, assumptions, and sometimes hidden power relations to their users and viewers, our experiences of the cinema or of a building exceed merely reading or decoding their signs and meanings. The visual experience of watching a film entails not only representation. It has a material nature that involves biological and molecular events taking place in the body of the viewer and in the physical and imagined space between the viewer and the film. Affect and sensation are material and part of that engagement. (2005, p. 4)

On cognition and affect, Ellsworth develops a theory of pedagogy as an interleaving of the materiality affect and subjective processes of cognition. She says:

> There is a difference . . . between the 'evidence of the ocular senses' in which one notices 'that the sensorium has been stimulated' and this other way of knowing, which he . . . describes as an interleaving of affect and cognition. (2005, p. 135)

On one level, then, affect is the concept of taking something on, changing in relation to an experience or an encounter. On another level an affect is a material entity: an aesthetic compound produced in relation to particular assemblages of space-time. As discussed elsewhere (Hickey-Moody, Windle, & Savage, in press), there are parallels between the notion of affect as the concept of taking something on, of changing in relation to an experience and the process of changing bodies that theorists such as Giroux (1999, 2004), Lusted (1986), Ellsworth (1997, 2005), and McWilliam and Taylor (1996) call 'pedagogy'. Just as the readings of affect discussed above each differ, so too do the theories of cultural pedagogy put forward by Giroux, Lusted, Ellsworth, and McWilliam.

Affect can thus be considered an emerging point of intervention and analysis in education, pedagogy and schooling. It expresses the embodied experience of learning, the places in which we learn, the histories and desires we bring to learning. Affect cannot be brought to bear on a lived situation – it is the lived reality of the situation – the feeling of learning and the excesses not captured through academics' frameworks for considering teaching, learning and disability. In this edition of *Discourse* we bring this site of intervention to disability education, which is, as noted in the early part of this introduction, an arena of emerging transformation.

The articles within this special issue of *Discourse* are drawn from scholars responding in various registers and contexts to questions of disability, pedagogy, affect, sensation and education. The articles appear in three sections, each of which explores disability, affect and pedagogy in different ways. These sections are 'Education and Schooling', 'Media and Pedagogy' and 'Art, Affect and Becoming'.

Section One: Education and Schooling

Section One opens with Julie Allan, who considers the practices and potentialities of the aspiring inclusive teacher educator in the contemporary climate of academic accountability and mistrust. Responding in part to disability activist and former academic, Mike Oliver, and his frustration with non-disabled academics, Allen traces the conflicted position of academics and the question of civic responsibility. Calling in Pierre Bourdieu's (1998) notion of 'serious play', Allan asks, 'how might teacher educators regain control, rediscover their civic duty and engage in serious play?' She responds to this through Michel Foucault's (1994) framework of ethics and James Joyce's (1963) epiphanies to argue that the aesthetic (sensory and sensual 'affects') and the epiphanic (the unforeseen and inaccessible aspects of ordinary life) are extremely productive practices for re-orientations and de-territorializations through which teacher educators can reinvent themselves in ways that might help recover civic duty through enactment.

Cassandra Loeser's article, 'Muscularity, mateship and malevolent masculinities: experiences of young men with hearing disabilities in secondary schools', brings us into the world of schools, education, young men, masculinity and hearing impairment. Designed around the question, 'How do young men with hearing disabilities simultaneously occupy their gender and their disability?' Loeser draws on Judith Butler's notion of performativity and Michel Foucault's '*techne* of the self' to explore the practices and techniques critical to understanding hearing disability and men as subjects of masculinities. From research conducted within contemporary Australian school sites, Loeser uses the stories and experiences of two young men with hearing impairment to demonstrate that the active construction of gendered subjectivity occurs through a variety of strategies mobilized to navigate and, at times, subvert aspects of the regulative mechanisms of masculinity – especially those deployed by the young men's peers. The article suggests that identity formation and practices of masculinity and disability are fragile, antagonistic and mediated productions, contingent upon approximate performances grounded in what different male peer cultures deem 'acceptable' or 'unacceptable'.

Continuing the exploration of education and schooling in, 'Mobile asylums: psychopathologisation as a personal, portable psychiatric prison', Valerie Harwood draws into contention the motif of the asylum, suggesting that the exercise of power can produce 'asylum type effects'. Bringing together popular culture, Michel Foucault's 'tokens of knowledge' (2006), and Irving Goffman's (1961) *Asylums*, Harwood formulates the concept of the 'mobile asylum'. To amplify the subtleties of her case for the 'mobile asylum', Harwood draws on the case studies of Elijah and Martin (relayed through a key informant) from her broader research on the psychopathologization of children. Here she details the experiences of two African-American children deemed through small events to be within the spectrum of Attention Deficit Hyperactivity Disorder (ADHD) and/or Oppositional Defiant Disorder (ODD) to be conveying the *effects of power*. It is the relationship between the power of diagnosis in these stories and the confinement that occurs in the classic psychiatrist–asylum couplet that points to the possibility of the existence of the mobile asylum.

The final paper in the first section is an opinion piece by Elizabeth Hayman describing the *UTS AccessAbility* project – the newly established, student-generated disability website at the University of Technology, Sydney (UTS). Hayman relates how the website evolved and grew organically through a process of ongoing, collaborative debate inspired by the commitment of its co-authors who were also intended users. The paper tours the construction of the website, via a 'geographical approach' to disability, in terms of practical, political, aesthetic and scholarly terrain, with a view to unpacking the cultural politics of disability as played out in the design and construction of the site. Hayman argues that the site generates a multiplicity of ways of relating to the all-too-often unexplored phenomenon of student life as it plays out in relation to disability. Further, she argues that the website became a nuanced political forum that, through its use of humour, politicizes the limitations of the institution. She concludes her analysis and commentary by way of ironic concession noting that the challenge to 'cripping' an institution 'would involve a pervasive infiltration of every aspect of the larger (university) website with a deep and complex understanding of the extreme value of the human differences already existing within the University community and the extended implications they present'.

Section Two: Media and Pedagogy

Gerard Goggin opens Section Two with an analysis of the reception of filmmaker Michael Noonan's doctoral research project, 'Laughing at the Disabled'. The film (its title was subsequently changed to 'Laughing with the Disabled') was a collaboration between Noonan and three people with intellectual disabilities. After its initial release, Noonan and the film became the subject of attack by two academics at the university in which the research was conducted, and the film then became a *cause célèbre*, not only in Australia but around the world. Goggin analyses the public record covering the criticisms of Noonan's research project, the disciplinary action taken by Queensland University of Technology, and the responses of those involved in the research in order to shed light on the place of disability in Australian culture, the role of power, questions of ethics – and, importantly, the cultural politics of disability in education. For many, including the editors of this issue, the furore was proof of the troubling status of disability in Australian universities.

The co-authored article by Elizabeth Christie and Geraldine Bloustien engages with the cultural and sonic experiences of Elizabeth's Cochlear Implant. 'I-cyborg: disability, affect and public pedagogy' brings the reader into the interior worlds of 'becoming more' through 'becoming cyborg'. Christie and Bloustien use Christie's Facebook postings and her personal navigations of her altered sonic world to trace affect and its utility as pedagogy. The article discusses neural plasticity (the brain's age-related – but not restricted – capacity to create new pathways), the daunting and physically painful experience of new sounds, the joys of altered sociality and the continued need to rely on old strategies for hearing and navigating degrees of deafness. We are taken into the world of hearing impairment, the world of digitized hearing and into Facebook as a means for enabling individual acquisition of critical knowledge and as a site of public pedagogy. In the language of Henry Giroux, Christie and Bloustien, 'bear witness to the ethical dilemmas that animate broader debates within the dominant culture' (2000, p. 355). As Christie notes to herself, and in the public arena of Facebook:

> Just as Lithium can make the bipolar patients just like themselves only a little less so, the Silicon chip allows those with a hearing loss to be 'themselves', only much more so.

Here Christie further demonstrates that, as Neil Marcus, poet and actor argues, 'Disability is an art. It is an ingenious way to live' (Hamilton, 2008, cited in Goggin, 2009, p. 490).

Anna Hickey-Moody's article takes aspects of Deleuze's writing on diagrams and revisits the 1997 Australian-made Rolf De Heer film – *Dance Me to My Song* – a film collaboratively devised with the late Heather Rose, a person with Cerebral Palsy, who also plays the lead character, Julia. While acknowledging that the film is problematic, and is seen as such by disability audiences and scholars in disability and media studies, Hickey-Moody engages Deleuze's concepts of the diagram to argue that an ethic of engagement is present and through diagrams, the film can be understood as opening up the potentiality of social relations and acts as a means of erasing cliché. In particular, it is the film's framing of disability through the use of diegetic sound (in Julia's breathing) and Madeline's emotional disability (Julia's carer) blur the boundaries of disable/able and enfold audience and character through affect. Hickey-Moody suggests that that the project of developing a cinematic ethics that is responsive to the disabled body is a question of inventing new diagrams, or models for feeling and thinking the disabled body. She concludes by suggesting that it is in 'hearing Julia and feeling Julia that the spectator/aurator feels their own body differently and the celluloid becomes modulated as flesh'.

Section Three: Art, Affect and Becoming

Section Three opens with Jessica Cadwallader's 'Stirring up the sediment: the corporeal pedagogies of disabilities'. Cadwallader takes up the workings of the Cartesian mind–body dualism in university pedagogy and her teaching of two courses, one on queer theory and the other on technologies of bodily alteration (primarily medical), that have a specific focus on disability, which acts as a lynchpin on which the rest of the course turns. Cadwallader argues that disability troubles a range of 'common sense' assumptions and in so doing troubles students' habituated styles of being-in-the-world. She suggests that the troubling can be a powerful pedagogical tool, and one that works through understanding students as *embodied* subjects, rather than simply minds tucked away within bodies. To this Cadwallader brings Maurice Merleau-Ponty's (1964) description of the subject as an embodied being always already thoroughly intertwined with the world, notions of syncretic sociability and 'syncreticothers', issues of intercorporeality and Lévinas's (1998) anachronistic sedimentary styles of being-in-the-world. Cadwallader concludes that troubling sedimented styles of being-in-the-world enables a reworking of the structures of habituated comportments and that this is critical to understanding university pedagogy as an embodied process. Certainly, such an understanding needs to be developed if tertiary education is to become more inclusive.

In 'Anxiety and niceness: drawing disability studies into the art and design curriculum through a live brief', Nicole Matthews argues that it is the responsibility of currently non-disabled teachers to provide space in the curriculum for their students to consider and interrogate the conventions of representing disabled people. Drawing on Sianne Ngai's (2005) understanding of affect and 'taste concept' and working through Sherry Adrian's (1997) strategies for raising the profile of disability studies across the arts and humanities, Matthews analyses the occurrence of absences, anxiety and niceness as they are experienced in a 'live brief' set for art, design, illustration and multimedia students at four UK universities. She contends that refocusing on affect underscores the complexity, unpredictability and inter-subjectivity of what happens in classrooms, studio spaces, libraries and all the other spaces where encounters that prompt learning occur. The emergence of both anxiety and niceness in the 'live brief' emphasizes that the experience that the bodies in the classrooms can draw upon shapes the movement and impact of intensities of affect.

In the final piece, 'A rhizomatics of hearing', Vicki Crowley stages a corporeal and affective trail through plateaus of 'Becoming deaf' in her workplace of academia. Crowley works through the unfamiliarity of deafness in a profession whose ability to speak and hear the written word is commonsense. In this piece, Deleuze and Guattari's 'rhizome' acts as a sensibility and motif for the experience of a body deafening. Crowley makes use of photography, poetry and poesis as multi-textual pedagogy of the disjuncture between advocacy and experience, and draws attention to the dysphoria of theorising affect and the multidimensionality of experiential relations of affect. Crowley asks her readers 'how to speak disability?' and she suggests the discursive domain of binary overcode between disabled and non-disabled, which is so often invoked in answering this question is, in fact, a catastrophe. The piece calls for us to listen to how, according to varying intensities and a multiplicity of material needs, dis/abled bodies labour in pedagogical spaces and practices. Such rhizomic becomings, in an ethico-aesthetic proliferation, might evoke both experience and experiment. Here deafness/becoming deaf is always a form of hearing and the 'strange label' (Kuppers, 2009, p. 228) of disability is brought into question just as it increasingly opens presence, tension, texture, and inter-dependence.

Questions of embodiment, affect and disability are woven throughout these contributions. The diverse ways in which these concepts appear emphasize both the utility of these ideas and the timeliness of their application. We very much hope that this collection prompts further consideration of the scholarly relationship between disability, affect and education.

Acknowledgements

We would like to sincerely thank Bridget Garnham and Dawn Butler for the help they have given in bringing this edition to fruition. Their editorial assistance has been greatly appreciated and has created space for the intellectual labour involved in conceptually arranging a special edition.

Notes

1. Restless Dance Company was formed in 1991 and became Restless Dance Theatre in 2008.
2. We would like to acknowledge the work of Leslie Roman (2009a, 2009b) in this area and particularly the leadership in disability arts in education demonstrated in the special issue, "Disability, arts, culture and politics: New epistemologies for qualitative research" in *International Journal of Qualitative Studies in Education* (2009).
3. More recently, *Body and Society* has published a special edition on the turn to affect, (see vol. 16, no. 29, 2010). Of particular interest is Patricia Ticineto Clough's 'Afterword: The future of affect studies' (2010).

References

Adrian, S.E. (1997). Disability, society, and ethical issues: A first-year experience for university students. *Intervention in School & Clinic, 32*, 178–185.

Albrecht-Crane, C., & Daryl Slack, J. (2003). Toward a pedagogy of affect. In J. Daryl Slack (Ed.), *Animations (of Deleuze and Guattari)* (pp. 191–216). New York: Peter Lang.

Bourdieu, P. (1998). *Practical reason*. Cambridge, UK: Polity.

CanDoCo Dance Company. (2010). *About us*. Retrieved January 23, 2010, from http://www.candoco.co.uk/general.php?tm = 1

Clough, P.T. (2010). Afterword: The future of affect studies. *Body & Society, 16*(1), 222–230.

Colman, F.J. (2002). Passaic boys are hell: Robert Smithson's tag as temporal and spatial marker of the geographical self. *Reconstruction: Studies in Contemporary Culture, 2*(3). Retrieved July 16, 2009, from http://www.reconstruction.ws/home2.htm

Colman, F.J. (2005). Deleuze's kiss: The sensory pause of screen affect. *The Warwick Journal of Philosophy, 16*, 101–113.

Deleuze, G. (1988). *Spinoza: Practical philosophy*. San Francisco: City Lights.

Deleuze, G. (1990a). *The logic of sense*. New York: Columbia University Press.

Deleuze, G. (1990b). *Expressionism in philosophy: Spinoza*. New York: Zone.

Deleuze, G. (2002). *Francis Bacon: The logic of sensation*. Minneapolis: University of Minnesota Press.

Deleuze, G., & Guattari, F. (1983). *Anti-Oedipus: Capitalism and schizophrenia*. Minneapolis: University of Minnesota Press.

Deleuze, G., & Guattari, F. (1986). *Kafka: Towards a minor literature*. Minneapolis: University of Minnesota Press.

Deleuze, G., & Guattari, F. (1987). *A thousand plateaus: Capitalism and schizophrenia*. Minneapolis: University of Minnesota Press.

Deleuze, G., & Guattari, F. (1994). *What is philosophy?* London: Verso.

Ellsworth, E. (1997). *Teaching positions: Difference, pedagogy and the power of address*. New York: Teachers College Press.

Ellsworth, E. (2005). *Places of learning: Media, architecture, and pedagogy*. Routledge: New York.

Foucault, M. (2006). *Psychiatric power: Lectures at the College de France 1973–1974*. New York: Palgrave Macmillan.

Foucault, M. (1994). A preface to transgression. In M. Foucault, *Aesthetics: Essential works of Foucault, 1954–1984* (Vol. 2). London: Penguin.

Gibbs, A. (2002). Disaffected. *Continuum: Journal of Media and Cultural Studies, 16*, 335–341.

Giroux, H.A. (1999). Cultural studies as public pedagogy making the pedagogical more political. In *Encyclopaedia of philosophy of education*. Retrieved May 15, 2005, from www.vusst.hr/encyclopaedia/main.htm

Giroux, H.A. (2000). Public pedagogy as cultural politics: Stuart Hall and the 'crisis' of culture. *Cultural Studies, 14*(2), 341–360.

Giroux, H.A. (2004). Cultural studies, public pedagogy, and the responsibility of intellectuals. *Communication and Critical Cultural Studies, 1*(1), 59–79.

Goffman, E. (1961). *Asylums, essays on the social situation of mental patients and other inmates.* New York: Anchor Books.

Goggin, G. (2009). Innovation and disability. *M/C: Media and Culture, 11.* http://journal.media-culture.org.au/index.php/mcjournal/article/view/56

Gregg, M. (2006). *Cultural studies, affective voices.* Basingstoke, UK: Palgrave Macmillan.

Hickey-Moody, A. (2009). *Unimaginable bodies: Intellectual disability, performance and becomings.* Rotterdam, The Netherlands: Sense Publishers.

Hickey-Moody, A.C., Windle, J., & Savage, G. (in press). Pedagogy writ large: Public, popular and cultural pedagogies in motion. *Critical Studies in Education.*

Joyce, J. (1963). *Stephen hero.* New York: New Directions.

Kuppers, P. (2009). Toward a rhizomatic model of disability: Poetry performance, and touch. *Journal of Literary and Cultural Disability Studies, 3*, 221–240.

Lévinas, E. (1998). *Otherwise than being: Or, beyond essence* (A. Lingis, Trans.). Pittsburgh, PA: Duquesne University Press.

Lusted, D. (1986). Why pedagogy? *Screen, 27*(5), 2–15.

Massumi, B. (2002). *Parables for the virtual: Movement, affect, sensation.* Durham, NC: Duke University Press.

McWilliam, E., & Taylor, P.G. (Eds.). (1996). *Pedagogy, technology and the body.* New York: Peter Lang.

Merleau-Ponty, M. (1964). *The primacy of perception: And other essays on phenomenological psychology, the philosophy of art, history and politics* (W. Cobb Trans.). Evanston, IL: Northwestern University Press.

Nancy, J.-L. (2000). *On being singular plural. Being singular plural* (Trans. R.D. Richardson and A.E. O'Byrne). Stanford, CA: Stanford University Press.

Ngai, S. (2005). *Ugly feelings.* Boston: Harvard University Press.

Northway, R. (2002). Integration and inclusion: Illusion or progress in services for disabled people? *Social Policy and Administration, 31*(2), 157–172.

Probyn, E. (2000). *Carnal appetites: FoodSexIdentities.* London: Routledge.

Restless Dance Theatre. (2010). *About us.* Retrieved January 23, 2010, from http://www.restlessdance.org/AboutUs.htm

Roman, L.G. (2009a). Disability arts and culture as public pedagogy. *International Journal of Inclusive Education, 13*(7), 667–675.

Roman, L.G. (2009b). The unruly salon: Unfasten your seatbelts, take no prisoners, make no apologies! [Special issue: Disability, arts, culture and politics: New epistemologies for qualitative research]. *International Journal of Qualitative Studies in Education, 22*(1), 1–16.

Seigworth, G. (2003). Fashioning a stave, or, singing life. In J.D. Slack (Ed.), *Animations of Deleuze and Guattari* (pp. 75–105). New York: Peter Lang.

Vincent, C., Evans, J., Lunt, I., & Young, P. (1996). Professionals under pressure: The administration of special education in a changing context. *British Educational Research Journal, 22*, 475–491.

Vislie, L. (2003). From integration to inclusion: Focusing global trends and changes in the western European societies. *European Journal of Special Needs Education, 18*(1), 17–35.

Watkins, M. (2006). Pedagogic affect/effect: Embodying a desire to learn. *Pedagogies: An International Journal, 1*, 269–282.

The inclusive teacher educator: spaces for civic engagement

Julie Allan

Stirling Institute of Education, University of Stirling, Stirling, UK

This paper is concerned with the teacher educator who is aspiring to be inclusive. It considers the obligations which arise within Higher Education Institutions and the extent to which these contribute to a loss of civic engagement and a lack of capacity to pursue inclusion, social justice and equity. The paper argues that this need not be the case and a reorientation for teacher educators is offered which affords teacher educators opportunities to, in Bourdieu's terms, 'play seriously'. This reorientation is in relation to three significant spaces – the ontological, the aesthetic and the epiphanic – and it is argued that operating within these spaces could enable new practices of inclusive teacher education to emerge.

Introduction

> Clov: What is there to keep me here?
> Hamm: The dialogue. *(Pause.)* I've got to get on with my story. *(Pause.)* I've got on with it well. *(Pause. Irritably.)* Ask me where I've got to. (Beckett, 1958)

Teacher educators concerned with issues of inclusive education, social justice and equity recognise the political dimensions of their work (Barton, 2004; Slee, 2004) and accept their responsibilities in this regard (Ferri & Connor, 2006). However, hostility towards teacher educators and other academics has come from disabled scholars who have been unimpressed by their failure to produce work which improves the material circumstances of disabled people and fosters greater social inclusion. Mike Oliver has been the most outspoken critic and ultimately decided to withdraw from the academy in frustration at his non-disabled colleagues, whom he accuses of '*shitting* disabled people' (1999, 187, original emphasis). He has expressed particular disappointment that the social model of disability, developed by disabled people, has not been used as a tool for change and wishes that 'people would stop talking about it' (Allan & Slee, 2008, p. 88). Finding the spaces in which one can engage with politics may be difficult to find, since, as Gates (1992) notes, 'it's in the gap between "is" and "ought" that politics hides out' (p. 330). This paper considers the role of the teacher educator in relation to inclusion, social justice and equity and identifies the spaces in which there is potential for political work. These spaces are ontological, aesthetic and epiphanic.

The donnish decline?

The role of the teacher educator, and the academic within universities more generally, has become increasingly constrained by the 'audit culture' (Strathern, 1997, 2000). What they write, and for whom, is more closely circumscribed than ever before, and the pressure to demonstrate 'impact,' whatever that may be, limits their capacity to have any real influence on communities and on their values. Halsey (1992) bemoans the 'decline of the donnish dominion' (p. 258), while Furedi (2004) wonders 'where have all the intellectuals gone?' (p. vii). The undermining of academic culture and autonomy (Paterson, 2003) and the regulatory practices within universities is 'producing fear and little else' (Evans, 2004, p. 63) and is 'killing thinking'.

Furthermore, as Lyotard (1986) notes, in a world in which success is equated with saving time, thinking itself reveals its fundamental flaw to be its capacity to waste time. Said (1994) argues that a further danger for the intellectual comes from the limitations and constraints of professionalism that encourage conformity rather than critique:

> The particular threat to the intellectual today, whether in the West or the non-Western world, is not the academy, nor the suburbs, not the appalling commercialism of journalism and publishing houses, but rather an attitude that I will call professionalism. By professionalism I mean thinking of your work as an intellectual as something you do for a living, between the hours of nine and five with one eye on the clock, and another cocked at what is considered to be proper, professional behaviour – not rocking the boat, not straying outside the accepted paradigms or limits, making yourself marketable and above all presentable, hence uncontroversial and unpolitical and 'objective'. (p. 55, original emphasis)

Pring (2008) notes that considerable fears were expressed in the early part of the twentieth century about the loss of academic respectability which might be produced by universities venturing into teacher education and other forms of professional education. These fears declined as the universities enforced greater academic rigour, removed the 'undifferentiated mush that passed for educational theory' (Peters, cited in Pring, 2008, p. 328) and introduced studies in the disciplines of philosophy, psychology, sociology, and history of education. However, as Pring points out, these moves did not necessarily resolve the troubling divide between theory and practice and may even have accentuated it, provoking continuing arguments about the appropriate contribution of universities to teacher education.

The civic duty which was behind the creation of universities in Scotland, other parts of Europe and the USA, in what was known as 'democratic intellectualism' (Paterson, 2003, p. 69), with a responsibility among academics for educating the public and promoting civil society, appears to have been lost. It might be questioned, however, whether UK and US universities have ever fostered the kind of intellectualism which could be seen in French universities, through for example the likes of Foucault, Derrida and Deleuze, or those in the Frankfurt school such as Habermas and Adorno. The contemporary German theorist Sloterdijk (1987), whose book, *Critique of Cynical Reason*, was bought in vast quantities by a public tempted into philosophy, has no parallels in the UK, USA or elsewhere, although writers such as Michael Apple, Terry Eagleton and Slavoj Zizek appear to have made some inroads into the public imagination through their engagement with the media. E.P. Thompson (1970) is somewhat damning of those who inhabit the UK universities:

> I have never ceased to be astounded when observing the preening and mating habits of fully grown specimens of the species Academicus Superciliosis. The behaviour patterns of one of the true members of the species are unmistakable. He is inflated with self-esteem and perpetually self-congratulatory as to the high vocation of the university teacher; but he knows almost nothing about any other vocation, and he will lie down and let himself be walked over if anyone enters from the outer world who has money or power or even a touch line in realist talk . . . Superciliosis is the most divisible and reliable creature in this country, being so intent upon crafty calculations of short-term advantages – this favour for his department, that a colleague who, next week, at the next committee, has promised to run a log for him, that he has never even tried to imagine the wood out of which his timber rolls. He can scurry furiously and self-importantly around in his committees, like a white mouse running in a wheel, while his master is carrying him, cage and all, to be sold at the local pet-shop. (p. 154)

Although Thompson's observations pertain to an earlier period, the simultaneous self-importance and willingness to be bought are sinister features of contemporary academic life. Zizek (2005) offers a more recent, but equally damming, account of the:

> prattling classes, academics and journalists with no specialist education, usually working in humanities with some vague French postmodern leanings, specialists in everything, prone to verbal radicalism, in love with paradoxical formulations that flatly contradict the obvious. (p. 23)

Such disenchantment with academics seems unfair and misplaced since the greater problem may be their unwillingness – or inability – to face up to their civic duty and to their responsibility to contribute to civil society.

The inclusive teacher educator

For teacher educators who seek to cultivate inclusive educational practices among their student teachers, and who promote values of social justice and equity, a number of pressures and dangers are evident. One significant pressure on teacher educators is the requirement to demonstrate ways in which inclusion, a concept which is under-theorised, lacking in empirical evidence and often used as a catch-all remedy for all kinds of inequalities, works in practice (Haug, n.d.; Hegarty, 2001). Gregoriou (2004), citing Lyotard (1993), notes that this operational imperative is part of an increasingly widespread demand for the simple, the practical and the reducible, and its negative effects are that it:

> threatens to totalize experience, to reduce language to Newspeak, to rob thinking of its childhood and pedagogy of its philosophical moment. It is the 'demand' for reality (for unity, simplicity, communicability) and remedy: remedy for the parcelling and virutalization of culture, for the fragmentation of the life world and its derealization into idioms, *petits recits*, and language games. (p. 233, original emphasis)

This demand for simplification is accompanied by a resistance to thinking and, as Colebrook (2006) suggests, 'all around us . . . we encounter the absence of thinking, the malevolence and stupidity that go well beyond error' (p. 2). Some of the material resources for teachers, in the form of packages of advice and support, appear to offer remedies to the 'problem' of inclusion. The plethora of handbooks, promising such goodies as '60 research-based teaching strategies that help special learners succeed' (McNary, 2005) or 'commonsense methods for children with special educational needs' (Westwood, 2002), construct inclusion as a technical matter and assail teachers with advice about *effective* inclusion. Brantlinger (2006) takes particular exception to the US hardback textbooks – 'big glossies' (p. 45) – that function as 'authoritative purveyors of technical knowledge' (p. 67) and portray idealised versions of classroom life and of children benefiting from interventions. These handbooks affect a sound theoretical base, but as Thomas (2008) observes, they amount to little more than 'theory junk sculpture' (p. 1), a 'cacophany of incompatible explanations', in which 'plausible homily, mixed with large portions of psychoanalytic and psychological vocabulary, take the place of a rational consideration of children's behaviour at school' (p. 1). The texts have been produced by learning disability scholars with a vested interest in the maintenance of special education, but as Gallagher (2008) notes, 'their implacability is matched only by the depth of their theoretical confusion' (p. 15). The realities presented in these texts bear little resemblance to the children whom the student teachers encounter and the certainty that they command (Allan & Slee, 2008; Brantlinger, 2006) make them irresponsible.

A further peril which confronts teacher educators cultivating inclusive practices, and which may be difficult to resist, is the descent into emotivism, which Alasdair MacIntyre (1984) describes as a confusion between two kinds of reply to the question 'why should I do …?' The first reply takes the form 'because I wish it' and is confined to the personal context of the utterance and the characteristics of the speaker. The second reply is unconditional and independent of who utters it, taking the form 'because it is your duty'. MacIntyre suggests that the second reply is often used to mean 'I like it and urge it on or recommend it to you' (Hernstein Smith, 1992). Inclusion, social justice and equity are thus urged and pressed upon people under the guise of a well-argued and moral evaluation, even though the arguments may be fallacious, in the sense of having an error in reasoning on material, psychological or logical grounds (Fearnside & Holther, 1959):

> Here is another trick, which, as soon as it is practicable, makes all others unnecessary. Instead of working on your opponent's intellect by argument, work on his will by motive, and he, and also the audience if they have similar interests, will at once be won over by your opinion, even though you got it out of a lunatic asylum. (Schopenhauer, 1896, p. XXXV)

Emotivism, according to MacIntyre, is a widespread phenomenon, but it leaves an overwhelming sense of confusion and of having been deceived:

> Now people still say 'It is good' and *think* they mean 'It is good', but, without knowing, they are really doing only what people used to do when they said 'I like it' or 'I want it,' namely expressing their own feelings and trying to get other people to feel, do, or believe certain things. And everyone is deceived: listeners are deceived about what speakers are doing; speakers are self-deceived about what they themselves are doing; and moral philosophers are either deceived, complacent, or complicitous. (Hernstein Smith, 1992, pp. 213–214)

It is difficult to see how teacher educators concerned with inclusion might resist these pressures and imperatives, but Bourdieu (1998) maintains that it is vital that they are protected from urgent duties and that they can be allowed to 'play seriously' (p. 128):

> *Homo scholasticus* or *homo academicus* is someone who can play seriously because his or her state (or State) assures her the means to do so, that is, free time, outside the urgency of a practical situation. (1998, p. 128)

So how might teacher educators regain control, rediscover their civic duty and engage in serious play? I want to suggest three possible kinds of re-orientations which they may be able to effect. These concern the ontological (their own selves and others) the aesthetic (sensory and sensual 'affects') and the epiphanic (the unforeseen and inaccessible aspects of ordinary life).

An 'other' ontology

On a basic level, teacher educators concerned with inclusion might ask 'what *can* we do'? To respond to that question effectively, I am suggesting that what is required is an ontological reorientation of themselves as political individuals who must *act* and who, in order to do so, will have to realign themselves in the academic and professional worlds. To achieve these realignments, inclusion might be conceived of as an ethical project, using the framework offered by Foucault (1994), and in which one's own self – and one's capacity to be in relation to others – is considered part of the material on which work has to be done. Foucault's framework of ethics could be used by teacher educators by, first of all, identifying the part of themselves as educators which they wished to work on (what Foucault calls determining the ethical substance). The second ethical dimension, the mode of subjection, could come from examining the rules which operate within Higher Education Institutions and which create barriers to inclusion and produce additional pressures. Self practice or ethical work, the third dimension, could be directed towards scrutiny of efforts to be inclusive and modifying these where necessary. Finally, teacher educators might work out the overall goal, the telos, of inclusive teacher education, either collectively or individually. Foucault's framework of ethics enables teacher educators to direct energy and resources towards themselves and may provide the means for rediscovering their civic duty (Allan, 2008).

Maxine Greene (2008) offers a helpful construction of the becoming nature of the self: 'I am what I am not yet', while Len Barton (2005) contends that it is necessary also to place hope – 'an informed recognition of the offensive nature of current conditions and relations and a belief that the possibilities of change are not foreclosed' (p. 23) – at the centre of the struggle for inclusion. Prerequisites are desire – for inclusion and the removal of exclusionary practices – and an undertaking to enact that desire on behalf of others. This moves the debate on from dichotomies of the universalists against the moderates or between homogenising and distinguishing tendencies (Cigman, 2007). To return to MacIntyre's question of 'why should I do', the inclusive teacher educator's answer may become a purposeful elision which avoids emotivism because the imperative is directed back towards themselves. In other words, 'because I wish it' and 'because it is *my* duty'.

Teacher educators may find it difficult to act politically within their own institutions, but there are multiple ways in which they might oppose institutional practices which create exclusion (Ballard, 2004; Brantlinger, 2006; Gallagher, 2006) and foster inclusion by 'communication across a multiplicity of cultures, identities and ways of thinking' (Booth, 2003, p. 55). More generally, teacher educators might 'resist and reject language that carries the ideology of exclusion' (Ballard, 2004, p. 103), foreground ideology and position (Gallagher, 2008) and challenge the appropriation of inclusive education by special education (Slee, 2004) and the 'easy sloganising' (Hegarty, 2001, p. 249) of inclusive education for all kinds of inequalities. Apple (2001) enjoins us to face up to the dynamics of power in unromantic ways and promotes the use of subversive tactics to challenge the hegemonic order, including tactical and counter-hegemonic alliances and heretical thought. He also suggests that while we might recapture our past to see what is possible, it is important not to romanticise dreams about the future. Corbett and Slee's (2000) depiction of academics as 'cultural vigilantes' (p. 134) is a useful starting point and the language of enmity is appropriate as a *casus belli*, an occasion of war for which there is just cause.

Evans (2004) suggests the kind of refusal of institutional power evoked by Virginia Woolf in *Three Guineas* which amounts to an 'attitude of complete indifference' (p. 309). Woolf envisaged this as a war against the 'pompous and self important' (Evans, 2004, p. 76) behaviour of males, but Evans suggests that this kind of resistance (by anyone) could be effective within universities and could lead to a different kind of politics, not of inclusion, but 'about, and in favour of, exclusion from those practices and processes which increasingly deform much of academic life' (Evans, 2004, p. 102).

There is a need also to refuse some of the closure in thinking that surrounds inclusion and education more generally – literally, by refusing the texts and preventing students' engagement with them – to begin to do justice (in both senses) to the complexity and messiness of the processes of inclusion and exclusion. The philosophers of difference – Foucault, Derrida, and Deleuze and Guattari – seem to offer some considerable promise in this regard (Allan, 2008; Biesta, 2001; Hickey-Moody, 2009; Olssen, 2009), in freeing up new ways of thinking, but Thomas (2008) has argued persuasively that instead of structured theoretical frameworks what we need are 'simpler and looser understandings' (p. 7), based on a Deweyan form of investigation and characterised by an acceptance of the inadequacy of existing knowledge. Biesta (2008) calls this as a 'pedagogy with empty hands' (p. 198), which requires that learners are approached without ready solutions or 'tricks of the trade', derived from research or elsewhere, and asked 'what do you think of it?'

Aesthetic affects

For Stephen, art was neither a copy nor an imitation of nature: the artistic process was a natural process. (Joyce, 1963, p. 171)

Deleuze (1998) testifies to the arts' transformative capacities, offering individuals sensory, and even sensual 'affects' and producing 'fragments, allusions, strivings, investigations' (p. 111) which create 'affirmative injunctions'. It is the role of the arts in affecting rather than being understood which is its most powerful feature and this takes place through expression, as opposed to emotion, and the unfamiliarity for individuals experiencing these affects is: 'capable of taking the ground away' (Uhlman, 2009, p. 64). It is the 'critical enmeshment of the newness' (Hickey-Moody, 2009, p. 172) which provides the content of expression and which removes the possibility of self-consciousness and the need for interpretation (p. 172). Within education, the arts can be seen as potentially producing a form of deterritorialisation, by altering the space in which education takes place, from one which is rigid, with lines of demarcation between the teacher and the learner, to one that is smooth and open to possibilities. The arts also offer scope for individuals to undertake learning that is, in Deleuze and Guattari's (1987) terms, rhizomic, moving in unanticipated directions and provoking new becomings (Allan, 2008). There is, however, a problem, as Deleuze (1981) notes, of harnessing forces for developing arts practices and this is caused, in part, by the very exclusionary and elitist nature of the arts themselves. There is also a limitation imposed by the 'major literatures' (Deleuze, 1986) through which academics are expected to communicate and which exclude, silence and subjugate.

Minor literatures, that have been created in major languages by minorities (Deleuze & Guattari, 1987), could offer academics a means of being inclusive, by enabling the articulation of new political subjectivities. These literatures could be used to help name minorities, marginalised groups, including disabled people, and those whose voices are normally subjugated, and to mobilise politically around these names, whilst at the same time working to undermine the sovereign subject. A minor literature has three features: the language used is affected by deterritorialisation, that is a smoothing out of space or a stripping out of syntax so that it loses all symbolism and signification; everything is political (and individuals are connected to a political immediacy); and everything has a collective value (Deleuze, 1998). Two great writers, James Joyce and Samuel Beckett, have been lauded by Deleuze and Guattari for their production of very different, but equally potent, minor literatures: Joyce achieves 'exhilaration and overdetermination' (Deleuze & Guattari, 1986, p. 19) while Beckett produces 'dryness and sobriety, a willed poverty' (p. 19) and both succeed in creating deterritorialisation that takes language to its limits, makes it stand still and forces a reterritorialisation. Kafka, observes Deleuze (1986), uses syntax on and against itself to render language inert:

> Kafka will turn syntax into a cry that will embrace the rigid syntax of this dried-up German. He will push it toward a deterritorialization that will no longer be saved by culture or myth, that will be an absolute deterritorialization, even if it is slow, sticky, coagulated. To bring language slowly and progressively to the desert. To use syntax in order to cry, to give a syntax to the cry. (p. 26)

The act of creating a minor literature is 'to find points of nonculture or under-development, linguistic Third World zones by which a language can escape, an animal enters things, an assemblage comes into play' (Deleuze & Guattari, 1986, p. 27).

The accomplishment – and use – of a minor literature is, as Deleuze and Guattari (1986) point out, against the dream by major styles, genres and movements of assuming major functions and aspiring to be authoritative, but is potentially at the heart of inclusive practice:

> Create the opposite dream: know how to create a becoming-minor. (Is there hope for philosophy, which for a long time has been an official, referential genre? Let us profit from this moment in which antiphilosophy is trying to be a language of power.) (p. 27)

The use of minor literatures to name and privilege particular voices and identities is described usefully by Rancière (2008) as a process of making a discourse of that which has formally been a noise and a process of rupture which renders certain identities visible:

> For me a political subject is a subject who employs the competence of the so-called incompetents or the part of those who have no part, and not an additional group to be recognised as part of society. 'Visible minorities' means exceeding the system of represented groups, of constituted identities... It's a rupture that opens out into the recognition of the competence of anyone, not the addition of a unit. (p. 3)

Critchley (2007) argues that the scope for political action has been reduced by the disarticulation of names which are inherently political, such as the 'proletariat' or the 'peasant', and cites the examples of 'indigenous' achieving the status of a force for change in Mexico and Australia. Critchley usefully advocates a kind of demonstration as demos-tration, 'manifesting the presence of those who do not count'. Minor literatures, because they take language beyond being merely representative, moving 'head over heels and away' (Deleuze, 1986, p. 26), offer great potential for academics to address inequalities. It does so productively and creatively, by 'setting fire to the unjust state of things instead of burning the things themselves, and restoring life to primary life' (Deleuze, 1986, p. 108).

Teacher educators seeking an aesthetic orientation may find inspiration from disabled dancers, who have experimented with affect. According to Hickey-Moody, disabled dancers can catalyse the construction of affect or sensation by virtue of their own disabilities, interacting in the performance space to enact a 'turning away' from a history of intellectual disability which imposes limitations upon them and in the eyes of a mainstream public. Through the act of turning away, disabled dancers can participate in an act of becoming other, an act which 'wrest[s] the percept from perceptions of objects and the states of a perceiving subject [and wrests] the affect from affections as the transition from one state to another' (Deleuze & Guattari, 1994, p. 167). There is possibly scope for inclusive teacher educators to model such affects, by creating performance spaces for beginning teachers to experience a 'turning away' from their own presumptions and misapprehensions about disabled people and other minorities, and to explore their becomings as teachers creatively:

> Creativity is always a becoming, a reterritorialisation and an establishment of new affective systems of relation. One cannot become-other unless there is something from which one turns away. (Hickey-Moody, 2009, p. 178)

Like the artist, the teacher educator may facilitate these affects among student teachers and privilege their experience and expression over the understanding of content. It implies a certain kind of work on the part of the teacher educator to constantly move the beginning teacher beyond the familiar, with experiences that are 'capable of taking the ground away' (Uhlmann, 2009, p. 64).

Epiphanies of the everyday

Although the pressures on teacher educators and the quest for certainty which has been a feature of inclusion may have clipped the wings of Socratic insight by insisting that all learning is tied down and rendered visible, there may be scope for opening learning up for colleagues and for stakeholders in the policy and practice communities. Specifically, teacher educators could help to create learning spaces which could allow exposure to what James Joyce has called 'epiphanies':

> The epiphany was the sudden 'revelation of the whatness of a thing', the moment in which the 'soul of the commonest object ... seems to us radiant'. The artist, he felt, was charged with such revelations, and must look for them not among the gods but among men, in casual, unostentatious, even unpleasant moments'. (Ellman, 1982, p. 83)

James Ellman (1982), the foremost biographer of James Joyce, explained how an epiphany, a sudden bringing into presence that which is otherwise inaccessible, was often achieved through great art and this view is endorsed by Taylor (1989):

> What I want to capture with this term is just this notion of a work of art as the locus of a manifestation which brings us into the presence of something which is otherwise inaccessible, and which is of the highest moral and spiritual significance; a manifestation, moreover, which also defines and completes something even as it reveals. (p. 419)

Hogan (2005) suggests that the practice of calling epiphanies into presence could be achieved by educators, but it would require a different orientation to one's work, that, above all, involves the 'ever alert acknowledgement of the possibilities and limitations which constitute our own way of being human among others' (p. 91). The gradual shift by public research funders from 'stakeholder engagement' to 'knowledge transfer' and now to 'knowledge exchange' (Ozga, 2006) reflects a more sophisticated understanding of the needs of different interest groups among researchers, funders and 'researched' and a recognition of the need for greater reciprocity in research relationships. This shift also creates a space into which teacher educators could position themselves as facilitators of 'everyday ephiphanies'. These would bring to attention 'the quality of what is actually experienced' (Hogan, 2005, p. 92), but which is usually bypassed because it is routine and therefore undertaken unreflexively, and invite a dwelling upon it.

  To produce these epiphanies, the teacher educator would need to work at convincing the participants not simply to engage in dialogue, but that they 'are a dialogue' (Hogan, 2005, p. 93). This means abandoning conventional approaches to stakeholder meetings which seek shared meanings and consensus (but which, of course privilege certain perspectives over others) and creating instead a smooth space for learning (a deterritorialised space in Deleuze & Guattari's, 1987, terms) in which partiality – or one's position and interests – is the material for discussion and incompleteness is a specific goal. Approaches such as Open Space Technology (www.openspaceworld/org/), developed by US businessman Harrison Owen, provide a smooth space for the participants to determine their own agenda for discussion.

It has been described as 'passion with responsibility' and as 'chaos and creativity' and is simultaneously loose, because the agenda is not set, and highly structured, using the responses of the participants to determine activities and outcomes. This technology has been used to try to bring student teachers and students together and to obtain insights from young people in relation to diversity (Allan, Smyth, I'Anson, & Mott, 2009). The approach appears to have been successful in altering the relations of the participants and the balance of power and, in our experience, has allowed 'epiphanies' to emerge.

Retrieving the civic

> I think what you'll find is, whatever it is we do substantively, there will be near-perfect clarity as to what it is. And it will be known, and it will be known to the Congress, and it will be known to you, probably before we decide it, but it will be known. (Rumsfeld, 2003)

The pressures faced by the present-day teacher educator are significant and the climate of accountability and mistrust gets at the souls of individuals and at their sense of capacity for civic duty (Ballard, 2004; Sennett, 1998): 'Operationally, everything is so clear; emotionally so illegible' (Sennett, 1998, p. 68). For the teacher educator committed to inclusion, the stresses are possibly even greater because of the imperatives for clarity, urgency and solutions and the difficulties of resisting these. The emphatic way in which disabled individuals have made clear their disappointment and frustration with teacher educators for doing little more than talking will inevitably heighten their sense of inadequacy. Teacher educators, and academics more generally, may have allowed themselves to be defined by 'the disfiguring language of performativity' (Fielding, 2001, p. 8) and may have used this to displace their civic duty. It need not be this way. The possibilities for reorientation by inclusive teacher educators, in relation to the ontological, the aesthetic and the epiphanic, are extremely productive. They offer new spaces in which teacher educators can revitalise some of the concerns that made them previously want to become teacher educators and reinvent themselves. Above all, it affords a means for teacher educators to recover their civic duty and to actively contribute to the building of civil society through the enactment, rather than the promoting, of inclusive values, putting that into practice in relation to themselves, their student teachers and, above all, those potentially facing exclusion.

References

Allan, J. (2008). *Rethinking inclusion: The philosophers of difference in practice.* Dordrecht, The Netherlands: Springer.

Allan, J., & Slee, R. (2008). *Doing inclusive education research.* Rotterdam, The Netherlands: Sense Publishers.

Allan, J., Smyth, G., I'Anson, J., & Mott, J. (2009). Understanding disability with children's social capital. *Journal of Research in Special Educational Needs, 9*(2), 115–121.

Apple, M. (2001). *Educating the 'right' way.* New York: Routledge/Falmer.

Ballard, K. (2004). Ideology and the origins of inclusion: A case study. In L. Ware (Ed.), *Ideology and the politics of in(ex)clusion* (pp. 89–107). New York: Peter Lang.

Barton, L. (2004). Politics of special education: A necessary or irrelevant approach. In L. Ware (Ed.), *Ideology and the politics of in(ex)clusion* (pp. 63–75). New York: Peter Lang.

Barton, L. (2005). Special educational needs: An alternative look. Unpublished discussion paper.

Beckett, S. (1958). *Endgame*. London: Faber and Faber.

Biesta, G. (2001). Preparing for the incalculable. In G. Biesta & D. Egéa-Kuehne (Eds.), *Derrida & education* (pp. 32–54). London: Routledge.

Biesta, G. (2008). Pedagogy with empty hands: Levinas, education and the question of being human. In D. Egéa-Kuehne (Ed.), *Levinas and education: At the intersection of faith and reason* (pp. 198–210). London: Routledge.

Booth, T. (2003). Views from the institution: Overcoming barriers to inclusive education? In T. Booth, K. Nes & M. Strømstad (Eds.), *Developing inclusive education* (pp. 33–58). London: RoutledgeFalmer.

Bourdieu, P. (1998). *Practical reason*. Cambridge, UK: Polity.

Brantlinger, E. (2006). The big glossies: How textbooks structure (special) education. In E. Brantlinger (Ed.), *Who benefits from special education? Remediating (fixing) other people's children* (pp. 45–76). Mahwah, NJ: Lawrence Erlbaum Associates.

Cigman, R. (2007). A question of universality: Inclusive education and the principle of respect. *Journal of Philosophy of Education, 14*, 775–793.

Colebrook, C. (2006). *Deleuze: A guide for the perplexed*. London: Continuum.

Corbett, J., & Slee, R. (2000). An international conversation on inclusive education. In F. Armstrong, D. Armstrong & L. Barton (Eds.), *Inclusive education: Policy, contexts and comparative education* (pp. 133–146). London: David Fulton.

Critchley, J. (2007). *Infinitely demanding: Ethics of commitment, politics of resistance*. London: Verso.

Deleuze, G. (1981). *Francis Bacon: Logique de la sensation* Vol. 1. Paris: Editions de la différance.

Deleuze, G. (1986). *Cinema 1*. London: Continuum.

Deleuze, G. (1998). *Essays critical and clinical*. London: Verso.

Deleuze, G., & Guattari, F. (1986). *Kafka: Toward a minor literature* (Trans. D. Polan). Minneapolis: University of Minnesota Press.

Deleuze, G., & Guattari, F. (1987). *A thousand plateaus: Capitalism and schizophrenia*. London: The Athlone Press.

Deleuze, G., & Guattari, F. (1994). *What is philosophy?* (Trans. H. Tomlinson & G. Burchell). New York: Columbia University Press.

Ellman, R. (1982). *James Joyce*. New York: Oxford University Press.

Evans, M. (2004). *Killing thinking: The death of the universities*. London: Continuum.

Fearnside, W., & Holther, W. (1959). *Fallacy: The counterfeit of argument*. Englewood Cliffs, NJ: Prentice Hall.

Ferri, B., & Connor, D. (2006). *Reading resistance: Discourses of exclusion in desegregation and inclusion debates*. New York: Peter Lang.

Fielding, M. (Ed.). (2001). *Taking education really seriously: Four years hard labour*. London: RoutlegeFalmer.

Foucault, M. (1994). *A preface to transgression*. In M. Foucault, *Aesthetics: Essential works of Foucault, 1954–1984* (Vol. 2). London: Penguin.

Furedi, F. (2004). *Where have all the intellectuals gone?* London: Continuum.

Gallagher, D. (2006). If not absolute objectivity, then what? A reply to Kauffman and Sasso. *Exceptionality, 14*(2), 91–107.

Gallagher, D. (2008, March). *Hiding in plain sight: The nature and role of theory in learning disability labelling*. Paper presented at the American Educational Research Association, New York.

Gates, H. (1992). Statistical stigmata. In D. Cornell, M. Rosenfield & D. Carlson (Eds.), *Deconstruction and the possibility of justice* (pp. 330–345). London: Routledge.

Greene, M. (2008, March). *From bare facts to intellectual possibility: The leap of imagination. A conversation with Maxine Greene*. Presidential address, American Educational Research Association.

Gregoriou, Z. (2004). Commencing the rhizome: Towards a minor philosophy of education. *Educational Philosophy and Theory, 3*, 233–251.

Halsey, A. (1992). *The decline of the donnish dominion*. Oxford, UK: Clarendon.

Haug, P. (n.d.). *Understanding inclusion in education: The example of Norway.* Unpublished paper.

Hegarty, S. (2001). Inclusive education: A case to answer. *Journal of Moral Education, 30,* 243–249.

Hernstein Smith, B. (1992). Judgement after the fall. In D. Cornell, M. Rosenfield & D. Carlson (Eds.), *Deconstruction and the possibility of justice* (pp. 211–231). London: Routledge.

Hickey-Moody, A. (2009). Becoming-dinosaur: Collective process and movement aesthetics. In L. Cull (Ed.), *Deleuze and performance* (pp. 161–180). Edinburgh: Edinburgh University Press.

Hogan, P. (2005). The politics of identity and the epiphanies of learning. In W. Carr (Ed.), *The RoutledgeFalmer reader in philosophy of education* (pp. 83–96). Abingdon, UK: Routledge.

Joyce, J. (1963). *Stephen hero.* New York: New Directions.

Lyotard, J. (1986). *The postmodern explained to children: Correspondence, 1982–1985.* Sydney: Power Publications.

Lyotard, J. (1993). *The postmodern condition.* Minneapolis: Minneapolis University Press.

MacIntyre, A. (1984). *After virtue: A study in moral theory.* Notre Dame: University of Notre Dame.

McNary, S. (2005). *What successful teachers do in inclusive classrooms.* London: Sage.

Oliver, M. (1999). Final accounts and the parasite people. In M. Corker & S. French (Eds.), *Disability discourse* (pp. 183–191). Buckingham, UK: Open University Press.

Olsson, L. (2009). *Movement and experiment in early childhood learning: Deleuze and Guattari in early childhood education.* Abingdon, UK: Routledge.

Ozga, J. (2006). Travelling and embedded policy: The case of knowledge transfer. *Journal of Education Policy, 21*(1), 1–17.

Paterson, L. (2003). The survival of the democratic intellect: Academic values in Scotland and England. *Higher Education Quarterly, 57*(1), 67–93.

Pring, R. (2008). Teacher education at Oxford University: James is alive but living in Karachi. *Oxford Review of Education, 34,* 325–333.

Rancière, J. (2008). Jacques Rancière and indisciplinarity: An interview. *Art and Research, 2*(1), 1–10.

Rumsfeld, D. (2003). *Department of Defense briefing.* Retrieved March 13, 2008, from http://www.slate.com/id/2081042/

Said, E. (1994). *Representations of the intellectual.* London: Vintage.

Schopenhauer, A. (1896). *The art of controversy.* New York: Cosimo.

Sennett, R. (1998). *The corrosion of character: The personal consequences of work in the new capitalism.* New York: W.H. Norton.

Slee, R. (2004). Meaning in the service of power. In L. Ware (Ed.), *Ideology and the politics of in/exclusion* (pp. 46–60). New York: Peter Lang.

Sloterdijk, P. (1987). *Critique of cynical reason.* Minneapolis: University of Minnesota Press.

Strathern, M. (1997). Improving ratings: Audit in the British university system. *European Review, 5,* 305–321.

Strathern, M. (2000). *Audit cultures: Anthropological studies in accountability, ethics and the academy.* London: Routledge.

Taylor, C. (1989). *Sources of the self: The making of modern identity.* Cambridge, MA: Harvard University Press.

Thomas, G. (2008, March). *Theory and the construction of pathology.* Paper presented at the American Educational Research Association, New York.

Thompson, E.P. (1970). *Warwick University Ltd.* Harmondsworth, UK: Penguin.

Uhlmann, A. (2009). Expression and affect in Kleist, Beckett and Deleuze. In L. Cull (Ed.), *Deleuze and performance* (pp. 54–70). Edinburgh: Edinburgh University Press.

Westwood, P. (2002). *Commonsense methods for children with special educational needs.* London: FalmerRoutledge.

Zizek, S. (2005, February 19). The empty wheelbarrow. *Guardian Comment.* Retrieved March 6, 2006, from http://www.guardian.co.uk/comment/story/0,3604,1417982,00.html

Muscularity, mateship and malevolent masculinities: experiences of young men with hearing disabilities in secondary schools

Cassandra Loeser

Learning and Teaching Unit, University of South Australia, St Bernards Road, Magill, Adelaide, SA, Australia

Across the analysis of interview fragments from two young men with hearing disabilities who attended secondary schools in Australia, this paper will demonstrate that masculinity in the schoolyard frequently emerges within and as a collective form of violence and malevolence against the disabled body. Yet while certain individuals or groups may constitute them as 'Other', the young men themselves do not believe that because they have a hearing disability, they are 'abnormal' or should tolerate acts of violence against their being. The young men's emphasis on the antagonistic nature of subjectivity in the context of dynamics of the schoolyard points to the uncertainty of settlements of what constitutes dominant masculinity in a given person between and within other groups. Their stories demonstrate the identities of masculinity and disability as fragile, antagonistic and mediated productions, contingent upon approximate performances grounded in what different male peer cultures deem 'acceptable' and 'unacceptable'.

Introduction

This paper attends to the experience and narratives of two young men with hearing disabilities who routinely attended secondary schools in South Australia. Their experience shows us that the making of masculinity is a labour-intensive achievement. Their stories draw attention to the cultural practices and techniques invoked that create and regulate hierarchies of masculinity. They suggest that the production of hearing disability and masculinity in and across school sites is profoundly contradictory, complex and uncertain, despite those literatures that mandate disability and disabled students as lacking and in need. The extent to which cultural limits that define hearing-disabled masculine subjectivities in schools are both liable to imposition, and open to exchange and re-articulation, is examined in light of Butler's and Foucault's claims about the production of subjectivity. The young men's stories reveal an important obligation for academics to give greater context and complexity to the positioning of disabled and masculine subjectivities in schools. They show the ways that disability and students with disabilities are understood and treated in school peer cultures is contingent on how gender is defined and performed.

Situating the bodies of young men with disabilities in schools

Many studies of the experiences of young men with disabilities in school systems analyze disabled male subjectivities in terms of social marginalization and subordination. Shereen Benjamin's work on the constitution of masculine identification for working-class boys with disabilities in a London special school, for example, found that boys with physical disabilities are positioned by current educational policy 'as the "failing/failed boys" of school effectiveness and similar discourses' (2001, p. 39). The 'only hope of success [for these] underperforming [boys] is to prove themselves as macho stars of the football pitch' (2001, p. 39) and attain a 'viable positioning in the school and classroom informal masculine cultures' (2001, p. 42). The characteristics associated with the normative forms of masculinity that the boys wished to attain was inaccessible. This is further illustrated in the following statement:

> The football business, as key mediator for them of working-class street culture, sets them up to crave stardom through physical prowess and acting tough, and in so doing, sets them up for failure. The education business emphasises excellence and achievement, constructed in terms of a tightly-defined notion of 'required levels' and thus also sets them up, as disabled working-class boys, to fail. (2001, p. 52)

Benjamin's work is important in highlighting the power of institutionalized masculinity as cultural ideal in schools. Masculine subjectivity for these boys is constructed in a permanent contestation with hegemonic norms. These norms, in turn, condemn the physically disabled working-class boys to failure. The only viable alternatives available to these boys in which they may have a chance to 'succeed' would be to make 'counter-hegemonic – "excluded" or "displaced" – actions and options available to them' (2001, p. 44). Australian studies, including the work of Gilbert and Gilbert, also find that boys with disabilities 'are subject to the same cultural images of masculinity as others; that it involves a denial of weakness, emotions and frailty' (1998, p. 145). Like Benjamin, Gilbert and Gilbert argue that '[b]oys with disabilities... are marginalised if they are unable to conform to the demands for competence in aggressive and competitive performance of play, or do not match the image of the masculine body' (1998, p. 45).

The work of both Benjamin and Gilbert and Gilbert identifies a range of elements associated with a dominant image of masculinity. Yet Benjamin's and Gilbert and Gilbert's point that 'boys with disabilities' only achieve subject positionings at the bottom of the hierarchy of masculinities in schools reiterates claims about the existence of an intrinsic masculine hegemony on which all other bodies are judged. In presenting a generic dichotomy of 'dominant' and 'Other', the complexities and possibilities of different masculine and disabled subjectivities in different schoolyard sites and contexts may be simplified.

There is a need to draw further on resources that can speak to the potential multiplicity of conceptual meanings, experiences, cultural elements and practices by which embodied masculine subjectivity is constructed. This is particularly pertinent because hearing disability, being a primarily 'hidden disability', means that young men with a hearing disability may possibly be read as masculine in different spaces and contexts. Lennard Davis, in his writings about disability, deafness and Deafness, claims that '[d]isability exists in the realm of the senses... the Deaf are perceived as such because one hears a different speech inflection' (Davis, 1995, p. 13), or sees a hearing aid:

> Without those sensory clues, the Deaf are embedded in the sensory grid of the 'normal' person. To the passerby on the street, the Deaf person is indistinguishable from anyone else until he or she begins to engage in communication. (Davis, 1995, p. 14)

Davis' contention can be used to suggest a variable experience. This is because hearing disability, as a primarily 'hidden disability', may not always already impact upon the visual relation of masculinity, which appears inevitably to assume the visibility of disability (see also Loeser, 2005).

The required level of attention to the possibilities of becoming and knowing for young men with hearing disabilities may be admitted through the selected works of Michel Foucault and Judith Butler. This article draws on selected elements of Foucault's work on ethics to explore some of the obligations and practices attending the construction of gendered identity for young men with hearing disabilities. Foucault elaborates his conceptualization of ethics in relation to what he calls the technologies of the self (1998a). Technologies of the self are 'an exercise of self upon self by which one tries to work out, to transform oneself and attain a certain mode of being' (Foucault, 1988a, p. 2), or the ways we *stylize* our embodied subjectivity. Foucault is clear that an analysis of the ethical constitution of the subject requires similar levels of attention to the task of self-stylization. Stylization implies an ongoing artistic construction of the self through acts, gestures and practices, as opposed to a stable and normative 'science of life' (Foucault, 1991a, p. 351).

Foucault is clear that the work of self-creation, which he describes as the 'techne of the self', requires a stylistics of existence that has no 'place . . . in the [universalist] body politic' (1991b, p. 42). Rather, '[i]t can only be produced in another, a different place [where there is] the permanent reactivation of an attitude' (1991b, p. 42). This attitude, what Foucault also refers to as a critical ontology of the self, involves the deployment of particular technologies that 'permit individuals to effect by their own means or with the help of others a certain number of operations on their own bodies and souls, thoughts, conduct, and way of being, so as to transform themselves in order to attain a certain state of happiness, purity, wisdom, perfection' (1988b, p. 18). Foucault's notion of subjectivity attends to the experimental practices that individuals perform on themselves.

Foucauldian ethics provides a useful theoretical resource through its shift away from universalist ontologies and grand narratives, towards personal and political economies 'styled' into embodied identities in everyday social and cultural domains. This ethical relationship of the self to the self – and so to others – hears the embodied subject as capable of navigating, challenging and resisting structures of domination. Moreover, Lennard Davis's (1995) proposition concerning the assumed visibility of disability is underscored by Foucault's contention that 'the techniques of the self do not require the same material apparatus as the production of objects' (1991a, p. 369). These techniques, Foucault asserts, 'are often invisible techniques' (1991a, p. 369). Foucault claims that identities are never unified or singular, inferring that the limits that constitute the social and identity mobility of hearing-disabled masculinities can be problematized, raising the possibility of constant, multiple traverses. For our purposes, it is important to analyze the ways that gendered identity created on the surface of the body can render masculine and disabled positionings as an encounter of exchange, built over both accurate and inaccurate readings. Masculinity and disability cannot be analyzed as fixed limits of subjective experience, but as co-ordinates of identity that drift across and into other co-ordinates. The subject is heard as combining a multiplicity of practices and a variety of discourses in its construction.

Judith Butler's notion of the performative provides another theoretical resource for analyzing the complex ways in which young men with hearing disabilities stylize their masculine subjectivities through bodily acts and gestures. For Butler, acts and gestures are '*performative* in the sense that the essence of identity they purport to express are *fabrications* manufactured through corporeal signs and other discursive means' (1990, p. 136). She writes 'gender proves to be performative...constituting the identity is purporting to be...by the very "expressions" that are said to be its results' (1990, p. 25). Considering gender as a corporeal style also involves an attention to the workings of power – for as Butler writes 'gender is a performance with clearly punitive consequences' (1990, p. 139). Butler's notion of the performative enables an exploration of the ways that both masculine and disabled identities become culturally intelligible through performances in social space. Her notion that there is no necessary causal relation between sex and gender incites attention to the potential discontinuities and divergences that occur in the project of creating the illusion of an abiding gendered self. It enables one to listen for the way the construction of identity is a multiple and conditional status of embodied experience that always involves assumptions about masculinity and disability. The trace of the ways in which masculinity and disability are shaped and contested gives an ear to the performative of gendered and embodied being (including disability) and where there can be a constant refusal of any fixed essence of identity.

Methods

The data discussed emerges from doctoral research that explored how young men with moderate to profound hearing disabilities, who communicate primarily in spoken English, construct their masculine embodied subjectivities in different spaces and locales of their everyday worlds. Two research questions are relevant to this paper: How do young men with hearing disabilities simultaneously occupy their gender and their disability? Which specific practices and techniques are significant for understanding hearing disability and men as subjects of masculinities within contemporary Australian spaces and sites? The empirical data were collected by means of exploratory in-depth semi-structured face-to-face interviews and on-line interviews conducted through e-mail. All interviews were conducted in the year 2000. Interviews sought the participant's reflections on matters including social interaction, friendships and personal relationships, sport, education, employment and manhood. The same interview schedule was used for both interviewing methods. In total, 19 formal interviews were conducted. Sixteen of these were face-to-face interviews, two were e-mail interviews and one participant chose to be interviewed by written mail. Follow-up interviews were conducted with five participants by telephone and two by e-mail.

Informants for the research were men aged 18–33 years who had a moderate to profound bilateral or unilateral hearing disability and lived in metropolitan or rural locations of Australia. Men with moderate to profound or unilateral hearing disability were specified as potential subjects for the research study because of the degree of difficulty associated with oral interaction described within these classifications of hearing disability. While a moderate hearing disability may result in difficulty understanding conversational speech and result in a speech impairment, people with a severe hearing disability may not be able to hear conversational speech at all, and rely on visual cues and hearing aids for communication and interaction (Australian Hearing®, 2000).

Advertising for the research project took the form of poster advertisements, letters of invitation and radio announcements. The poster advertisements were placed, with the permission of the relevant organizations and committees, in a variety of regional, local and national Australian newspapers, magazines, websites and noticeboards. In total, 19 men responded via e-mail and phone messages to the call for volunteers to participate in the research. With the exception of six participants, the young men had responded to the poster advertisement and letter of invitation sent out to the mailing list clientele of the South Australian service provider for people with hearing disabilities. A poster advertisement placed in a newspaper yielded three participants. One participant responded to a poster advertisement placed in a local newspaper circulated in the Riverland region of South Australia. A colleague provided me with the name of a male friend with a hearing disability. One participant was a personal associate.

Eleven of the participants had speech impairments. Most of the men identified as heterosexual, one participant identified as bisexual, and two did not speak about their sexual identities in the interviews. With the exception of two men who identified as Italian-Australian and Vietnamese-Australian, the interviewees are primarily white Westerners. All participants use spoken English as their main form of everyday communication. Young men who use sign language as a major component of their everyday interactive encounters were not interviewed. This is despite three of the men being fluent in sign language and who identified as having participated in some activities in their local Deaf communities. Two of these young men stated that they no longer attended activities in their local Deaf communities and did not elaborate on why. The other young man who had recently lost all his hearing said that he had just begun participating in activities in his local Deaf community and planned to become more active in the future. The three young men were not excluded from the study because they use spoken English as their main form of communication. At the time the interviews were conducted, the world in which the participants lived was largely devoid of a sense of community that involved ongoing interactions with other young people with a hearing disability.

Excerpts from the interview transcripts were chosen for inclusion in the dissertation because of their capacity to reflect the workings of discursive and embodied complexity, interchange, encounter and ambiguity that constitute the lived actualities and commitments attending each of the participants' everyday lives. All 19 young men who participated in the study spoke about their experiences of male-to-male friendship relations in the space of the schoolyard. Excerpts from interviews with Andrew and Seth are included in this paper because they best exemplify the power of institutionalized masculinity as cultural ideal in the construction of their gendered subjectivities (see Loeser, 2005, for the detailed analyses of interviews with all participants). The two men's stories give insight into their located and culturally contextualized experiences of negotiating and formulating peer relations in the schoolyard. Their stories reveal different practices and processes employed in and across male peer group cultures in the schoolyard as a way to negotiate reflexively the prescribed codes accorded to masculinity.

The schoolyard: Andrew's story

Andrew's story demonstrates the contradictions inherent in the (re)negotiation of a masculine positioning and the antagonistic nature of subjectivity in the context of male peer dynamics in schoolyard space. He is 21 years old, white, identifies as heterosexual and has a severe hearing disability in both ears. Andrew attended a secondary college in a prestigious suburb near the central business district. He draws attention to the role of his friend James and the way James's behaviour influenced the way boys related to Andrew in the schoolyard. He also speaks about a friend called Adam who introduced him to this male peer group:

Andrew: I did have a bit of trouble with it [bullying] for a while and I just learnt to deal with it ... There were a few people that were different. There was one guy who had big problems hearing. He had no luck at all. There were a few people who got paid out worse than me ... Someone was paying me out [about the hearing] so bad one day I just cracked and told a teacher about it but it didn't really help because everything happened behind the teachers' backs anyway ... They just tell the student off and that's it ... So once I learnt that was a no-go I didn't do that. I just put up with it, just walked past them ... That's when I was most prone to it when I was by myself. This guy James I mentioned ... he would actually stand up for me when people where picking on me and he used to get in a lot of trouble for that ... Yes, he would throw people around ... [and] Adam he helped me a lot when I had trouble in social situations and that. You know, like he'll introduce me to someone before I'll try and introduce myself to someone. He [Adam] is the same age as me ... and we went to the same primary school together and he helped me into the group.

Cassandra: Okay, how did your group of friends, like the guys you were hanging around with ... at high school, how did they respond to people picking on you?

Andrew: People wouldn't pick on me when I was with them ... All my mates, you know, treat me normal ... If I started [school] all over again I would do things a bit differently, like be a stronger person and ... I'd handle the [bullying] situation earlier so it just doesn't keep going. Just put a stop to it straight away like physically.

Australian writers including Connell (1987, 1989, 1992, 1993, 1995, 2000), Kenway and Fitzclarence (1997), Martino (1999, 2005), Martino and Pallotta-Chiarolli (2003) argue that schools are involved in the making of masculinities that are often implicated in forms of violence. Andrew identifies oppressive practice and locates the source of that practice: bullying and discrimination against people who are categorised as 'different' or 'not normal'. The targeting of Andrew when he is alone demonstrates the fragility of masculinities in schoolyard space. The bullies enacted this particular form of violent masculinity only when there was little chance of resistance. Masculinity emerges within and as a collective performance of violence against the disabled body – a body that must be isolated and alone in order for this mode of masculinity to be (re)established and maintained. The violence mobilized towards Andrew's 'disabled body' can therefore be read as an intrinsic aspect of what constituted masculinity for this group of bullies. Normative and Othered masculine identifications are elucidated in a context of social rejection and expulsion. This explanation is reinforced when Andrew says that the school bullies were cautious about teasing him when he was with his male peer group. The presence of James who 'stood up' for Andrew by physically assaulting others worked as a mechanism to counteract the violence of others. Violence also worked as technique for consolidating Andrew's position as a member of a peer group.

Andrew's interview provides a significant insight into the way male power and social positioning can be negotiated and contested. The threat of humiliation, pain and bodily injury was mobilized as a divisive strategy to work out male power relations in schoolyard space. Andrew's attention to James's use of physical violence to counteract bullying further works to demonstrate how modes of contestation can become implicated in the reproduction of certain modes of relating. The use of violence is a compelling mode for masculine conformity. While James acted to resist the denigration of Andrew's status as a hearing-disabled male student, his violent behaviour was still caught up within a normalizing regime of fashioning particular forms of masculine subjectivity through the violation and oppression of others.

It was within such normalizing regimes of violent practice that many of the boys went about the business of fashioning their masculinities, in the interests of establishing their status as 'normal' or 'proper' boys. This explanation is reinforced when Andrew says that if he started school 'all over again' he would utilize his knowledge of the power of physical violence to stop other boys bullying him.

Another issue that is pivotal to the case of James's insulation of Andrew from other men's verbal assaults is the assertion that 'the care of the self . . . can only be conceived of and performed within the exigency of caring for others . . . within our distinct communities' (Probyn, 1993, p. 169). When James inflicted violence on other males as a mechanism to control their abuse of Andrew, he simultaneously re-enacted and reinforced his own 'popular' status amongst his school peers. This status was grounded in his being an exemplar of physical prowess through fighting. James was working to construct and reinforce Andrew's membership within the group, as well as his own gendered status, as dominant, powerful and authoritative. The tactic of violence was the condition of possibility by which James simultaneously asserted his socially exalted status and performed Andrew's social transition from the 'outside' to the 'inside' group. Through this process, a blurring of identificatory boundaries occurred that, in Lloyd's terms, 'involves rejecting the outside–inside alternative . . . replacing it with a mode of thinking the two together' (1997, p. 84). Although power operated within James's relationship with Andrew, masculine positioning and status could never be finalised. The violence mobilized toward Andrew's gendered status impacted on that of James.

The friendship of Adam, James, and other members of the male peer group, performed for Andrew an understanding of his masculine status as socially desirable. The dynamics of this friendship in which Andrew's peers 'treat him normal' was the vehicle through which he understands his gendered subjectivity. Andrew's interview points to the power of male friendship for shaping how young men can come to understand themselves as 'acceptable' and thus 'normal'. Later in the interview, Andrew infers this very important point when he says:

I looked back and I thought, like some people clash and they just don't get on. Even though a lot of people didn't like me, I think that I'm normal when it comes to that.

The possibilities of accessing the normative parameters that determine masculine signification are obtainable for Andrew despite his hearing disability being incited and rejected by certain boys in his school. The production of friendship relations in the schoolyard simultaneously recreated a space in which Andrew could rethink ideas concerning his gendered positioning in social contexts.

Fuss maintains that the fear of the Other, 'which continually *rubs up against*' (1991, p. 6, original emphasis) that which is socially deemed as 'natural' and 'normal', 'concentrates and codifies the very real possibility and ever present collapse of boundaries' (1991, p. 6). The gendered identities of the 'able-bodied' young men were threatened by Andrew's presence. That Andrew's peers and James needed to mobilize violence as a modality by which to establish the specificity of their own gendered identifications, reveals that it is only through practices of disavowal of the 'Other' that their own positionings may be established. Andrew's story highlights the ways that the normalizing regimes for fashioning a particular style of masculinity are negotiated through and governed by relationships with peers. Masculinity is an antagonistic and mediated production, contingent upon approximate performances grounded in what different male peer cultures deem 'acceptable' and 'unacceptable'. In the next section, Seth's narrative demonstrates the aesthetic appearance and performance of the male body as intrinsic to the shaping of what he understands a 'powerful' form of masculinity that is joined to forms of social belonging.

The schoolyard: Seth's story

Seth attended a public secondary school in a working-class suburb. He is 23 years old, white, identifies as heterosexual and has a moderate hearing disability in both ears. Seth says that he experienced ongoing bullying on the football field and basketball court during school recesses. The regime of abusive practices enacted by boys denigrated Seth's gendered status. This experience compounded Seth's school-yard relations to that of social marginalization and expulsion:

Seth: I never had any friends at high school. I never had anybody really close. I didn't hang around with anybody in particular. I just went out and just played sport whether it was with the Year 12s... Yes, or at basketball... I'd just go and play basketball even though I'm in Year 8, I'm playing basketball with the Year 12s sort of thing, you know, I was always out there, you know, doing my bit, playing footy, playing basketball, whatever was playing at the time and I didn't give up even then.

Cassandra: You know how you said within men there's a hierarchy, a pecking order, was one source of status at school people who were good at sport?

Seth: Yes, being good at sport, you were a jock, yes. There were a few things I did well in and yeah, I didn't give up and I tried to accomplish as much as I can... I think it's just personal satisfaction... and yeah, discipline and also looking after yourself, showing that, you know, I am healthy. I believe that, you know, muscularity does lead to masculinity.

It is important to recognise in Seth's narrative that the concept of social margin-alization refers to his exclusion from the establishment of friendship relations with boys of his own year. Seth says he 'never had any friends in high school . . . anybody really close'. This contention is reinforced by Seth's reference to his association with the Year 11 and 12 students by way of sporting activities where he 'didn't hang around with anybody in particular'. The consensus of the notion 'close' with 'friend' therefore designates the company of the boys he interacted with through sport to the realm of informality, boundaries and distance. For Seth, the company of the Year 11 and 12 boys on the sports field enabled interactive participation that he was excluded from amongst students from his own year level. The provision of social linkages imparted by sport allowed his participation in performances of sporting athleticism and ability proscribed to the masculine positioning of 'jock status'.

The pursuit of sporting activities by Seth was situated within an ongoing quest to 'accomplish' masculinity. By way of demonstrating through his muscular physique that he *is* healthy and he *is* masculine, sport was a technique that moved Seth beyond the binary frame of disabled signification and containment. Outward corporeal compliance to the privileged status accorded to the 'jock' role was a technique deployed to affirm a personally ascribed gendered status. What is of further significance is the way that Seth stories his gendered status as being in contrast with those 'other' boys who did not, or could not, participate in this highly competitive gendered arena. The ritual forms of sociability attained through competition, teamwork and the construction of the exterior surface of the body were crucial loci around which dominant constructions of masculinity operated.

Although Seth says that his participation in sporting activities did not lead to the construction of intimate relations with other men, the legitimacy and consent he gave to the symbolism accorded to the competitive and muscular male body can be read as technique implemented in the interest of investing in a particular form of powerful masculinity. Seth's interview is therefore significant in bringing attention to the importance of personal meaning and self-comprehension in the ascription of certain modalities of masculine being. It demonstrates how his knowledge of masculine signifiers was contextualized in schoolyard space. This initiated his desire to perform a sporting masculinity that could enable his participation in the 'pecking order' of male sporting relations.

Seth's interview reveals sport as a strategy implemented to counteract the experience of alienation through conformity to collective Year 11 and 12 schoolyard male practices. Unlike preconceptions that determine the power of masculinity as repressive and working to fix disabled subjects in ongoing relations of identifactory exclusion and lack, the cultivation of a muscular body was a way that Seth attempted to situate himself in the hierarchy of masculine positions based on physical sporting ability. Seth's participation in these activities, however, remained largely problematic amongst young men in his own year level. This is because gendered positionings in the male relational hierarchy were actively worked out through the use of physical violence:

> Seth: I'm not violent. I know that. I know that much . . . I'd walk away and yeah, that sort of thing. I'd give them as much as they gave me . . . I actually got into a fight with a kid at school and I broke his jaw and he gave me a black eye and I was suspended for two weeks . . . It was the only time I ever got – I never got detention or anything like that. I always managed to, you know, wriggle my way out of, you know, fights and stuff and this one time I broke the kid's jaw.

Cassandra: Did you find, Seth, that it was certain people through high school that did the bullying?

Seth: Yeah always, always the top person because it's, I mean, it's some ways classical the top person always picks on the weakling and I guess they viewed me as a weakling because I was hearing impaired.

Seth excerpt demonstrates that his subjectivity, as positioned within the male peer relations in his year level, is imbricated in ongoing acts of violence and renunciation. These acts of physical assault were mobilized by the 'top person' in the schoolyard social network, who attempted to situate Seth in the identifactory position of the hearing-impaired 'other'. Seth's status as 'hearing impaired' allocated him the label of 'weakling' among male students in his year level. According to Seth, 'weakling' is an emasculating definition that correlates with hearing impairment and is antithetical to the 'hardness' of 'top' or high-status male social practice. The acts of physical and verbal assaults that were mobilized by the 'top' person rendered Seth's masculine status something to be disavowed. Writers such as Martino argue that 'a public form of masculinity is enacted through a regime of discursive practices ... at the expense of those boys who are designated as the "other" and who are clearly unable or refuse to engage in such practices' (1999, p. 246). Yet Seth retaliated to physical taunts in this example by breaking the perpetrator's jaw.

Seth is specific that his choice to engage in violence was a mechanism of self-defence, rather than a pronounced characteristic of his masculine being. His story is consistent with Louie's (2002) work on the *wen-wu* [cultural attainment – martial valour] dyad for conceptualizing masculinities in Chinese culture. Louie writes that Chinese masculinity is partially structured through the archetype of *wu*, a martial masculinity symbolized through physical strength and skill, the characteristics of loyalty, righteousness and brotherhood, and conformity to the maxim of being able to bear provocation and not resort to fighting unless necessary. The act of physical retaliation was an occasion for the incitement and intensification of masculine 'strength' that shaped the way Seth related to himself as a gendered subject. Here, Seth's excerpt is significant in that it reveals that in being socially constituted and categorised as the Other, Seth did not *become* the Other. Rather, the social and personal ascription of the 'Othered' category of hearing-impaired onto his gendered being propelled an ethical impulse to provoke a contestation of disability as weakness and inferiority.

Seth's description of his schoolyard experiences illustrates an environment where he, at all times, needed to be ready to face the ongoing potential of legitimate violence in sports and the illegitimate violence of brawling. In this environment, he came to experience his body as a means of serviceable hardware. Such an instrumentalist conception of the masculine body transformed aesthetic concerns to the level of technical efficacy and the desire to signify a 'healthy masculine' image by looking taut and hard. Feats of bravery and the capacity to 'never give up' were essential to Seth's participation in this schoolyard – a site he felt he could not participate in without such performances because of the socially subordinate meanings associated with being 'hearing impaired'. Contrary to the assumption that people with disabilities 'find themselves trapped in a world of non-communication' (Wacquant, 1998, p. 337) and live in 'silent denial' (p. 337), the physical violence and brutality in sport offered Seth a rich vocabulary for personal valorization. The rules for developing a culturally exalted status in schoolyard sports through the coordination and development of his muscular body, and the ability to 'hold one's own', effected a heroic celebration of school life, and offered Seth the opportunity to become an exemplar of the masculine characteristics of independence, physical competence and health. Seth is actively working the discursive contradictions of masculinity. He has developed his own ethics of everyday life – a stoic attitude where you have to suffer to become strong. Strength through suffering facilitates a becoming of what one 'ought' to be.

Conclusion

The stories of Andrew and Seth are crucial and valuable contributions to future analyses of disabled boys in secondary schools. Their stories demonstrate that the active construction of their gendered subjectivity took place through a variety of strategies mobilized to navigate and, at times, subvert aspects of the regulative mechanisms of masculinity deployed by their peers. Often, the young men's tactics were reproductive and aimed at survival and assimilation. Other tactics drew on certain prerogatives of masculine behaviour in an attempt to disrupt the power of others to subordinate and violate their gendered bodies. The mobilization and deployment of such tactics were always contingent on the location or site where a range of differentiated masculinities was made available.

These stories of young male students with hearing disabilities illustrate the power of institutionalized masculinity as cultural ideal in the construction of their gendered subjectivities. Their stories also allow for the identification of different practices and processes employed in and across the schoolyard as a way to negotiate reflexively the prescribed codes accorded to masculinity. Their interviews enable us as observers to distinguish how meaning is accorded to their gendered understandings of self in secondary school, even when their attempts were not always 'successful' or continuous. Their stories also show that while certain individuals or groups may constitute them as 'Other', the young men themselves do not believe that because they have a hearing disability that they are 'abnormal' or should tolerate acts of violence against their being. The men's emphasis on the antagonistic nature of subjectivity in the context of dynamics of the schoolyard points to the uncertainty of settlements of what constitutes dominant masculinity in a given person between and within other groups. It reveals the ruptures and breakages inherent in the ambiguous experience of masculine identification, preventing disabled and masculine identity from being assured as ontologically given of the subject.

This paper demonstrates that framing studies of and about disabled masculine subjectivities at the level of epistemic generalities ignores the comprehensive work and labour required for such subjectivities to appear and disappear in schooling environments. Complicit in this assumption is the way identities of disability and masculinity are not 'natural'. Disability and masculinity are instead the reiterated effect of discourses produced by embodied actors in an attempt to delimit the possibilities by which hearing-disabled young men might experience their masculine subjectivities differently.

It is suggested that other researchers recognize the contestations which hearing-disabled male students enact in the sites of secondary school when developing policies or writing literatures that aim to work against the many forms of oppression in educational institutions. The acts of contestation are acts that can problematize and possibly unsettle the discourses of 'normalcy' and 'Otherness' that can be seen to materialize in respective school communities. Working through the spaces of uncertainty and instability in which young male students with hearing disabilities construct their subjectivities can help work against the repetition of assumptions that often hinder anti-oppressive change in schools. Exploring different ways of becoming masculine and disabled across and through different school sites can help identify those practices that demarcate disabled bodies as already on the outside.

References

Australian Hearing® (2000). *Understanding hearing loss.* Information sheet (NFR2145). New South Wales, Australia.

Benjamin, S. (2001). Challenging masculinities: Disability and achievement in testing times. *Gender and Education, 13,* 39–55.

Butler, J. (1990). *Gender trouble: Feminism and the subversion of identity.* New York: Routledge.

Connell, R.W. (1987). *Gender and power.* Cambridge, UK: Polity Press.

Connell, R.W. (1989). Cool guys, swots and wimps: The interplay of masculinity and education. *Oxford Review of Education, 15,* 291–303.

Connell, R.W. (1992). A very straight gay: Masculinity, homosexual experience, and the dynamics of gender. *American Sociological Review, 57,* 735–731.

Connell, R.W. (1993). Disruptions: Improper masculinities and schooling. In L.Weiss & M. Fine (Eds.), *Beyond silenced voices: Class, race, and gender in United States schools* (pp. 192–208). Albany: State University of New York Press.

Connell, R.W. (1995). *Masculinities.* St. Leonards, Australia: Allen & Unwin.

Connell, R.W. (2000). *The men and the boys.* St. Leonards, Australia: Allen & Unwin.

Davis, L. (1995). *Enforcing normalcy: Disability, deafness and the body.* London: Verso.

Foucault, M. (1988a). The ethic of care for the self as a practice of freedom: An interview with Michel Foucault on January 20, 1984. Conducted by R. Fornet-Betancourt, H. Backer, & A. Gomez-Muller. In J. Bernaur & D. Rasmussen (Eds.), *The final Foucault* (pp. 1–20). Cambridge, MA: MIT Press.

Foucault, M. (1988b). Technologies of the self. In L. Martin, H. Gutman & P. Hutton (Eds.), *Technologies of the self: A seminar with Michel Foucault* (pp. 16–49). Amherst: The University of Massachusetts Press.

Foucault, M. (1991a). On the genealogy of ethics: An overview of work in progress. In P. Rabinow (Ed.), *The Foucault reader: An introduction to Foucault's thought* (pp. 340–372). London: Penguin.

Foucault, M. (1991b). What is Enlightenment? In P. Rabinow (Ed.), *The Foucault reader: An introduction to Foucault's thought* (pp. 32–50). London: Penguin.

Fuss, D. (1991). Inside/out. In D. Fuss (Ed.), *Inside/out: Lesbian theories, gay theories* (pp. 1–10). Routledge: New York.

Gilbert, R., & Gilbert, P. (1998). *Masculinity goes to school.* St. Leonards, Australia: Allen & Unwin.

Kenway, J., & Fitzclarence, L. (1997). *Masculinities, violence and schooling: Challenging poisonous pedagogy.* Working paper 96047, Deakin Centre for Education and Change, Deakin University, Geelong, Australia.

Lloyd, M. (1997). Foucault's ethics and politics: A strategy for feminism? In M. Lloyd & A. Thacker (Eds.), *The impact of Michel Foucault on the social sciences and humanities* (pp. 78–101). New York: St. Martins Press.

Loeser, C. (2005). *Embodiment, ethics and the ear: Constructions of masculine subjectivity by young men with hearing disabilities in contemporary Australia.* Unpublished doctoral dissertation, University of South Australia, Australia

Louie, K. (2002). *Theorising Chinese masculinity: Society and gender in China.* Cambridge, UK: Cambridge University Press.

Martino, W. (1999). 'Cool boys', 'party animals', 'squids' and 'poofters': Interrogating the dynamics and politics of masculinities in school. *British Journal of Sociology of Education, 20,* 239–263.

Martino, W. (2005). Issues in boys' education: Encouraging broader definitions of masculinities in schools. *Curriculum Leadership: An Electronic Journal for Leaders in Education, 3*(33), 1–6. Retrieved July 7, 2009, from http://www.curriculum.edu.au/leader/issues_in_boys%E2%80%99_education:_encouraging_broader_def,12017.html?issueID=9796

Martino, W., & Pallotta-Chiarolli, M. (2003). *So what's a boy? Addressing issues of masculinity and schooling.* Maidenhead, UK: Open University Press.

Probyn, E. (1993). *Sexing the self: Gendered positions in cultural studies.* London: Routledge.

Wacquant, L. (1998). The prizefighter's three bodies. *Ethos, 63,* 325–352.

Mobile asylums: psychopathologisation as a personal, portable psychiatric prison

Valerie Harwood

Faculty of Education, University of Wollongong, Wollongong NSW, Australia

Psychopathologisation, broadly understood as processes that lead to the effects of being psychopathologised, can have considerable consequences for isolating students from education. This can be especially the case for children and young people affected by the racialisation of behaviour and/or socio-economic disadvantage. Drawing on Foucault's analysis of the relationship between the psychiatrist and the asylum in his lectures 'Psychiatric Power', the argument is made that these effects can be tantamount to being institutionalised in a mobile asylum. Portrayal of the asylum in the American television series *House MD* is used to highlight how, if we rely on classic depictions of the asylum–psychiatrist couplet, we risk missing – or minimising, the mobile asylum that some young children experience when they are psychopathologised in schooling.

Introduction

Cut to the Mayfield Psychiatric Hospital parking lot. Dr Nolan is leaving. He pulls out his car keys and sees House sitting on a railing close to his car.

Dr Nolan: Not the most exciting use of the overnight pass I've ever seen.
House: She left.
Dr Nolan: And ...
House: I'm lost.
Dr Nolan: [*Sits next to House*] I'm going to write your letter ... to the medical board, recommending that they give your license back.
House: You can't just console me by giving me a lollipop when I skin my knee.
Dr Nolan: Well, two things just happened. You got hurt, which means you connected to someone else strongly enough to miss them. And more important ... You recognized the pain and came to talk to me, instead of hiding from it in the Vicodin bottle. The fact that you're hurting and you came here, the fact that you're taking your meds and we're talking right now ... Come inside and get some sleep. Tomorrow you can start saying your good-byes.
[Transcript from *House MD* (Friend, 2009)]

The asylum is the psychiatrist's body, stretched and distended to the dimensions of an establishment, extended to the point that his power is exerted as if every part of the asylum is a part of his own body, controlled by his own nerves. (Foucault, 2006b, p. 181)

The centrality of the psychiatrist to the asylum is evocatively portrayed in the above statement by Foucault (2006b). Made during his 1973–74 Lectures at the Collège de France, the discussion where he offers this remarkable amalgam is concerned chiefly with the desire to account for the 'stamp of medicine' on 'asylum power' (2006b, p. 181).[1] This very same necessity is evident in the depiction of the psychiatrist–asylum couplet in a recent double episode of the television drama *House MD* (Friend, 2009). The dialogue provided above is one of several scenes with interactions between new patient, Gregory House, and chief psychiatrist, Dr Nolan. Throughout this medical drama the power of the psychiatrist is evocatively aligned with the asylum in such a manner that the two are veritably indistinguishable.[2] Portrayal of the psychiatrist and asylum in *House MD* echoes Foucault's analysis of the two, even though this was directed toward the asylums of the nineteenth century. This representation, with its uncanny capturing of Foucault's historical sketch of the asylum is exactly my point of departure in this essay.[3]

My intention is to mount the argument that psychopathologisation can result in confinement in a mobile asylum. From this perspective asylums do not exist only where there are walls, locked doors and where the long-held identifiable systems of incarceration and domination prevail. While internment in a recognisable asylum was a pre-eminent feature in the depiction of House's madness, what I hope to outline is how for children and young people, a mobile asylum can arise. Though speculative, this essay seeks to respond to an uncomfortable doubt that arose in recent research into psychopathologisation and disadvantage. Psychopathologisation can be understood as occurring when children and young people experience being subjected to the truth and power of psychopathology (Harwood, 2004). Existence of psychopathologisation is evident in the diagnosis (or suspicion) of a mental disorder and via being subject to the array of practices tied to or invoking questions of psychopathology (for instance: medication, exclusion from school, school assessments, attendance at psychiatric or psychological clinics, child welfare, police, juvenile justice). Initially devised for Australia, the study focused on sites in four Australian states where there were both high rates of prescription medications for Attention Deficit Hyperactivity Disorder (ADHD) and significant social and economic disadvantage (Harwood, 2010). In these sites key youth services were targeted, and semi-structured interviews were held with youth service professionals.

Troubled by the findings that suggested the extent of psychopathologisation evident in these young people's lives, the study was broadened to include interviews from two locations outside of Australia: in Cambridgeshire, England and in the Greater Bay Area of San Francisco.[4] The youth professionals interviewed in these locations (two in England and three in the USA) were working in areas of socio-economic disadvantage that had comparatively high rates of child and youth behavioural problems. In this essay, due to the restriction of space, I have elected to draw exclusively on two stories from one of these interviews. These are stories that compellingly suggest why we might pause to rethink how we understand the asylum.

Asylum walls

The dialogue between Dr Nolan and House that opens this essay is taken from a scene near the end of the two-part movie-length episode that launched season six of *House MD*, the award-winning US medical drama televised in several countries worldwide (Wicclair, 2008). In these opening episodes Gregory House (known as 'House'), the main character of the popular series, is voluntarily committed to Mayfield Psychiatric Hospital for Vicodin withdrawal and for delusions. Waking from drug withdrawal, the story unfolds as House fights succumbing to the care of the chief psychiatrist, Dr Nolan. This relationship between the two doctors (one now a psychiatric patient, the other, the psychiatrist) is pivotal because House is dependent upon Nolan's recommendation if he is to return to his career as a medical doctor. However, a problem arises because 'Dr. Nolan refuses to sign a recommendation to the board of medicine saying he is able to return to work', for this reason, 'House resigns to stay at the hospital and get his clearance' (Fox, 2010). In the scene cited in this essay House had just been granted an overnight pass, the purpose of which he had used to visit the woman with whom he had formed a romantic attachment; but the woman had rejected him. Sitting outside of the hospital, House encounters Dr Nolan, who assesses him favourably, and ushers him 'inside', where he can 'get some sleep'. Returning to the looming architecture of the hospital to 'sleep' conjures a surprising juxtaposition of tranquillity; one synchronised with House's newfound accommodation of his psychiatrist's advice. This linking of asylum building and psychiatrist is a recurring feature of this episode, and invites us to draw together the inseparability of the two.

Mayfield Psychiatric Hospital figures at the epicentre of these episodes. Filming in this fictional hospital took place on site at Greystone Park Psychiatric Hospital in Parisappany-Troy Hills, New Jersey. Originally named the State Asylum for the Insane at Morristown, Greystone Park was opened in 1876 'as a state-of-the-art mental health facility' that covered over 700 acres. Although designed for around 500 patients, in the mid-twentieth century this number rose to more than 7000 (Santiago, 2009). These numbers reduced significantly in the latter part of the twentieth century, with the hospital finally closing its doors to patients in 2007 (New Jersey Department of Human Services, 2007). In Figure 1,

STATE ASYLUM FOR THE INSANE, AT MORRISTOWN, N. J.
(PERSPECTIVE VIEW.)

Figure 1. Artist's depiction of the proposed State Asylum for the Insane at Morristown, New Jersey, Perspective View. The name was changed in 1925 to New Jersey State Hospital at Greystone Park, and it was later known as Greystone Park Psychiatric Hospital. The image is estimated to be circa 1850. It is a depiction of the building, and was reproduced in the *Report of the Commissioners Appointed to Select a Site and Build an Asylum for the Insane of the State of New Jersey* (1872). This image is sourced from Images from the History of Medicine, United States National Library of Medicine, National Institutes of Health (A010535; http://ihm.nlm.nih.gov/luna/servlet/view/search?q=A010535). Reproduced with permission.

Figure 2. Main Building, State Asylum for the Insane at Morristown, photo circa 1891–1908, Department of Institutions and Agencies, 1876–1965 (New Jersey State Archives, Department of State). Reproduced with permission.

the iconographic front of the main building is discernible (which also figured in frequent scenes in the two episodes of *House MD*).

That the hospital exterior is striking goes without saying (Figure 2). The buildings are extensive, indeed, elaborate, and built to the 'distinctive' Kirkbride Plan that was used only in the USA. Named after the psychiatrist Thomas Kirkbride (1809–1883) and designed by the architect Samuel Sloan, Greystone Park incorporates pavilions, using an 'echelon arrangement' with the structure forming a 'linear plan ... made up of short but connected pavilions, arrayed in a shallow V' (Yanni, 2007, p. 14).[5] Greystone Park was what Erving Goffman would call a total institution, with an:

> encompassing or total character ... symbolized by the barrier to social intercourse with the outside and to departure that is often built right into the physical plant, such as locked doors, high walls, barbed wire, cliffs, water, forests, or moors. (1961, p. 4)

Within such a mental institution, as Foucault commented referring to Goffman's work, 'a patient ... is placed within a field of fairly complicated power relations' (Foucault, 2000a, p. 356).

The visual spectacle created by filming *House MD* at Greystone Park presents the power of the asylum, one that is intricately bound up with its structure. In these two episodes, the psychiatrist personified by Dr Nolan does not yield. Although challenged by the infamously controlling and conniving House, the message is clear: it is the psychiatrist, accompanied by the mechanisms of the asylum apparatus and underpinned by the quintessential building that triumphs.

This example from the recently screened episode of *House MD*[6] clearly conveys the powerful way in which the asylum functions as a signifier *par excellence* for madness and its treatment in our culture. The influence of this architecture is not surprising given the presence of asylum structures over the last 200–300 years in western culture, the more recent closures following the publicised de-institutionalisation movements of the mid-twentieth century (Fakhoury & Priebe,

2007). What Foucault's assessment reminds us of and why it is so valuable, is that it pinpoints the relation *between* the asylum and the psychiatrist as what assures asylum power. When Foucault (2006b) set out to analyse psychiatric practices in these lectures he highlighted the shift made from his previous analyses in the *History of Madness* (Foucault, 2006a). The move is from one focused upon the examination of representations via 'the perception of madness' to an analysis that emphasises power. Concern with psychiatric power in these lectures is reflective of the view that grasping this form of power assists in understanding the mechanisms of normalisation (Foucault, 2000b). Attentiveness to power is an insight that has had a good deal of influence for critical studies into medicine and mental illness (Bunton & Peterson, 1997; Rose, 1989, 1998) and psychiatry (Bolton, 2008), and is one that can assist in the development of another conception of the asylum.

Power, the clinic and token knowledge

The necessity of the relationship between the psychiatrist and the asylum raises a crucial problem for my argument in this paper.[7] Namely if Foucault's line of reasoning is adhered to, what is the relation that exists for the mobile asylum (is it between the psychiatrist, or is it more than that individual specialisation?) and does this relationship underwrite the power of the mobile asylum? Contrary to commonplace depictions such as in popular media like *House MD*, in the mobile asylum neither walls nor the sole figure of the psychiatrist are central. Yet, to think of an asylum without walls is to expunge one of its principal features, and to cleave the psychiatrist from a central position could, arguably annul if not reduce the potency of asylum-power. A way forward in the conceptualisation of the mobile asylum is to seize on the weight that Foucault placed on the clinic in these lectures, and to explore how the clinic, envisioned as interconnecting networks of knowledge-power, may constitute a relationship that produces asylum-type power.

In his analysis of the specific points at which power is exercised effectively in the asylum, the clinic is identified as *the* fundamental site in the propounding of psychiatric power:

> The enormous institutional importance of the clinic in the daily life of psychiatric hospitals from the 1830s until today is due to the fact that the doctor constituted himself as a master of truth through the clinic. (Foucault, 2006b, p. 187)

Here the reference is not restricted to the asylums of history, but right up to the present moment. But what is the clinic? On the one hand, as Long logically concludes, it 'is first a place to diagnose and treat sick persons' (1992, p. 137). It is however more than that, it is 'also a way of thinking and speaking; it is a discursive practice that links health with knowledge' (Long, 1992, p. 137). Combining these it is feasible to challenge the privileged position of the clinic as a site (the doctor's office, for example) and extend it outward. The clinic then could be conceived as a form of power, a network that 'diagnoses and treats sick persons' via the 'discursive practices that links health and knowledge'.[8] The prominence to the asylum that Foucault attributed to the clinic can be applied to the mobile asylum, even withstanding the sweeping changes that have occurred since deinstitutionalisation. The proposition being, firstly, that in our contemporary moment, and especially with deinstitutionalisation and the increases of community-orientated services, the clinic–mobile asylum may function in lieu of the psychiatrist–asylum. It may well offer a means to conceptualise how the figure of the psychiatrist has been displaced. Secondly, this relationship may well underwrite the power of the mobile asylum.

To conceive of the clinic as not tied to a specific asylum, and yet functioning in a manner that produces mobile asylum power onto children appears unworkable. Turning to the 1973–74 lectures presents a decisive route to establish how such a clinic may operate: 'tokens of knowledge'. These 'the tokens of knowledge are magnified in the clinic . . . The tokens of knowledge, and not the contents of science, allow the alienist to function as a doctor within the asylum' (Foucault, 2006b, p. 187). It is, however, what these 'tokens of knowledge' allow, that is essential:

> These insignia of knowledge enable him to exercise an absolute surplus power in the asylum, and ultimately to identify himself with the asylum body. These tokens of knowledge allow him to constitute the asylum as a sort of medical body that cures through its eyes, ears, words, gestures and machinery. (Foucault, 2006b, pp. 187–188)

Returning to the problem at the heart of this essay, which is the power of the proposed mobile asylum, it is possible to use this analysis to suppose how a surplus of power might be manifested. Points of analysis from these lectures where Foucault emphasised psychiatric power and how it functions offers a means to theorise the power that acts upon young individuals who are interred in ways that are tantamount to confinement.

In the remainder of this essay my objective to work with this idea of the centrality of the clinic as a means to tease out this notion of the mobile asylum. To do this I draw on two case studies of children described by Nancy, the US interview participant who had considerable expertise and experience in the field of child and youth disability. While this interview does focus on issues in the State of California, the insight to be gained is of consequence in other regions experiencing alarming rates of child and youth psychopathologisation (for instance, the UK, Australia, Canada and several European countries) (Scheffler, Hinshaw, Modrek, & Levine, 2007). The first case study, describing Elijah's confinement in the family apartment, demonstrates how the tokens of knowledge enable the action of a clinic that can occur between institutions (the school, the hospital, welfare agencies). In the second case study, the emphasis is on legislation: another form of token knowledge that serves to make a clinic between institutions possible. The aim in presenting these stories is to convey the *effects of power* as these manifested toward and acted upon these two children. The marked difference between these stories and the confinement that occurs in the classic psychiatrist–asylum couplet (as demonstrated in the example from *House MD*) points to the possibility of the existence of the mobile asylum.

The mobile asylum[9]

Diagnostic categories[10] such as ADHD are tokens of knowledge that are connected to an extensive array of cultural practices of psychopathologisation, many of which are associated with diverse coercive mechanisms. A case in point is the distinction between having ADHD and being ADHD:

There's this shift and I've been hearing it in the last two to three years, where now it isn't that you *have* ADHD, suddenly you are ADHD. I'm starting to hear 'My child's ADHD', not my child *has* it. (Nancy interview)[11]

To be ADHD as opposed to having ADHD is a subtlety that could well pass as nothing more than a slight change in language. How can a child 'be' ADHD, and how can such psychopathologisation be so effective, when, compared to the weight of internment in an institution, it is little more than a diagnostic category? A clue can be found in the tokens of knowledge that are readily available, and make possible, a clinic that can exist between institutions. These tokens of knowledge include far more than categories. While categories have a central role, how these translate into power needs to be carefully investigated. In the cases discussed below, categories lend support to other tokens of knowledge such as pieces of legislation that make it legal to detain children and young people on the basis of the degree of their psychopathology. Because these tokens of knowledge are so readily available and all too straightforwardly applied, internment within the solid walls of one institution is not necessary. A clinic can thus operate between institutions and draw on token knowledge such as categories and legislation that both supports and gives power to these categories. This can operate in ways that can *effect* a production of power that is uncannily like the asylum power synonymous with the psychiatrist–asylum couplet.

A clinic between institutions: Elijah's story[12]

The story of Elijah, a nine-year-old African-American child, offers a poignant example.[13] Elijah's story was told to me in an interview by Nancy who had come into contact with the nine-year-old and his 23-year-old mother because of considerable difficulties that were occurring in school. Elijah had been sent home by his teacher on 'the very first day of school . . . after 30 minutes or so because he's throwing papers and he won't sit down and he's openly defiant'. Psychopathologisation can occur when a teacher speaks of a child 'having behaviour problems'. In this instance, whilst an official diagnosis is not conferred, the spectre of diagnosis is raised (Harwood, 2006). Attribution of diagnostic categories does more than invoke an allusion to something that is of little consequence because it is purely speculative, or even an aside in a school staffroom. To assume that there are no effects without diagnosis is to miss the power of psychopathologisation (Harwood, 2006, 2010). When a child is spoken of as having a mental disorder, these words could come from a number of people, some are associated with institutions such as schools, clinics, hospitals, family drop-in centres and others are not. They may be in line at the supermarket, in the family, friends, other children, or in the media. When commenting on a child's behaviour, this could possibly function as token knowledge, that given the action of power, could have the propensity to contribute to the psychopathologisation of a child that in some instances could result in what is, in effect, a mobile asylum.

In Elijah's case, the teacher that suspected psychopathology was in her first year of teaching, and Nancy commented on how she sympathised with the difficulties that the teacher faced in a 'room full of kids'.[14] One day when he threw paper and ran from the room refusing to do as asked, the school sent Elijah for psychiatric evaluation at the Children's Hospital. The hospital did not detain Elijah, since according to their assessment 'he's not a danger to himself or others, so therefore doesn't meet the criteria that would allow us to keep him involuntarily here at the hospital' (Nancy interview). The hospital did recommend, however, that he could benefit from assessment for special education.

Assessment for access to special education provisions required Elijah's mother to complete a questionnaire. Nancy explained that when 'mum is filling out a questionnaire about her child, she feels like the school already hates her child, they think he's a horrible child, so she minimises all his behaviours at home'. Based on the mother's responses, Elijah did not satisfy the requirement of being 'cross context', which meant he did not qualify for special education. This led to the decision that Elijah had social maladjustment, which 'is not the same as disability, it is cultural or socio-economic' (Nancy interview). Failure to qualify for special education provision meant the school refused Elijah entry, and he ended up out of school for several months. With the school refusing to have Elijah, and being a single mother who needed to work, there was little else to do but leave her son at home. She did her best and organised for Elijah to have the phone number of a neighbour in case of any emergencies. School days were spent like this, for several months on end: day after day, at home in an apartment, while his mother went to work to support them both.

John, a hospital social worker, was in contact with Elijah and his mother, and reported to Nancy that the young boy was now 'horribly depressed and suicidal' (Nancy interview). He had contacted Nancy to inform her that he had 'diagnosed Elijah with ADHD and ODD [Oppositional Defiant Disorder], because "I've gotta give him a label cause I've gotta get him some help"' (Nancy interview). As she recounted, John had expressed exasperation because 'Elijah's been on waiting lists to get these medical assessments that the school said he had to get' (Nancy interview). With ADHD and ODD, Elijah was eventually given a behavioural support plan, and access to a psychologist, and, as Nancy pointed out, 'there will be immense pressure on mum to medicate him'. As these psychopathologising interventions proceeded, the school principal commented to Nancy that 'part of the problem might be that he's kinda bored "cause he tests high school on his verbal"'. Nancy had reviewed the behaviour checklists completed by the classroom teacher, and on 'every single thing he was the most extreme worst case'. Armed with this information, Nancy questioned the teacher, asking her, 'Is there nothing likeable about this child? Is he Satan? Because when you read this you would think Satan has come to your school'. The teacher's response to this question was that they did not really know Elijah, because 'he's never lasted more than 30 minutes in my classroom'. Nevertheless, Elijah was barred from school and confined to the family apartment.

Elijah was in a mobile asylum. When he had attended school, he was taken from that school to a Children's Hospital for psychiatric evaluation. He spent four months at home, alone. Days were lived in an apartment with no access through the boundaries of the school. Later, when he was not permitted to attend school, he had been assessed by a social worker, which led to the diagnosis with ADHD and ODD. Elijah was later put on a behaviour support plan and allocated a psychologist. Next he was a candidate for referral to a more restricted school, and there was the spectre of medication (alongside the practices medication routines). The isolation endured by Elijah appears to be the obvious point at which the asylum appears, and in this respect there is the risk of attributing the asylum on the basis of the presence of walls.

However, this would be to err on an analysis that emphasises the *perception of madness*. In this case, this means recourse to recognisable representations of the asylum. Relying on the apartment as the indicator of the asylum additionally could lead to overlooking the effects of what Priebe (2004), drawing on Goffman (1961), terms 'institutionalisation without walls'. This form of institutionalisation can be identified in community populations of psychopathologised[15] adults where for example assertive outreach services 'can develop phenomena of institutionalization such as forms of persistently bizarre interactional behaviour between staff and patients' (Priebe, 2004, p. 81). If Elijah's story is analysed from the standpoint of power, the effects of institutionalisation can be witnessed both within and outside of the apartment. It is this surplus of power generated by the clinic–mobile asylum (and not the psychiatrist–asylum) that came to affect Elijah, preventing him from attending school and confining him to solitude in the family apartment.

As Elijah's story demonstrates, the surplus power of the clinic can directly act on a young person, causing them to be interred in new ways. For Elijah, the token knowledge of his suspected psychopathologisation led to his confinement, and this occurred independently of an asylum such as Greystone Park Psychiatric Hospital. From one angle, it could be maintained that he was excluded from school, and not confined. Although this interpretation is correct, because it does not seek out power, it misses assessing the effects of what can so easily pass as only exclusion from classes. The danger of this assessment is that Elijah's very real and very distressing experience of confinement remains invisible. Calling upon the idea of the mobile asylum permits a view that has the potential to ascertain the workings of power, and thereby more closely appreciate the experiences of this child.

The token knowledge of 5150 legislation: Martin's story

The power that produces the mobile asylum relies on many elements, the foremost of which is the diagnostic category. These categories are not only significant as token knowledge to be applied to an individual. In Elijah's story, the spectre of behaviour, and the recourse to diagnosis loomed large. When he was not diagnosed due to the lack of 'cross context' the effects were stultifying, with his banishment from school and the consequent virtual incarceration in the family apartment. When he was diagnosed he moved from the apartment and into psychological treatment and educational remediation, with both serving to inscribe psychopathology. Although forming an integral token knowledge that can be directly applied, these categories also inform a range of contemporary practices, such as schooling provision and legislation for psychiatric intervention.

Elijah's story draws our attention to power, provoking reconsideration of the form an asylum can take and where it may occur. The second story is concerned with the operation of power again; but this time, power that was wielded via recourse to the token knowledge of legislation. The token knowledge of this legislation formed part of the rationale that led a principal to use a SUV (sport utility vehicle) to give chase to and contain Martin, a six-year-old African-American child. Martin had been sent to the principal's office.[16] In this office, when he was told that his mother was being called, Martin ran out, running from the school into the busy neighbourhood and down a busy road. The principal, together with his secretary, for reasons of concern, quickly sought to follow the boy. They got into 'this big, black SUV, he's a white principal, big guy, and he's chasing after this little kid' (Nancy interview). When they did get to Martin they tried to pull him into the SUV. The effort to pull him into the vehicle resulted in Martin becoming bruised, an indisputable fact evidenced by the photos taken by his mother after the incident.

Deciding 'he's a danger to himself', the two school personnel called the police. A 5150 is the term for a piece of legislation contained in the State of California's Welfare Institutions Code. This legislation authorises involuntary incarceration under psychiatric care, for a period of up to 72 hours. The code depends on two conditions; the identification of a mental disorder and that the individual with this disorder 'is a danger to others, or to himself or herself, or gravely disabled'.[17] The Code allows for a 'peace officer' or authorised psychiatric staff (of the institution or, for example, a mobile crisis team) to take the individual into custody for a period of 72 hours in order to provide for evaluation and treatment. When the 'peace officers', the police, arrived, they proceeded to take the young boy into custody. Mistakenly, the frightened child was relieved, believing that the police were there to help him. To the child's surprise, the police handcuffed him explaining that this was the official procedure. In the report on the incident the police made positive comments about the child, which Nancy described as something to the effect 'the child was very agreeable and compliant to everything that I asked him to do'. The child was handcuffed, even though the police car had a protective screen, and the report states that the child was 'compliant'. Nancy was of the view that 'I would not have believed that they would have handcuffed a white child in a suburban school'.

Handcuffed, the child was taken by police vehicle to the Children's Hospital for psychiatric assessment. After two to three hours in the hospital the staff decided that 'while he may have ADHD or something like that, there isn't any reason to hold him'. Although he was sent home, the school did not permit him to return, stipulating that he was not safe there, because he 'ran off'. The boy was put on a '45 day interim placement while they figure what to do' (Nancy interview). Over this period the school organised 'one hour per week of home instruction'. The mother, 'who was the only breadwinner' and had 'other children' ended up losing her job. At the same time, the Children's Hospital continued to assess the child, investigating possible diagnoses. As with Elijah, these were the pathway to returning to school since it would provide for special education funding provision. Medication was also likely to accompany the diagnosis, even though, as Nancy points out, 'parents don't ever seem to be told that the medication doesn't seem to have any impact on learning . . . parents are willing to medicate because maybe he will do better at school'. Two instances of token knowledge tied to the category are apparent: the connection between diagnosis and special education provision, and with medication. Both Elijah and Martin were barred from their schools and both were subjected to diagnostic processes with the purpose to establish a disorder. The presence of which would secure the funding support that was demanded by the schools to allow the children to return to class.

Martin would not, according to Nancy, have been put on the interim placement order had the family had 'significant financial resources'. If that had been the case, 'there would have been a placement'. Nancy, and the other child and youth professionals interviewed in the study indicated that children from racial minorities and/or poor backgrounds had markedly different experiences in relation to perceived behavioural problems (Harwood, 2010). It is not an accident that both of the stories told by Nancy were of black children: there is much cause for concern regarding the racialisation of diagnosis, with black children over-represented in the special education classroom (Ferri & Connor, 2005; Fitzgerald, 2009). Evaluating these experiences as instances of a 'mobile asylum' affords countenance of the institutionalising – and racialising – effects that may be occurring. Recalling the insights from Goffman's (1961) *Asylums*, it is wise to remember that behaviours that would appear to belong to madness are arguably the product of institutionalising effects.[18] Following Goffman then, there are very real *institutionalising effects* occurring for children such as Elijah and Martin confined in their own home. These effects can be missed if the asylum and institutionalisation are not recognised.

Confinement within one institution did not occur for Elijah and Martin. At least, not in the way that confinement and internment in traditional asylums are understood, whether from the eighteenth century of Foucault's analysis, or from the twentieth century of Goffman's famous sociological study. Broadly speaking, these asylums were a distinct entity, and the inmates belonged to, and were identified with, a singular institution. Whether it be the Bicêtre of Phillipe Pinel in late eighteenth-century Paris, or the Washington mental institution in the ethnography by Erving Goffman in the mid-twentieth, the asylum held true as a rigid structure. Although the apartments that the boys were contained within had a rigid structure, the walls that held them are not analogous to the asylum–psychiatrist couplet described by Foucault and so aptly portrayed in *House MD*. Nor can the apartment be considered as an asylum in and of itself. Neither Elijah nor Martin were 'free' once they could move beyond those walls, for they remained very much subject to the token knowledge of a clinic, albeit one that seems somewhat intangible compared to the clinic that is easily perceptible in the asylum setting. This clinic that administers a power that can produce the mobile asylum can position children with mental disorders, and effectively prevent school attendance. This clinic operated between institutions, ensuring that confinement did not cease with movement out of an apartment. This suggests the importance of a distinction between the 'institution without walls' proposed by Priebe (2004) and the mobile asylum. More than institutionalisation happened to the children: they were physically blocked, prevented from entering places. Their movements were restricted, and these impositions were particularly effective by virtue of their status as children, where their choices were drastically closed down.

Conclusion: a case for the mobile asylum?

Integral to the function, indeed the identity of the asylum, is the type of power; a power intimately controlled by the 'psychiatrist's nerves' (Harwood, 2006), and that produced the psychiatrist–asylum. The asylum, portrayed to stereotype in *House MD*, is surrounded by walls and contains a plethora of recognisable idiosyncrasies. It is a place characterised by the enmeshing of architectural boundaries with the psychiatrist's all-knowing persona. While some grandiose asylum structures remain, and some feature in popular broadcasts that serve to enshrine the psychiatrist–asylum couplet, it would be mistaken to believe that asylums exist solely in this form. To contend the existence of a mobile asylum is to depart from this evocative image, and to look instead to the exercising of power that can produce asylum-type effects. The stories of Elijah and Martin reveal certain powerful practices that deserve reconsideration.[19]

There is, however, a response to be made to an invisible interlocutor who would be more than justified to ask, 'why asylums?' The rationale for this choice is twofold. First, what might be missed if we assume a tidy demarcation between psychopathologisation of child behaviour and what Erving Goffman (1961) called the 'total institution'? Would the latter exist to serve a relational purpose of extremity, symbolic of the sobering finitude of mental disorder? Second, has the emphasis that has continued to be placed on the asylum as the marker of the extreme caused us to be unaware of the extremes that can and do exist via the psychopathologisation of child behaviour?

For this reason it is crucial to revisit the orthodoxy of the asylum. This requires a shift in focus from the perception of madness (for instance, the ADHD child) to one concerned to interpret the effects of power. To argue for the mobile asylum is to argue for the need to be alert for and recognise power and the frightening effects that certain practices, regardless of their intent, can engender. If the psychiatrist–asylum couplet is challenged we may well be better positioned to appreciate the workings of a power that can confine children and young people. The psychiatrist is no more orchestrating from a site positioned above and beyond us than the asylum is the only place to which the psychopathologised are confined. In our contemporary experience of psychopathologisation, the asylum as motif of madness needs to be re-evaluated. It can no longer be identified by distinction from the world of the everyday, but rather, by its faint assimilation amongst us.

Acknowledgements

My thanks to the editors of this special issue, Anna Hickey-Moody and Vicki Crowley, for their kind support of this paper. My thanks also to the two universities that hosted me during my sabbatical in 2008: The Beatrice Bain Research Group, University of California, Berkeley, and the Department of History and Philosophy of Science, University of Cambridge.

Notes

1. This discussion occurs in Lecture Eight, 9 January 1974.
2. For a fascinating discussion on the increasing use of biologically based interpretations of the mind in literature see Marco Roth's (2009) essay 'The rise of the neuronovel'.
3. For a discussion that departs from Foucault's account of the rise of the asylum and the psychiatrist see Wright (1997).
4. Details of the locations have been altered to maintain confidentially. Due to budget constraints the international site selection was made to reflect the original aims of the project (to investigate the occurrence of the high diagnostic rates of behavioural disorders in areas of disadvantage) and to coincide with the locations whre the author took sabbatical leave in 2008 (University of California, Berkeley and University of Cambridge).
5. The Kirkbride Plan was based on 'moral treatment' of the insane, an approach that was enthusiastically endorsed by Thomas Kirkbride (Yanni, 2007). Moral treatment, developed in the late eighteenth century, and popularised in the nneteenth, departed from what was viewed as punitive and cruel treatment of the insane. The approach stresses 'respectful and kind treatment under all circumstances, and in most cases manual labor, attendance on religious worship on Sunday, the establishment of regular habits and of self control, diversion of the mind from morbid trains of thought' (Brigham, 1847, p. 1).
6. Premiered in the USA on 21 September 2009; screened in Australia on 31 January 2010.

7. The argument in this essay has benefited from the contributions and criticisms made by the two anonymous reviewers. My thanks for their input.
8. See also my discussion of biopower and biopedagogies (Harwood, 2009).
9. This discussion is tentative, and is presented as a first attempt to theorise the power that can confine and detain psychopathologised children.
10. Mental disorders such as ADHD are defined in the *Diagnostic and Statistical Manual of Mental Disorders* (American Psychiatric Association, 2000). Disorders that are associated with behaviour problems can include, but are not restricted to ADHD, Conduct Disorder, Oppositional Defiant Disorder. With the application of the concept 'co-morbidity', terms may also include such disorders as Bipolar Disorder (Masi et al., 2006) or depression (Brown, 2008).
11. From an interview conducted by the author in 2008. All names and identifying information has been changed.
12. The stories of Elijah and Martin are challenging because of the issues that they convey. The re-telling of these stories by Nancy could be questioned for its veracity, and to what extent it can be taken as plausible. My view is that these stories, from a highly respected professional who has developed close contact with and the respect of the individuals with whom she works, are valuable and are significant. In this sense, both Nancy's re-telling of these stories, and my own attempt to present them here, is an effort 'to prick the consciences of readers by inviting a re-examination of the values and interests under-girding certain discourses, practices, and institutional arrangements found in today's schools' (Barone, 1992, p. 143).
13. All names and potentially identifying material has been altered or removed.
14. Preservice teachers and newly qualified teachers rate behaviour problems as a high cause for concern (McMahon, 2008, McMahon in press), a point that deserves careful attention if the issue of speculating about behaviour problems and the associated psychopatholo-gisation is to be addressed.
15. The phrase 'psychopathologised adults' is used to displace the emphasis *from* the individual as having a mental disorder and *to* the processes that identify them.
16. While from the perspective of the principal and his secretary, the rationale for giving chase to Martin may appear sound, the point here is to bring to the fore the power that enabled this to occur, particularly the suspicion that Martin was a danger to himself and may need to be in psychiatric care. This suspicion, and the possibility that it could be acted on, was only possible because of the 5150 legislation.
17. California Law, Welfare and Institutions Code, Section 5150, Retrieved November 2, 2009, from http://www.leginfo.ca.gov/cgi-bin/waisgate?WAISdocID=5431285642+0+0+0&WAISaction=retrieve.
18. This is a point that deserves to be further explored empirically, since it could add a valuable perspective on institutionalising interpretations of child and youth behaviour. This is especially important from the point of view of the mobile asylum. For example, how might behaviour be differently understood if the institutionalising effects of the mobile asylum are taken into account?
19. While these two stories are from the USA, given the accounts from the participants in the Australian interviews, previous research by the author, together with anecdotal evidence, it is likely that comparable stories exist in Australia and elsewhere. This is an area that could benefit from further research with children and their families.

References

American Psychiatric Association. (2000). *Diagnostic and statistical manual of mental disorders, fourth edition, text revision (DSM-IV-TR)* (4th ed.). Washington, DC: Author.

Barone, T. (1992). Beyond theory and method: A case of critical storytelling. *Theory into Practice, 31*(2), 142–146.

Bolton, D. (2008). *What is mental disorder? An essay in philosophy, science and values.* Oxford, UK: Oxford University Press.

Brigham, A. (1847). The moral treatment of insanity. *American Journal of Insanity, 4*(1), 1–15.

Brown, T.E. (Ed.). (2008). *ADHD comorbidities: Handbook for ADHD complications in children and adults.* Arlington, VA: American Psychiatric Publishing.

Bunton, R., & Peterson, A. (1997). Foucault's medicine. In R. Bunton & A. Peterson (Eds.), *Foucault, health and medicine* (pp. 1–11). London: Routledge.

Department of Institutions and Agencies. (1876–1965). *New Jersey State Hospital at Greystone Park annual reports, 1876–1965.* Trenton, N.J.: State of New Jersey Archives.

Fakhoury, W., & Priebe, S. (2007). Deinstitutionalization and reinstitutionalization: Major changes in the provision of mental healthcare. *Psychiatry, 6,* 313–316.

Ferri, B.A., & Connor, D.J. (2005). In the shadow of brown. *Remedial and Special Education, 26*(2), 93–100.

Fitzgerald, T.D. (2009). Controlling the black school-age male. *Urban Education, 44,* 225–247.

Foucault, M. (2000a). Space, knowledge, power. In J.D. Faubion (Ed.), *Power, the essential works of Michel Foucault* (Vol. III, pp. 349–364). New York: The New Press.

Foucault, M. (2000b). Truth and juridical forms. In J.D. Faubion (Ed.), *Power, the essential works of Michel Foucault* (Vol. III, pp. 1–89). New York: The New Press.

Foucault, M. (2006a). *History of madness* (J. Murphy & J. Khalfa, Trans.). Abingdon, UK: Routledge.

Foucault, M. (2006b). *Psychiatric power: Lectures at the College de France 1973–1974.* New York: Palgrave Macmillan.

Fox. (2010). *House MD* [Television series]. Retrieved February 1, 2010, from http://www.fox.com/house/recaps/s6_e01.htm

Friend, R. (Writer) (2009). House MD – 6.02 Broken, part 2. *House MD* [Television series]. USA: Fox.

Goffman, E. (1961). *Asylums, essays on the social situation of mental patients and other inmates.* New York: Anchor Books.

Harwood, V. (2004). Subject to scrutiny: Taking Foucauldian genealogies to narratives of youth oppression. In M.L. Rasmussen, E. Rofes & S. Talburt (Eds.), *Youth and sexualities: Pleasure, subversion and insurbordination in and out of schools* (pp. 85–107). New York: Palgrave.

Harwood, V. (2006). *Diagnosing 'disorderly' children: A critique of behaviour disorder discourses.* London: Routledge.

Harwood, V. (2009). Biopower and biopedagogies. J. Wright & V. Harwood (Eds.), *Biopolitics and the 'obesity epidemic': Governing bodies* (pp. 15–30). New York: Routledge.

Harwood, V. (2010). The new outsiders: ADHD and disadvantage. In L.J. Graham (Ed.), *(De)Constructing ADHD: Critical guidance for teachers and teacher educators* (pp. 119–142). New York: Peter Lang.

Long, J.C. (1992). Foucault's clinic. *The Journal of Medical Humanities, 13*(3), 119–138.

Masi, G., Perugi, G., Toni, C., Millepiedi, S., Mucci, M., Bertini, N. et al. (2006). Attention-deficit hyperactivity disorder – bipolar comorbidity in children and adolescents. *Bipolar Disorders, 8,* 373–381.

McMahon, S. (2008). *Ready and rearing to diagnose: A study of preservice teachers' response to and participation in discourses of ADHD in school settings.* Unpublished honours thesis, University of Wollongong.

McMahon, S. (in press) Doctors diagnose, teachers label: The unexpected in pre-service teachers' talk about labelling children with ADHD. *International Journal of Inclusive Education.*

New Jersey Department of Human Services. (2007). *A new beginning: Greystone Psychiatric Hospital* (2nd ed.). Trenton, N.J.: V. Harwood.

Priebe, S. (2004). Institutionalization revisited – with and without walls. *Acta Psychiatrica Scandinavica, 110,* 81–82.

Rose, N. (1989). *Governing the soul, the shaping of the private self.* London: Routledge.

Rose, N. (1998). *Inventing ourselves: Psychology, power, and personhood.* Cambridge, UK: Cambridge University Press.

Roth, M. (2009, October 19). The rise of the neuronovel. *n + 1, 8.* Retrieved January 28, 2010, from http://www.nplusonemag.com/rise-neuronovel

Santiago, K. (2009, April 14). TV show 'House' to film at Greystone Park Psychiatric Hospital. *The Star-Ledger.*

Scheffler, R.M, Hinshaw, S.P., Modrek, S., & Levine, P. (2007). The global market for ADHD medications: The United States is an outlier among developed countries in its high usage rates of these medications among children. *Health Affairs, 26*, 450–457.

Wicclair, M.R. (2008). Medical paternalism in House M.D. *Medical Humanities, 34*(2), 93–99.

Wright, D. (1997). Getting out of the asylum: Understanding the confinement of the insane in the nineteenth century. *Social History of Medicine, 10*(1), 137–155.

Yanni, C. (2007). *The architecture of madness: Insane asylums of the United States.* Minneapolis: University of Minnesota Press.

Re-thinking disability in public: the making of the *UTS AccessAbility* website project

Elizabeth Hayman

Faculty of Design, Architecture and Building, University of Technology, Sydney, Harris Street, Ultimo, NSW, Australia

Introduction

Moves are afoot at the University of Technology, Sydney (UTS) to acknowledge disability within the overall experience of student life. Scheduled to launch in time for UTS Orientation 2010, *UTS AccessAbility* is a student-generated web presence[1] addressing the significant additional layer that experiences of disability add to study experiences. Over 1000 students across both UTS campuses have personal experiences of studying and disability, yet prior to *UTS AccessAbility* there had been a lack of direct engagement with disability within the University's online presence. Covering both practical and cultural dimensions, the site operates as a first-stop location for disability-relevant information intended to enhance the experience of those studying, and about to study, at UTS. Given this intention, the site needs to be able to reach and find relevance with a potentially highly diverse audience. Its underlying ethos is to reflect, encourage and generate a multiplicity of ways of relating to the all-too-often unpacked phenomenon of student life as it plays out in relation to disability. This article will outline how the *UTS AccessAbility* website has evolved, some of the issues that have emerged during its creation and go on to speculate about how the project might be extended in the future.

Genesis of the project

This latest phase of the *UTS AccessAbility* website project has been co-authored by two UTS students who had previously founded the Disability Action Group of Students (DAGS).[2] DAGS was approached during a sitting of the Disability Action Planning Committee early in 2009 and asked to continue an existing project. The group was specifically approached because the UTS Web Team considered it important that 'students who are in the user group ... generate the content'. DAGS considered the website an effective and appropriate means by which the diverse experiences of students living and studying with disabilities could gain cultural recognition, acknowledgement, a sense of value, and networking opportunities.

Then known as *Launchpad*, the first incarnation of the website had been initiated by the UTS Web Team, with support from UTS Equity & Diversity Unit and from

UTS Student Services Unit. The funding application to the UTS Disability Fund[3] ('Providing an Inclusive Virtual Environment for staff/students with disabilities or an interest in accessibility') outlined a number of potential objectives and goals. A former UTS Masters degree student, Emily Parkinson, took on the project towards completion of her Masters degree. Parkinson's work addressed the acknowledged lack of disability presence throughout the UTS general website identified in the 2008 review of the UTS Disability Action Plan (UTS Disability Action Plan Committee, 2008). The work to seek ways of 'securing compliance' in providing government-determined online accessibility standards was also begun.[4] Parkinson devised a number of strategies to address these issues and her recommendations were considered by the UTS Disability Action Plan Committee. After the approval of a UTS Disability Fund Application, initial funding was allocated in 2008 to build a user-centric website 'to increase awareness of accessibility as well as promote and retain knowledge within the UTS community' (Ward & Doust, 2008, p. 1).

The project, which has now become known as *UTS AccessAbility*, was co-written over a 12-week period from mid-November 2009 guided by the initial content audit of the co-authors which enabled the project to remain within scale and within the resources and time available. *UTS AccessAbility* has drawn upon the support of various internal UTS departments. Further funding was obtained early in 2010 from UTS Equity and Diversity to implement a promotions and marketing strategy via the UTS Marketing and Communication Unit. Specially commissioned promotional launch material, comprising posters and postcards, have been used during UTS Orientation and on notice boards and postcard racks around the University (Figure 1).

The project has thrived and evolved in the midst of on-going collaborative debate. The depth and extent of how 'things grew organically' has surprised both site authors and has come to mean a great deal on a personal level to each of them: '*AccessAbility* . . . has consumed most of my waking day for the past three months. It has been a bit of a passion; reigned in by working to a deadline'. The personal relationship each co-author has with disability inevitably informed a combined approach. Much of the site material, for example, was developed jointly in the midst of close consultations which

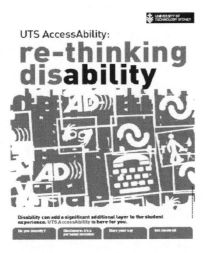

Figure 1. Design by Hoc Ngo for posters and postcards distributed throughout the City Campus, February and March 2010. Credit: UTS Marketing and Communication Unit.

at times bordered on 'heated discussions' about key subject areas. The intention was to capture the sense that there is a multiplicity of views and debates that have coalesced around issues such as disclosure, discrimination and confidentiality.

The creation of 'The Essentials' folder was deliberately prioritized based on the assessment that, as the 'backbone' of the project, it would consume the most planning time of all the proposed sections of the site. On-going debate during this phase ensured a sense of accountability and justification for organizing the material in this folder into eight distinct pages. A great deal of effort was expended to ensure that the content of 'The Essentials' folder would be quick and 'snappy' for its users whilst developing a realistically up-beat pitch underscored with humour where appropriate. To present information in well-organized, containable loads, we effectively used separate pages within the folders rather than expecting users to sift through and waste time on irrelevant information and potentially lose interest in the site. Keen to achieve a cultural dimension within the pages of the 'The Essentials', we wanted the robust debate and joint-writing style used to create the pages to counter much about the way in which this type of resource information is traditionally aimed at intended disability-related audiences. This subtle introduction of an overall style, and therefore sense of culture, was a deliberate intention to off-set what could have become the driest and most information-loaded section of the site. Future updates could further this experience of writing from within personal insight and explore how other people and their uniquely informed views can be included.

Aims of the project

From its inception, the aims of *UTS AccessAbility* have been developed through on-going debate. The intention was to infuse the site with political, academic and cultural engagement with an eye to what kind of community might already be in existence at UTS and what it might become in the future. As indicated above, an online-appropriate writing style has been jointly developed. This style is one that is approachable yet openly questioning and avoids concluding statements in favour of presenting the conundrums that disability often brings with it. Another intention agreed upon from the beginning was that the website act as a central 'sign-post' to other resources through the inclusion of hyperlinks to relevant and appropriate online sources. This 'sign-posting' intention is both a cultural-political issue and a practical maintenance issue. Through hyperlinks, the sheer variety of sources that the site is linked into is more clearly indicated at the same time as granting space to each of their unique cultural-political qualities. These two points are important in an area in which there are a variety of political and cultural positions, both established and emerging.

Audience

In light of the perceived complications of who *UTS AccessAbility* should appeal to and the complexity of the subject area, potential audiences have been approached from an unusual position. With audience appeal crucial to the success of *UTS AccessAbility*, there was a perceived need to consider what could make the experiences of students living and studying with disabilities a 'difficult subject to present to a number of audience groups' and think though why it might be thought of as 'hard to know what is needed and what isn't'. This confusion arises in part from the fact that 'the disability community can claim no geographical site or recognized language in a definition of cultural origins' (Mitchell & Snyder, 2000, p. 212).

The joint decision was made to focus on the everyday experience of a significant proportion of any population that is often misrepresented, unacknowledged, or at worst, hidden. Rather than presume experiential knowledge about these multi-faceted experiences, the focus has been placed on creating material written from a UTS-based position that looks at what has already been created as 'disability-related', first at UTS, then within the local Sydney area, and on as far as the wider New South Wales context. This geographical approach avoids the commonly experienced, yet often unnecessary, outsider need to specifically identify actual audience member 'types'. Importantly, though, we have not allowed this local geographical parameter to limit that which might also inform potential avenues for re-thinking disability and so links have been made within the site to concepts emanating on a global scale. The website has been structured to encourage personalized journeys through cutting-edge information and locally accessible resources for anyone who passes through the UTS infrastructure. The intention of the co-authors was for users to self-navigate through the site, enabling them to stop and select what they decide is relevant rather than presume the needs of those who visit. The site makes use of two rolling galleries of images to extend a sense of what the University can be like. Various viewable shots of the Disability Resources Room, described as 'our space', and the UTS Library's Special Needs Room create possibilities for envisaging participation for that part of our audience as yet unfamiliar with University culture.

Disability scholarship

Various extracts from scholarly works emanating from the field of Disability Studies have been included to indicate that disability is a complex and contested area of academic debate. The introductory page to the initial 'Do you identify?' folder intentionally fractures neat definitions of the concept of disability. In so doing, the website operates as a way of opening debate about disability within the overall UTS online presence. Disability is presented as a human situation that is potentially 'transitory and unpredictable' (Corcoran & Hayman, 2010), and something that can be political in nature. Through this problematization, *UTS AccessAbility* introduces disability to the university community as a potential 'space of provocation' (Titchkosky, 2007, p. 9) that not only stirs up multiple identity issues but has the potential to fundamentally 'reconsider the meaning of identity politics' (2007, p. 16). From this position the complexity of disability can be acknowledged in terms of its capacity to simultaneously offer positives and carry predicaments. This provides a basis for understanding that situations may arise that require strategic disclosure within university and social circumstances. Quotations from two well-respected Disability Studies scholars have been included to illuminate this complexity. That lifted from Fiona Kumari Campbell's recent *Contours of Ableism* (2009) explores the notion of 'disability as a state of ambivalence', where 'people with disability negotiate and experience internal ambivalence in their own lives as well as negotiate the ambivalence towards disability in society' (p. 160). In order to open up ideas about what disability might mean for our various potential audiences it was important to capture and demonstrate Campbell's questioning style of writing, quote her questions directly and introduce what, for many, will be new terms for referring to the context in which disability is framed in our society:

> How does the person with a disability negotiate the expectations and compulsions of ableism? In other words, do they choose to conform or hypermimic ableism or do they go it alone and explore other ways of being? (2009, p. 160)

Disability Studies scholar Tom Shakespeare is quoted in order to challenge the dominant perception that disability is an unvaryingly negative state of being:

> The predicament of impairment – the intrinsic difficulties of engaging with the world, the pains and sufferings and limitations of the body – mean that impairment is not neutral. It may bring insights and experiences which are positive, and for some these may even outweigh the disadvantages. (2008, p. 242)

All attempts to avoid simplistic, label-orientated references to our audience members have been balanced with a style that is both understandable, without needing a grounding in current Disability Studies academic discourse, and generally appealing to an audience which might be encountering disability-related thinking for the first time.

Aesthetic representation

The visual presentation of *UTS AccessAbility* has been as much a part of the political intent motivating this website's creation as that behind the creation of its written content. With calls having long been made for ways in which disability can be made appropriately visual in western culture, it was decided that a clearly aesthetic quality, within the limits of budget and institutional context, was most important (see Hevey, 1992 and Thompson, 2001). A new, relatively limited and relatively rare breed of disability representation has emerged, marked initially by the 1998 *Dazed & Confused* fashion shoot, 'Access-able', created by the late fashion designer Alexander McQueen (1998) and acclaimed fashion photographer Nick Knight.[5] Though not without some inherent complications (see Thompson, 2004), this photoshoot offered ready material with which some in the Disability Studies field could develop a postmodernist understanding of how visual 'meaning is created in acts, and is neither fixed nor stable or unitary, but part of the shifting, realigning field of simulacra' (Kuppers, 2002, p. 186). Kuppers was keen to assess how images, created when there is a 'media love affair with (some) stylish disabled people' (p. 185), such as those in the *Dazed & Confused* shoot, work to give 'attention to the playing field of meaning, the realms of the legible, [and which] can help focus on the mechanisms that complicate attempts to categorize images into specific social and political agencies' (p. 186). Images of model and athlete, Aimee Mullins, and her beautifully carved legs (see Pullin, 2009, p. 32), complicate traditional notions of what we might visually, culturally and politically expect from realms addressing disability:

> rather than concealing, normalizing, or erasing disability, these photos use the hyperbole and stigmata traditionally associated with disability to quench postmodernity's perpetual search for the new and arresting image. Such a narrative of advantage

works against oppressive narratives and practices usually invoked about disabilities. First, Mullins counters the insistent narrative that one must overcome an impairment rather than incorporating it into one's life and self, even perhaps as a benefit. Second, Mullins counters the practice of passing for nondisabled that people with disabilities are often obliged to enact in the public sphere. Mullins uses her conformity with beauty standards to assert her disability's violation of those very standards. As legless and beautiful, she is an embodied paradox, asserting an inherently disruptive potential. (Thompson, 2004, p. 97)

Sydney-based photographer Belinda Mason has worked to create highly polished and stylized images of 40 people who live with disabilities and some of their partners. Touring since 2004, the focus of her *Intimate Encounters* exhibition remains on sexuality, in both its subject matter and the visual vocabulary it employs.[6] Stereotypical representations of disability typically fail to account for this aspect of life and render it taboo. They also tend to focus primarily on the 'disability' aspect to the exclusion of any other element being portrayed. Mason's work encounters sexualities which are more usually overlooked, or even quashed, thereby exposing the type of underlying prejudices which typically negate more comprehensive, varied and realistic visual representations of people with disabilities. Mason's sensually constructed images work to ensure that 'disability is shown as part of a normal continuum of life experience, an aspect of someone's life, rather than the full definition'.[7] *UTS AccessAbility* has a similar intention and insistence on 'open[ing] enquiry to questions that need to be answered if we want to move on representational politics, and address the representational economics of our times' (Kuppers, 2002, pp. 186–187). Indeed, this need to 'transfigure disability within the cultural imagination' has been considered as 'the central goal of what might be called the New Disability Studies of the last decade' (Thompson, 2000, p. 181). A new visual reconception of disability is underway, picked up in projects such as the '*Don't DIS my ABILITY*' and *Made You Look* campaigns during the past two years[8] in their, at times, luxurious and lush photographic and print qualities. In particular the 2008 *Made You Look* front page image of Tracy Barrell, styled, made up and with skateboard in hand, demonstrates the possibilities that this type of 'of-the-moment' visual representation, which so often fails to extend to encompasses human difference, can offer for re-thinking disability.[9] Without recourse to the same creative photography and sophisticated post-production to generate a similar high-end aesthetic, the smaller-scale and more modestly-budgeted *UTS AccessAbility* project has had to be more lateral in its visual contribution towards reconceptualizing disability.

A strategic and lateral approach to the visual approach of *UTS AccessAbility* has drawn, first, upon existing visual material, second, on the core 'sign-posting' intention mentioned above and, third, upon visual material specifically created for this project where none had existed before. The project was kindly offered the use of some recent professional photoshoot material created for the redevelopment of the UTS Equity and Diversity website, taken at an international student recruitment day. Images of groups and crowds of people have been selected from this already created body of work with none of the images depicting anyone with an obvious disability. As such, this choice of imagery only partially addresses the move towards reconceptualizing disability and depends heavily on being read within the context of the overall site. Nonetheless, it was felt this was a pertinent way, within the limited means of the project, to challenge expectations of how disability is portrayed. One of the visual agendas for the site was set in the following way: if the familiar international blue wheelchair symbol for disability lies at one end of a visual continuum the project aimed to explore its opposite end.[10] Rather than allowing this wide range of human experience to become abstracted – and by implication unmentionable, distant, generic and ultimately dehumanized – the chosen images retain a strong sense of human scale, variety and uniqueness. Most of the images have been cropped to concentrate the focus on the spontaneous interaction and energy captured within the group rather than on any one individual. There is opportunity within these strategies to challenge the expectations of already visually adept website audiences visiting the site. Since none of the images depict anyone with an obvious disability, 'hidden' disabilities are more likely to be accounted for. Moreover, the collective sense of humanity engendered by the images go some way towards addressing both the temporary nature of ablebodiedness and opens questions about ratios and proportions of those of us who are, or one day shall be, living with disability. Crowd scenes also negotiate the politics of inappropriate staring by avoiding the visual isolation of any particular individual and their body, thereby avoiding any unwanted sense of 'traffic[ing] in otherness by fetishizing the bodies of people from groups traditionally associated with the body's processes: women, the disabled, people of color' (Thompson, 2000, p. 187).

The second method used to sustain a visual reconceptualization of disability is the site's exploitation of its 'signposting' strategy, explained above, as a way of connecting with externally created imagery. Other sites containing appropriately challenging imagery have been both referred to and inserted into *UTS AccessAbility* by hyperlink. The project was not of a scale to commission beautifully crafted imagery, but, by including an online news image at the beginning of *UTS AccessAbility*'s 'Creative hub' folder, it has been able to co-opt the super-scaled white marble voluptuousness of Marc Quinn's *Alison Lapper Pregnant* (Figure 2). The sheer impact of this temporary art installation, by an internationally acclaimed artist, which inhabited one corner of Trafalgar Square in London between 2005 and 2007, has been knowingly used as a way to both signal the challenge represented by much of the contents of *UTS AccessAbility*'s 'Creative hub' folder and to set a tone for the type of re-thinking debate the website has the potential to become part of.

The third visual strategy within the website takes the form of images taken by the co-authors which have been made into online galleries of automatically revolving images (Figure 3). Two such galleries have been made to showcase two specifically disability-orientated areas of the UTS City Campus: the Special Needs Room in the Blake Library and the Disability Resources Room on the 16th floor of the Tower Building. Images of equipment and resources, with an overall sense of what the two spaces consist of, aid site users to envisage what these spaces can mean and enable. The reconceptualization possibilities offered by these galleries of images lie in the establishment of tools by which personal involvement with the University can be imagined in order to then be enacted in individual real time.

The highly visual quality of the website medium has been exploited in this project to embed an approach that challenges how disability is generally represented and seen. Exploring the same visually challenging territory, Kuppers asks, 'What new maps emerge?' (2002, p. 187). More than any other section of the website the 'Creative hub' folder has most potential to do this exploratory work. The words of

Figure 2. Introductory page to *UTS AccessAbility*'s 'Creative hub' folder, including the image of Marc Quinn's sculpture installation. Credit: UTS Web Team, N. Corcoran and E. Hayman.

comedian and actor, Philip Patston, introduce the initial page of the 'Creative hub': 'The creative expression by disabled people of what it is to be a disabled person is ultimately about creating social and political change' (Patston, quoted in Rix, 2008, p. 8). A video collage of various performances of Patston's are included in the 'Creative hub'. His 'sharp, pithy and completely unsentimental' comedy style (Rix, 2008, p. 8), along with his savvy, highly styled personal appearance demonstrate how new cultural space is being mapped out and how disability is being re-imagined and, most importantly, re-valued.

Deep engagement

Not only does *UTS AccessAbility* present the intellectual and aesthetic engagements to be had with disability, but also the deeply experiential ones. The website has been developed to work several stages beyond any facile label that a generic treatment of 'disability' can so easily become. Within the constraints of project time and website space, the content has been written from positions that have gone further into the disability experience than the co-authors have tended to find in similar

Figure 3. The gallery of 13 images showcasing the Disability Resources Room on the UTS City Campus. Credit: UTS Web Team, N. Corcoran and E. Hayman.

circumstances. Typical terminologies and disability concepts have been unpacked further than is usually found in a constant attempt to 'go beyond the label'. Refusing to remain with commonly used terminologies has entailed detailed and, at times, personal attempts to unpack the knowledge that both authors have garnered from having lived othered lives in relation to their own experiences of university study.

Despite the level of time involved, it was decided that it was vital to fully investigate all internal UTS or external online presences to ensure total relevance, appropriate tone, context and vision before embedding them as hyperlinks within *UTS AccessAbility*'s text. All sites linked in throughout the website make direct contributions to the points being made on each page. Any unnecessary or misleading 'fillers' are avoided given that this has emerged as an issue of respect with an audience that is more likely to be dealing with additional online interaction methods. Not only does this help to ensure a more comfortable experience for *UTS AccessAbility* users, it also importantly maximizes their chances of becoming involved in what are already more restricted opportunities than for most. Where users are sent within and from the website, is part of *UTS AccessAbility*'s cultural intention and part of generating the right sort of expectations about what is possible when we re-think disability/ability constructs.

Tanya Titchkosky addresses how we enact disability and uses Judith Butler's deployment of 'performativity' to 'pursue the possibility of scrutinizing what we *are doing* to make disability' (Titchkosky, 2007, p. 17), finding that 'the meaning of disability lies "between" people and not merely in people' (p. 18). The imperative to monitor and utilize this relational aspect of disability-making shaped the approach to selecting external and internal online content to interlink with *UTS AccessAbility*. A network of hyperlinked sites has been embedded into the co-authored content which serves to complement and build the ethos of the site. As far as possible, within a forever-changing web-scape, time has been taken to link *UTS AccessAbility* to currently viable, technically-advanced and accessible sites which are based in sophisticated, currently-formulated thinking. However, links have also been included which have a narrower conceptualization of how disability is enacted. This is an inevitability in light of the fact that:

> The construct of disability represented in the media culture is generally a limited one. [People with disabilities] do not participate on equal terms as workers in media industries, and, unfortunately with few exceptions, mainstream journalists, editors, producers, film and video makers, scriptwriters, computer games designers, multimedia content producers, and those devising cultural material online and mobile phones do not produce the diverse representations of people with disabilities across various genres that are expected of other groups. (Goggin & Newell, 2005, pp. 34–35)

The resulting 'ableism', rife within the wider web context, can easily undermine the empowering cultural and political ethos that has been promoted throughout the site. As long as 'media plays a central role in culturally embedding the profound sense of otherness that many people with disabilities experience' (Goggin & Newell, 2005, p. 35), it seems appropriate to selectively encourage other sites which also 'work beyond the label' to challenge stereotypical thinking, and somewhat steer our audiences' experience with *UTS AccessAbility*. A subtle play of power, perhaps, and one all the more effective for consisting 'in guiding the possibilities of conduct and putting in order the possible outcomes' (Tremain, 2005, p. 8), rather than acting more obviously and repressively. A realization of how 'the exercise of power ... is a total structure of actions brought to bear upon possible actions; it incites, it induces, it seduces, it makes easier or more difficult' (Foucault, 1983, p. 220) is important here. This conscious use and exercise of authorial power is partially mitigated by the very structure of the website medium, within which content and hyperlinks mix, since not only can audiences negotiate their own way around individual pages and links but can navigate entirely away from any of its authorial content and link choices.

Those sites not able to manage the conceptual leaps that *UTS AccessAbility* attempts to present are clearly demarcated in the way they are included in the site. Many websites still demonstrate the common tendency to narrowly conceptualise the lives of those they are intending to reach with inappropriate medical definitions. This is indicated as an issue on the occasions when it has been crucial for *UTS AccessAbility* to include links to such sites. Our introduction to the Companion Card scheme is a case in point: 'Culture vulture on a budget? Two tickets for the price of one: the qualifying criteria are rather narrow, but it's worth checking out the exciting new Companion Card (opens an external site) scheme' (Corcoran & Hayman, 2010). This deliberate disruption and undermining of structures within which disability is often created, enacted and governed is a potentially effective counter-balance to an all-pervasive ableism which forms the inevitable context in which *UTS AccessAbility* and its audience members operate. It also takes into account the disparity of including sites less developed in their approaches alongside more nuanced sites, allowing them to work in relation to each other to produce an implied and emerging debate for our university-based audience to pick up on.

The importance of using the website format to present a re-thinking of disability is worth noting. This is especially effective when different routes to presenting that challenge are collected together in their various forms and formats. For example, a unique synergy can be generated from any individual journey between, say, the call to action of *UTS AccessAbility*'s media watch page, the moving image content of the comedy page and the editorial pages that discuss the strategic disclosure of personal information. An equally creative re-imagining of disability could steer between the geographic (for instance, the gallery of images introducing the Disability Resources Room in the City Campus), the indefinably cultural ('Beyond categories' page in *UTS AccessAbility*'s 'Creative hub') and the legislative implications of the United Nations Convention on the Rights of Persons with Disabilities in the 'Knowing your rights' page. This last example of interlinked potentiality is pertinent as we increasingly take cultural concepts on board as we look beyond the now-limiting social model with its 'juridical conception of power that has prevailed in disability studies' (Tremain, 2005, p. 9). As a medium, the website format can have the potential to be open to input and interaction. 'Inspired to comment?' opportunities are available at various points through *UTS AccessAbility*'s overall site. The collaborative opportunities of the website format also allow for a range of views to inform and determine its parameters. The educational potential of stumbling across the website is unrivalled, extending well beyond any intended audience group. However, there is one website-related concern about going one stage further in the site's keenness to go beyond usual terminology. As a website, *UTS AccessAbility* needs its content to attract, not exclude, the undeniable potential that Google and other search engines offer. It can be difficult to ascertain in the initial instance whether it has enough of the 'right' material to catch their attention. It is too early in the process to tell whether the Web is too 'ableist' to pick up on *UTS AccessAbility*, or whether the site might already be aptly placed and worded to contribute to any existing wider project of re-thinking disability. This concern can be addressed in subsequent website maintenance.

Theoretical concerns

Beneath the more obvious aims of the project, is the concern that ableism inadvertently frames a project of this nature. No matter how *UTS AccessAbility* might aim to 'embrac[e] disability at the level of beingness (i.e., as an intrinsic part of the person's Self)' (Campbell, 2009, p. 20) through various means, such as the intention to 'unpack the label' mentioned above and the insistence on developing strategies of visual representation, it exists as a project that nonetheless holds disability apart. Disability here inhabits its own clearly marked out territory (as '*UTS AccessAbility*') within a larger institutional system (in this case the overall UTS website). Disability is presented as a concept distanced from the rest of the UTS online presence, paradoxically perpetuating a human othering that it indeed is attempting to challenge.

This well-defined website behaves, in essence, as an ableist response conceived within 'the compulsion to emulate ableist regulatory norms' (p. 3). If 'the presence of disability upsets the modernist craving for ontological security', *UTS AccessAbility* has acted to conveniently identify, relocate and maintain disability, albeit, in rather boisterous and challenging form in just yet another conveniently understandable form of institutional sense-making. The *UTS AccessAbility* website project could be seen as hopelessly subject to an insidious form of bio-power, acting to 'inadvertently extend those arrangements' by which 'the identity of the subject of the social model ("people with impairments") is actually formed in large measure by the political arrangements that the model was designed to contest' (Tremain, 2005, p. 10). Higher educational structures have been constructed to be difficult for the majority to access. *UTS AccessAbility* may go some way towards soothing the more obvious difficulties and barriers, even challenge people to re-think what they believe disability to be, yet it ultimately leaves problematic structures unchallenged.

A separately defined site of disability can also be seen to be historically problematic. Ring-fenced as this website is from the rest of the university website, *UTS AccessAbility* perpetuates a troubled association that disability has had with deliberately isolated, institutional confinement (see Atkinson, Jackson, & Walmsley, 1997; Humphries & Gordon, 1992). A more effective approach could instead have worked to infiltrate the larger UTS website, working to 'crip' (McRuer, 2006) the existing site at every necessary turn. This of course would have been a much larger project, and one less likely to attract sufficient funding, but one which more accurately reflects the ethics and ideals of at least one of the co-authors of the current project.

Perhaps this undeniable tension is an outcome of the context in which *UTS AccessAbility* has been created. The undeniable othering effect, of a separate website within a larger website, needs to be balanced with the previous silences within the UTS web presence that *UTS AccessAbility* now begins to fill. In a head-on challenge to the idea that 'for systems of thinking to be maintained, certain ways of imagining need to remain unspeakable and unspoken' (Campbell, 2009, p. 20), *UTS AccessAbility* is a collection of ideas which have been previously absent within the University's public presence. It proudly infiltrates space that has previously ignored the cultural and social presence of students who live the concepts that are constituted as 'disability'. *UTS AccessAbility* may currently sit in its separate webspace, it may stand alone, but it has the great advantage of being in an overview position from which it can drop snippets of information which we hope form an overall cultural response that has not been seen here before. Apart from endorsements implied by the hyperlinks we have made from the site to other carefully selected bodies, the only allegiance *UTS AccessAbility* will later make is with the UTS Equity and Diversity Unit, once their website re-design process has been finalized. The wide-reaching, cross-faculty quality of *UTS AccessAbility*'s intent will be maintained. It may even be enhanced in its aim to provide a political, cultural and social context to disability, where none has been given before, and to the numerous educations individually determined by those involved with this university.

Cripping the institution

From the start of the project, and despite the (perhaps necessary) structural limitations that underscore its overall conception, the authors have been keen to apply thinking developed in recent Disability Studies. The important process of re-thinking established institutional space *through* positions of experienced disability has begun and we have evidence now of what that can begin to look like in practice. Ultimately, it is very difficult to create something that will be both currently acceptable to all its expected audiences and its funding source and able to carry out the full implications of a truly critical approach to the inherently structural 'ableism' (Campbell, 2009) that all educational systems are currently formulated within. Ultimately, the time-scale of the 12-week project has defined that in some respects the site, for now, remains within an expected university system and operates despite an awareness that bio-politics have controlled how this project has formed.

The need for educational institutions to re-think how they might relate to what they might think disability experiences are, can be illustrated by one example the authors dealt with when writing the 'Getting around campus' page. An elaborate process has been constructed and established by unknown persons employed by UTS, and clearly living without experience of disability, to control physical access to the UTS main Library. After much debate it was decided that it would be best to make light of this embedded ableist approach with a rather deliberately chirpy, 'You'll need a proximity pass at the Blake Library (City Campus) if you need to avoid the swipe-through entry gates' (which is required in addition to the library card carried by all students and despite the constant presence of a human security guard with the ability to swipe users through when this is more convenient). The phrase 'proximity pass' is hyperlinked directly to the page where its apparent need is outlined in the Library's own terms. This is employed as a means of creating distance by referring users directly to the source that has constructed a complication which achieves nothing other than an additional process of othering for all concerned. At times like this, the website has become a nuanced political forum where, as in this case, subtle alerts can be placed for those who will also wonder why such 'ableistly' constructed interior space, and the scenarios which develop in response to them, need to be in place at all.

Conclusion

UTS AccessAbility is an attempt to generate a space within a large higher education institution in which a multiplicity of nuanced understandings of disability can be explored. It is intended to be a readily consumable framework of ideas, support and provocation, through which users self-navigate. Co-authored by intended users, it has been infused with an eclectic mix of political, practical, academic and cultural engagement to encourage a dialogue which moves beyond general understandings of disability. Generalist assumptions about disability are further fractured and made thoughtful by introducing ideas drawn from disability scholarship. The aesthetic quality of the site has been carefully considered in light of the importance of working with visual representation. Despite budget limitations, we have developed a visual context in which we encourage a re-think of student-based experience of disability. By acting as a 'sign-post', *UTS AccessAbility* has maintained the integrity of the sites it has linked with, forging connections which are sometimes strongly endorsed, sometimes more tactically tentative. This faceted approach to *UTS AccessAbility*'s wider context comes from a deeply experiential position. By unpacking what is already out there, at the same time as encouraging a critique of that which is enacted as disabled, we have tried to generate a new level of grounded expectations. This is political work of a certain subtlety and not without a certain level of authorial audacity, hopefully tempered by the debate that has collaboratively informed the site and the part played by users themselves in their individual pathways through the content and hyperlinks. Concerns remain about how the very separateness of *UTS AccessAbility*, within the context of a larger site, effectively undermines its challenge to all-pervasive ableism. Beyond rethinking disability, a more effective 'cripping' of the institution would involve a pervasive infiltration of every aspect of the larger UTS website with a deep and complex understanding of the extreme value of the human differences already existing within the University community and the extended implications they present. Until the go ahead for a project of that scale, there is long list of maintenance issues, new collaborations to enlist, pages to be created and updated, links to be checked and established, and a formal action planning and funding process to tackle, suggesting that we already have our work cut out in the immediate future.

Notes

1. *UTS AccessAbility*, http://www.AccessAbility.uts.edu.au, launched 18 February 2010.
2. A University of Technology Sydney (UTS) Student Association collective.
3. Administered by the UTS Equity and Diversity Unit.
4. The long-awaited Web Content Accessibility Guidelines (WCAG) 2.0 were endorsed in the days after the launch of *UTS AccessAbility*. See Media release 05/2010, *Dealing with government online to become easier for Australians with disabilities*, from the office of The Hon Lindsay Tanner MP, 23 February 2010 (retrieved February 23, 2010, from http://www.financeminister.gov.au/media/2010/mr_052010_joint.html).
5. An image of Aimee Mullins from this shoot is viewable at http://www.nickknight.com/main.html
6. Belinda Mason's photographic exhibition *Intimate Encounters* can viewed at http://www.belindamason.com/
7. Belinda Mason, exhibition notes to *Intimate Encounters*, 2010, http://www.belindamason.com/
8. The *Don't DIS my ABILITY* campaign and its official publication, the *Made You Look* magazine, are joint initiatives of the New South Wales Government and the Department of Ageing, Disability and Home Care. They have been timed to coincide with International Day of People with Disability in December of the past three years. See http://www.dontdismyability.com.au/publications
9. See http://www.dontdismyability.com.au/publications for downloadable versions of the 2008 and 2009 *Made You Look* magazines.
10. Evidence of how pervasive this older way of conceptualizing disability remains in collective consciousness can be seen within the publicity material generated to promote *UTS AccessAbility*. Although the exploratory 'continuum' visual agenda idea was clearly stated in the brief to the publicity design team the result does not encompass our suggested visual re-think and remains with abstracted, symbol-based imagery.

References

Atkinson, D., Jackson, M., & Walmsley, J. (1997). *Forgotten lives: Exploring the history of learning disability*. Kidderminster, UK: Bild.

Campbell, F.K. (2009). *Contours of ableism: The production of disability and abledness*. Basingstoke, UK: Palgrave Macmillan.

Corcoran, N., & Hayman, E. (2010). *'Do you identify?' UTS AccessAbility*. Retrieved February 18, 2010, from http://www.accessability.uts.edu.au/identify/index.html

Foucault, M. (1983). The subject and power. In H.L. Dreyfus & P. Rabinow, *Michel Foucault: Beyond structuralism and hermeneutics* (pp. 208–226). Chicago: University of Chicago Press.

Goggin, G., & Newell, C. (2005). *Disability in Australia: Exposing a social apartheid*. Sydney: University of New South Wales.

Hevey, D. (1992). *The creatures time forgot: Photography and disability imagery*. London: Routledge.

Humphries, S., & Gordon, P. (1992). *Out of sight: The experience of disability, 1900–1950*. Plymouth, UK: Northcote House.

Kuppers, P. (2002). Image politics without the real: Simulcra, dandyism and disability fashion. In M. Corker & T. Shakespeare (Eds.), *Disability/postmodernity: Embodying disability theory* (pp. 184–197). London: Continuum.

McQueen, A. (1998, September). Access-able (styled by Katy England with photographs by Nick Knight). *Dazed & Confused, 46*, 68–83.

McRuer, R. (2006). *Crip theory: Cultural signs of queerness and disability*. New York: New York University Press.

Mitchell, D.T., & Snyder, S.L. (2000). Talking about talking back: Afterthoughts on the making of the disability documentary 'Vital signs: Crip culture talks back'. In S. Crutchfield & M. Epstein (Eds.), *Points of contact: Disability, art, and culture* (pp. 197–217). Ann Arbor: University of Michigan Press.

Pullin, G. (2009). *Design meets disability*. Cambridge, MA: MIT Press.

Rix, P. (2008, September). *Enabling people with disabilities to participate in mainstream*. Paper presented at the ARATA (Australian Rehabilitation & Assistive Technology Association) Conference, Adelaide. Abstract retrieved from http://www.tutti.org.au/uploads/file/Keynote_ARATA_conference_Sept_2008.pdf.

Shakespeare, T. (2008). Disability: Suffering, social oppression, or complex predicament? In M. Düwell, C. Rehmann-Sutter & D. Mieth (Eds.), *The contingent nature of life: Bioethics and the limits of human existence* (pp. 235–246). Berlin: Springer.

Thompson, R.G. (2000). The beauty and the freak. In S. Crutchfield & M. Epstein (Eds.), *Points of contact: Disability, art, and culture* (pp. 181–196). Ann Arbor: University of Michigan Press.

Thompson, R.G. (2001). Seeing the disabled: Visual rhetorics of disability in popular photography. In P.K. Longmore & L. Umansky (Eds.), *The new disability history: American perspectives* (pp. 335–374). New York: New York University Press.

Thompson, R.G. (2004). Integrating disability, transforming feminist theory. In B.G. Smith & B. Hutchison (Eds.), *Gendering disability* (pp. 73–103). New Brunswick, NJ: Rutgers University Press.

Titchkosky, T. (2007). *Reading and writing disability differently: The textured life of embodiment*. Toronto: University of Toronto Press.

Tremain, S. (2005). Foucault, governmentality, and critical disability theory. In S. Tremain (Ed.), *Foucault and the government of disability* (pp. 1–24). Ann Arbor: The University of Michigan Press.

UTS Disability Action Plan Committee. (2008). *Review of UTS Disability Action Plan 2003–2007*. Unpublished document available from UTS Equity and Diversity Department.

Ward, N., & Doust, S. (2008). *Providing an inclusive virtual environment for staff/students with disabilities or an interest in accessibility*. Unpublished application document to UTS Disability Fund.

'Laughing with/at the disabled': the cultural politics of disability in Australian universities

Gerard Goggin

Journalism and Media Research Centre, University of New South Wales, Sydney, NSW, Australia

In 2007 the film-maker Michael Noonan embarked on a project initially entitled 'Laughing at the Disabled' (a title then changed to 'Laughing with the Disabled'), a collaboration between himself and three people with intellectual disabilities. A doctoral candidate in the Creative Industries at Queensland University of Technology (QUT), Noonan's film was the subject of a furious attack by two QUT academics – and then became a *cause celébrè* not only in Australia but around the world. The 'Laughing at/with the Disabled' project became a touchstone for the futility and contempt inherent in much contemporary academic research and teaching – but especially was viewed by many as proof of the troubling status of disability in Australian universities. While it has been widely discussed in the press, and with the furore continued online via blogs, YouTube, and email lists, there has been an absence of critical discussion of the case. Accordingly, in this paper, I analyze the public record covering the criticisms of this research project, disciplinary action by QUT, and responses by those involved in the research. Rather than making judgments on the project, I explore this case for the light it sheds on the place of disability in Australian culture, the role of power, questions of ethics – and, perhaps most importantly, the cultural politics of disability in education.

Introduction

On 11 April 2007, two academics from Queensland University of Technology (QUT), John Hookham and Gary MacLennan, published an article in *The Australian* newspaper, deploring a doctoral thesis underway in their Creative Industries Faculty. The thesis in question was entitled 'Laughing at the Disabled', undertaken by a student and film-maker called Michael Noonan. Hookham and MacLennan had been present at Noonan's PhD confirmation hearing, and their stringent critique of the 'Laughing at the Disabled' project lit the fuse of controversy that gained national and international attention and notoriety for months to come. As the outcry and debate ensued, Noonan modified the title of the project to 'Laughing with the Disabled' – but criticism did not abate. Nonetheless in early 2010, Michael Noonan and his collaborators finished their film (now entitled *Down Under Mystery Tour*), and Noonan submitted his thesis. *Down Under Mystery Tour* is being shown at film festivals, with a wider international release planned (including a television version).

Three years after the outcry concerning 'Laughing at/with the Disabled', it is timely to consider the significance of this episode. With the imminent release of the final film, audiences and scholars can view and debate a unique text that advances our understanding of the discourses and cultural politics of disability. Such a reflection is the purpose of this paper.

My argument is that this *cause célèbre* has much to tell us about the relations and politics of disability. However, little such insight featured prominently in the various discourses that played out during 2007 and 2008 regarding Noonan's project, and still continue. In many respects, disability itself – and the diverse views, investments, and experiences of people identifying with disability, and those who are not regarded as disabled – was overlooked here. Accordingly, my content is that it is the discourses of disability themselves in the 'Laughing' episode that have the most to tell us about social relations and cultural locations of disability in Australian universities – and how disability figures in wider society.

Academic institutions, knowledges, practices, identities – the habitus of academic and intellectual work – rely still on particular notions of bodies, abled and disabled ones. This situation deeply frames and structures the field of disability, what its issues are seen to be, and what the possibilities for alternative approaches to disability in disciplines like disability studies, education, cultural studies or sociology might be. The work of assembling and sustaining contemporary culture crucially engages and depends upon the relations, relays, and assemblages of disability. So too does a cultural studies that seeks to register, explore, research and transform disability; as does the even more fragile project of critical disability, which seeks to fundamentally change the power relations of expertise, knowledge and research concerning disability (Goggin & Newell, 2005; Meekosha & Dowse, 2007; Meekosha & Shuttleworth, 2009).

To explore this controversy and its meanings, the paper falls into three parts. First, I discuss the overarching environment for disability in Australia, and note the difficulties in sustaining critical conceptions of, and research into, disability. Second, I discuss the discourses of disability at play in the controversy over the preliminary stage of Michael Noonan's doctoral project 'Laughing at/with the Disabled'. Third, I briefly explore the fertile area of collaborations traversing disability by disabled people and others. Indeed this is the very topic as well as condition of Noonan's final project of his thesis, so a brief reading of *Down Under Mystery Tour* highlights such questions.

Disability, research and criticism in Australia

At roughly the same time that the 'Laughing' controversy unfolded, there were important developments in disability rights and policy in Australia and internationally. The landmark United Nations Convention on the Rights of Persons with Disabilities (CRPD) and its optional protocol were adopted on 13 December 2006, opened for signature in March 2007, and came into force on 3 May 2008. The Australian government relatively quickly ratified the Convention in July 2008, seeing it as a mark of its embrace of disability as an important political issue. While the Rudd Labor government, with its adoption of a human rights approach to disability, has made important progress in a number of areas, disability still remains an area of great need (Deane & National People with Disabilities and Carer Council, 2009; Goggin & Newell, 2005).

In Australian higher education, there has been a significant rise in participation by students who identify as having (a) disability. The number of identified domestic students with a disability has risen from 17,574 in 1998 to 30,872 in 2008, or from approximately 2.8% to 4.1% of all students (Department of Education, Employment and Workplace Relations, 2009). There are issues about how well such statistics – and the surveys or questionnaires that underpin them – accurately capture the diverse population of students with disability. (Although at least we do have some reliable figures on students, whereas data on numbers and participation of university staff with disability are less well captured). While there has been an intensifying interest in the various facets of disability in education in universities, schools, and other settings (for instance, see Christensen & Rizvi, 1996; Newell & Parmenter, 2005; Newell & Offord, 2008), the participation of students with disability in Australian universities lags well behind the proportion of people with disabilities in the general population (usually measured at one in five Australians or approximately 20% of the population – Australian Bureau of Statistics, 2004; Australian Institute of Health and Welfare, 2009, pp. 137–185; Ryan, 2007). The 2009 National Disability Strategy Consultation Report notes that '[l]ow participation rates in higher education, training and employment would suggest that few young people with disabilities are able to access the support required to successfully make this transition [into an independent adult life]' (Deane & National People with Disabilities and Carer Council, 2009, p. 50).

Moving from the broad scene of disability in Australia, and that of the general profile of students and staff in Australian universities, it is important to briefly consider the status of academic research regarding disability – especially critical research (Meekosha & Dowse, 2007; Meekosha & Shuttleworth, 2009; Social Relations of Disability Research Network, 1999). As a field, disability studies faces various challenges – as it does in gaining acceptance and legitimacy in cross-fertilizing other fields and disciplines (Goggin, 2003, 2009; Jakubowicz, 2003; Meekosha, 2004). There remains a lack of understanding of or acceptance of cultural or social approaches to disability. Ironically, the idea that the social nature of or context of disability is vital to approaching this area has steadily gained influence in policy. This has been not unproblematic, but the recent emphasis on this in the UN CRPD, in the definition and statistics regarding disability (registered in the work of the Australian Institute of Health and Welfare), and in Australian government policy, is encouraging. In the area of theory, the social model of disability, derived from the British disability movement and disability studies, still has an strong, if not dominant, influence (Dowse, 2001; Shakespeare, 2006), though Australian disability studies has always drawn from both the UK and US modes of disability theory (Siebers, 2008; Snyder & Mitchell, 2006), as well as non-metropolitan accounts (Goggin & Newell, 2005; Meekosha, 2004).

In Australia, disability studies is quite fragmented or dispersed as a field (which, of course, can be a strength as well as weakness). There is no general Australian journal of disability studies (though there are efforts underway to establish such a venue for publication). There is also still a lack of good international journals for social and cultural work in disability, though there are now various new endeavours, such as the *Journal of Literary & Cultural Disability Studies* (recently moved to

Liverpool University Press). In academia, as elsewhere, the lion's share of resources still are invested in the traditional disability knowledge professionals, institutions, and academic fields – from health sciences, 'caring professions' (such as social work), to areas such as special education. These researchers into disability are deeply invested in power-knowledge regimes surrounding disability, which are only slowly transforming themselves (or indeed decolonizing). There is a small cadre of relatively established critical disability studies scholars in Australia, but what gives hope for the future is the rich, vibrant work being produced by emerging scholars, especially those at the doctoral and post-doctoral area (Campbell, 2009; Dowse, 2001, 2002, 2009; Ellis, 2008; Hickey-Moody, 2009). Early-career researchers face real challenges, given weak state of field, no annual cross-disability conference, let alone regular meetings, seminars, and resources for connecting researchers and developing dialogue, collaboration, providing outlets and support for research. In media and cultural studies, disability remains a relatively new topic of interest but innovative work in creative practice and research is appearing.

This brief sketch of the general conditions of disability in Australia, and in universities and research in particular, is important. It provides a context for understanding some of the strange features of the discourses of disability in the controversy over disability research at QUT. It also suggests the need for theorization of the place of disability in Australian public culture, and the university's connection to such public spheres that I cannot fully address here – but hopefully preliminary aspects of which unfold in the rest of the paper.

The politics of laughing and research

When Hookham and MacLennan raised their concerns about Michael Noonan's project in the pages of *The Australian* in April 2007, they did so through a continuation of an earlier entry into the lists deploring the putative relativism of post-structuralism, and its pernicious effect on the humanities – the case in point being the barbarians inside the gate of their own Creative Industries Faculty:

> A time comes when you have to say: 'Enough!', when you can no longer put up with the misanthropic and amoral trash produced under the rubric of postmodernist, post-structuralist thought. The last straw, the defining moment, came for us when we attended a recent PhD confirmation at the Queensland University of Technology, where we teach. (Hookham & MacLennan, 2007)

In the view of Hookham and MacLennan, such research not only rested on questionable intellectual foundations, but more seriously it was morally repugnant. They maintained here and subsequently that universities should not be supporting or approving such research as such an enterprise was not conducive to a trusting and respectful relationship with the disability community. In making their case, Hookham and MacLennan firstly criticized the project for its exploitation of the two men with intellectual disabilities who worked with Noonan on the project:

> Candidate Michael Noonan's thesis title was 'Laughing at the Disabled: Creating Comedy that Confronts, Offends and Entertains'. The thesis abstract explained that 'Laughing at the Disabled is an exploration of authorship and exploitation in disability

comedy, the culmination of which will be the creation and production [for sale] of a six-part comedy series featuring two intellectually disabled personalities.

'The show, entitled [Craig and William]: Downunder Mystery Tour, will be aimed squarely at the mainstream masses; its aim to confront, offend and entertain.' [Editor's note: the subjects' names have been changed to protect their privacy.] Noonan went on to affirm that his thesis was guided by post-structuralist theory, which in our view entails moral relativism. He then showed video clips in which he had set up scenarios placing the intellectually disabled subjects in situations they did not devise and in which they could appear only as inept. Thus, the disabled Craig and William were sent to a pub out west to ask the locals about the mystery of the min-min lights.

In the tradition of reality television, the locals were not informed that Craig and William were disabled. But the candidate assured us some did 'get it', it being the joke that these two men could not possibly understand the content of the interviews they were conducting. This, the candidate seemed to think, was incredibly funny … Humour undermines the rich and powerful, and it can be politically subversive. But we don't think it's funny to mock and ridicule two intellectually disabled boys. We think we, and the university, have a duty of care to those who are less fortunate than us. (Hookham & MacLennan, 2007)

More so than Noonan, however, the target of Hookham and MacLennan's ire was the cultural studies professors holding court at QUT:

It is not our intention here to demolish the work of Noonan, an aspiring young academic and filmmaker. After all, ultimate responsibility for this research rests with the candidate's supervisory team, which included associate professor Alan McKee, the faculty ethics committee, which apparently gave his project total approval, and the expert panel, which confirmed his candidacy.

Let us be clear: we are not blaming students. In our line of fire are the academics who have led the assault against notions of aesthetic and moral quality in cultural studies … Lest the reader think we exaggerate, let us turn to the views of McKee, the enfant terrible of the post-structuralist radical philistines within the creative industries faculty at QUT … by elevating Big Brother to the level of Shakespeare, the radical philistines have taken the high culture v low culture distinction and inverted it. Low culture is the tops and anyone who so much as refers to high culture becomes the enemy and is subjected to the politics of abuse and exclusion. This is what has led us to Craig and William: Downunder Mystery Tour. (Hookham & MacLennan, 2007)

Hookham and MacLennan's jeremiad ignited a furious debate about universities, ethics, research, doctoral education, academic freedom, and disability that culminated with an out-of-court settlement. Squarely under attack (again) was cultural studies – and the contemporary university. *The Australian* newspaper, of course, has well-established form in fomenting outcry about contemporary cultural theory and its deformation of universities. I do not propose to dwell on this thread of the debate, in which Hookham and MacLennan received brickbats and rebuttals as well as bouquets:

The authors attack a video for mocking two of the intellectually disabled. This is very politically correct. But doesn't being PC define postmodernists? They trash their former dean, John Hartley, for putting Big Brother and Shakespeare's The Taming of the Shrew in the same framework. Via tenuous links such as this they accuse cultural studies of 'undermining the moral fabric of the university'.

But the issue of Shakespeare v popular culture in the curriculum is different from moral relativism … Awareness of the complexity of moral and political issues is a traditional academic value Hookham and MacLennon should be defending. The only thing justifying their publication is their anti-postmodernist ideology. That shouldn't be enough. (Hodge, 2007)

QUT took disciplinary action against Hookham and MacLennan leading to their six-month suspension with pay, and debate raged further about whether academic freedom was being depreciated or upheld through this penalty (given their strenuous advocacy against Noonan continuing his project) (Livingstone, 2007a; O'Keefe, 2007a, b). The two academics took their case on appeal to the Federal Court, and eventually resigned and settled with the university (Healy, 2007; Livingstone, 2007d). Subsequently the film-maker also faced a legal action taken by an indigenous woman upset at her portrayal (Healy, 2009; Lane, 2008).

The debate played out in newspapers and television. It also was continued in email lists, the blogosphere – much commentary as well as Noonan posting the offending excerpts from the doctoral confirmation hearing of the Brisbane *Courier-Mail* newspaper blog for all to see (Livingstone, 2007b, c) – and YouTube – with Hookham and MacLennan's supporters uploading videos (Lane, 2007; Strong, 2007). The leading disability organization that spoke out against Noonan's project, and supported Hookham and MacLennan was Queensland Advocacy Incorporated which held many concerns as their highly respected director Kevin Cocks explains:

> The abstract for the confirmation seminar itself suggests a number of potential ethical pitfalls. Exploring authorship and exploitation in disability comedy is a legitimate academic aim. However it is not legitimate to explore this by reproducing relationships which are exploitative, by representing vulnerable people with disability in offensive ways or by exposing them to public mockery by the 'mainstream masses'. Further, the abstract makes the fallacious assertion that there is a 'fine line between laughing at and laughing with'. To claim this in the context of reactions to people with disability is to be ignorant of the powerlessness of people with disability and the extremely detrimental impact of historical social constructions of disability ... It would appear that we as a society have lost our sense of decency when it comes to demonising and public ridiculing people based primarily on difference and deeply held assumptions that are ignorant and flawed. (Queensland Advocacy Incorporated, 2007)

In this distinctively multi-platform circulation of views and pro-am media productions concerning the 'Laughing at/with the Disabled' project, what is especially interesting is the representation of disability – the kinds of discourses of disability we can observe, and what they tell us about how disability features in public culture.

This case has some curious features, and there is certainly more to it than meets the eye. It was a painful episode for all involved, yet the 'Laughing at/with the Disabled' case is also an important one for thinking about disability in Australia. The main reason why analysis of the discourses of disability around 'Laughing at/with the Disabled' is a helpful way to proceed is because it helps us understand the ways in which the case functioned to close down, rather than open up, discussion about disability.

It is probably important that I make clear what I mean here: I'm not so much referring to the furore over academic freedom, which Hookham and MacLennan, and their defenders, saw as central – for instance, their arguments that their own academic freedom was being extinguished by the disciplinary action taken by the university. I think this is a narrow notion of academic freedom, but even on these terms its invocation is dubious here given their own critique of Noonan's work.

Hookham and MacLennan had a right in principle to express their view on his work, and in doing so to seek to underpin their critique with reference to their expertise (in film-making and research on documentary-making). However, in their own terms, they do need to face the various criticisms in response: that their critique was poorly conceived, and made without due engagement with, or knowledge of, the ideas they sought to discredit (notably, post-structuralism and cultural studies); that they expressed their views inappropriately and breached their duty of care to a doctoral student; they were not prepared to extend the same conditions of academic freedom to Noonan to allow him to continue to develop his ideas.

There is a further problem in Hookham and MacLennan's position as their notion of academic freedom does not come so much out of a liberal philosophic tradition – though they, and certainly their supporters, rely on this as their agonistic struggle with QUT goes on – as a radical, left, critical realist position. There is central tension between balancing the activation of academic freedom and then countervailing claims of ethics, morality, respect to other communities, claims of truth – and, of course, the question of who is the arbiter or indeed legislator of these.

So we find in the style of Hookham and MacLennan's stance – the way they articulate their key concerns and concepts – a recurrent sense of absolute certainty. This manifests itself in supreme confidence to speak on behalf of the 'disabled', who are imagined as the 'afflicted', evident in two early instances:

> And now, when we say that in civilised society it is repugnant to mock the disabled, most academics in our field appear to disagree with us. When we say it is morally wrong to laugh at the afflicted, our colleagues seem indifferent to the truth of this statement. Presumably for them it is just our 'narrative'. (Hookham & MacLennan, 2007)

> It's quite simple, Michael, I was brought up by my mother – one of the uneducated Irish peasantry. She was the best human being I have ever met. She taught me not to mock the afflicted. I had to go to a university to see the mocking of the afflicted being celebrated under the spurious rubric of 'post-structuralism'. (e-mail from MacLennan, quoted in Fraser, 2007)

The word 'afflicted' jars for many of us, part-and-parcel as it is of the charity discourse of disability (Fulcher, 1989). Many important and good things have, and do, come out of charitable approaches to disability. Yet this discourse and its institutions have also been historically a central part of oppression, and have caused much injustice and pain too. Hookham and MacLennan also put an emphasis on 'mocking' – rather than 'laughing', or even recognizing the subversive claims of genres of comedy, satire, or irony – which itself is a telling way to frame what Noonan's project entailed.

Interestingly one response from QUT directly responded to – and perhaps inadvertently mirrored, or at least accepted such rhetoric. In a letter to *The Australian* defending the ethics process of the faculty and university, Professor Brad Haseman wrote:

> Hookham and MacLennan were not part of the formal committees that have ruled that Noonan's study will now progress to completion. Given their distance from these deliberations, it is neither reasonable nor acceptable for them to judge their fellow academics as being indifferent to the belief that it is morally wrong to laugh at the afflicted. Their fellow academics are just as sensitive to such matters and recognise that

guarantees are in place to ensure that everyone involved will be treated justly and with integrity. (Haseman, 2007)

Note here that Haseman's statement has a number of telling qualifications, the most important being that he terms their moral prohibition not to 'laugh at the afflicted' as 'their belief'. He suggest that fellow academics are not 'indifferent' to their 'belief'. A number of other commentators do recoil from the patronising terminology of 'affliction'. On the left-of-centre group blog Larvatus Prodeo, Kim remarks that 'it's worth noting in passing that the so-called concerns expressed appear to deny all agency to people with disabilities, and construct us as poor souls in need of protection' (Kim, 2007).

These kinds of distinctions are not simply a quibble with the language used to discuss disability. These locutions are crucial operators in the discourses that construct disability here – as well as the surprising lacunae in these debates. The obvious things missing in action in the 'Laughing at/with the 'Disabled' case were: the two actors with intellectual disabilities; people with disabilities, with only a few exceptions (notably Kevin Cocks, and Queensland Advocacy Incorporated); academics and researchers with disabilities; any mention of the existence of something called disability studies, or critical disability studies; any suggestion that cultural studies might also include a fertile strand of disability inquiry.

Three years on, there are key elements that still have been little discussed. First, while the ethics process in this case appears to have been followed correctly, that there are deeper issues about both the broader frameworks for ethics in research in universities, as suggested by Christopher Newell, among others. Such concerns are not restricted to disability studies. The application of the physical scientific framework for ethics regulation and approval is problematic across the humanities and in the social sciences too (see, for instance, Atkinson, 2009; Dingwall, 2008).[1] Second, there remain real issues about how the enterprise of research on disability is conceived – notably the absence of researchers with disabilities in conceiving, undertaking, and shaping disability research. Third, there still are significant issues about how universities engage with disability communities. Fourth, that there is a lack of general understanding of different approaches to disability; for instance, that the views and requirements of an advocacy and service provider organization, such as Spectrum in this case, may be quite different from other disability groups, or indeed the wider movement, as expressed by Queensland Advocacy Incorporated. Here, for instance, the view of Queensland Advocacy Incorporated is quite consistent with approaches informed by the social model of disability, regarding the *sine qua non* of people with disabilities undertaking research about disability. Further, the disability community is neither a pan-disability entity, nor a monolithic, unitary grouping – with a wide range of views on this film, and other projects, of course to be expected and demonstrated (if not widely acknowledged or represented). Fifth, in this regrettable episode there is a lack of open discussion and acknowledgement of the creative collaborations and dialogues by people with disabilities and others in research – yet there is an important, emergent debate about what just and sustainable models might be (Dowse, 2002, 2009; Ellis, 2008; Ferrier & Muller, 2008; Hickey-Moody, 2009). Sixth, there is no public acknowledgement here that there is something called disability studies; that disability studies has theories of power, including those from Marxist, feminist, critical race, queer, and, even, post-structuralist perspectives; and disability studies is interacting with cultural studies – yet another thing that merits debate and discussion.

Models for collaboration: reading *Down Under Mystery Tour*

The serious debate and critical assessment of the meaning of the 'Laughing at/with the Disabled' case has not yet begun. Perhaps this is a good thing, because the product of this furore is now available – in the form of the film *Down Under Mystery Tour*. At the time of writing, Noonan, his collaborators and the supporting organization Spectrum were preparing to release it as a DVD, with an educational forum discussion (in which this author participated), and notes. Noonan was also in negotiation over festival release and broadcast versions of the film. Thus the public reception of *Down Under Mystery Tour* still lies ahead, and will be very interesting in its own right. What is fascinating about the film is that it is a genuine, thought-provoking, funny and intelligently wrought meditation in its own right on film, disability, genre, and the ethics of disability and authority. While its origins may lie in the maladroitly titled predecessor project 'Laughing at the Disabled', it is a very long way from the unsubtle framing that brought Noonan such grief (partly an outcome of the debate that was sparked by the reductive critiques of Hookham and MacLennan). In this final part of the paper, then, I want to briefly discuss *Down Under Mystery Tour*, and suggest why is it an important film in its own right.

Down Under Mystery Tour features three actors with intellectual disabilities – Malcolm Bebb, Darren Magee and James Bradley (the latter two had previously starred in Noonan's 2007 film *Unlikely Travellers*). Malcolm is a budding director who is keen to make a film about love and romance. He teams up with an opportunistic film producer, a young female industry professional, Simone Cahill, who has a gift for gaining government film support for production – and is especially keen because disability ticks the box when submitting an application. The two stars of the show are Darren and James, who tour to different places to try to solve the various mysteries of Australian locales – such as the Yowie, Min-Min lights, and the Big Cat. Along the way are threaded various encounters and tales that come from the part-quest, part-picaresque loosely woven structure of the film. Malcolm is frustrated about the inability of the 'knuckleheads' to deliver entertaining material, and, keen as he is on injecting sex into the mix, eventually replaces them for a time with two blondes. Malcolm's production team includes a cameraman and a sound recordist, Warren Williams. The latter is not especially keen to be typecast as the guy who does 'disabled boom operating', and delivers some of the most shockingly disablist lines in the show – for instance, how 'watching disabled people on television' is a real turn-off and 'just ruins the whole night'. Ironically, the boom operator would quite like to be friends with James, at least as long as his other friends are none the wiser.

There are two other important disabled characters who feature in the film. There is the blind assassin, David Roosje, hired by Malcolm to do a hit on Darren and James. He is never able to escape the loving, smothering embrace of his carer, Carla McLeish, who idolizes him – delighted to be able to enjoy a picnic with him, when he has work to do (namely rub out the two actors Malcolm can no longer stand). Then there is the disability activist, Cyril Turner, from the 'Committee for the Protection of Disabled People on Film'. Turner rather resembles Bruce Ruxton, the infamous former national president of the Returned Services League (RSL). This sanctimonius character arrives on the filmset in a helicopter, with music and vision straight from *Mission Impossible*. He announces his presence, and first invigilates the production, to protect the two disabled boys, and eventually banishes Malcolm to direct the film himself. An inspired idea the disability rights director has is to bring in two professional actors to play Darren and James. Two well-known, even iconic, Australian actors, Alan David Lee and John Jarratt respectively play Darren and James, with cringe-worthy results. The film ends with the blind assassin massacring the disability-activist-turned-director and crew, a bloody end reported on the nightly news – while Darren, James, and Malcolm manage to escape unscathed to resume their lives.

Here I can convey the briefest sense of some key parts of the film. Suffice to say that it contains much else that makes it a rare, confronting, but often subtle and ironical text about disability, gender, and power in society. I have concentrated on the direct challenges – indeed provocations – it offers that go to the heart of issues of representing disability in film. It provides a gleeful, no-holds-barred retort to the critics of the project. In its depiction of the many manipulative, controlling relationships between the heroes (Darren, James, and also, in his own way, Malcolm) and those with a vested interest in film and disability (producers, production crew, and others who invoke the disability community to influence cultural production), the film pillories problematic, exploitative collaborations. *Down Under Mystery Tour* unsettles the viewer further in rather more subtle ways, in part because it is such a hybrid of genres. It really is not just a comedy, it also is mockumentary, reality television, melodrama, satire, cinema verité, splatter flick, and even records the everyday tragedies of the experience of people living with disabilities (institutionalization, the search for intimacy, discrimination, and disablism). There are formal intricacies too, in its highly wrought scripting, filming, and editing, and in structural features – such as the fact that Darren and James often pursue their own adventure, much to the frustration of Malcom, in a kind of film-within-a-film.

There is ample evidence that the film really is a genuine, respectful collaboration among, and creation of, Noonan, and the three actors, Malcolm, Darren and James. The concerns, often genuinely held and understandable, raised by critics in 2007 regarding the ethics of this collaboration, can now be very substantially put to rest. Difficult questions still remain that Noonan discusses openly in his own account of the film (contained in his dissertation), about the acquisition of film-making and narrative skills and experience, and how projects can proceed with the mix of expertise and backgrounds needed – without film professionals dominating, or without aesthetic, production, and other values being short-changed. There are other questions too that can be much more productively posed now – such as what is the relationship between this film, and its various models of collaborations, and those suggested by other exemplary Australian films about disability, that this film stands alongside such as Rolf de Heer's *Dance Me to My Song* (1998) or Penny Fowler Smith and Kath Duncan's *One-legged Dream Lover* (1999). There is a dissonance, for instance, in *Down Under*'s portrayal of the disability rights activist making his directorial debut by pressing non-disabled actors into service that does not reflect the long, complex, and rich tradition of artists, actors, directors, and writers with disability engaging in a range of collaborations that have also bequeathed important models of how to represent disability differently (regarding intellectual disability especially, see Hickey-Moody, 2009).

Conclusion

From an unpromising, bitter and apparently irremediable battle over whether or not people with intellectual disabilities could in their own right collaborate with a director to create a film that deploys comedy to provoke reflection disability, we have come a long way. With the release of *Down Under Mystery Tour*, we now have an important film explicitly about the representation of disability – that offers us new visions, scripts, challenges, and ideas about the cultural politics of education. We can now genuinely start the process of taking up the 2007 controversy about whether Noonan had the right to make such a film, in the groves of the new humanities in Brisbane academe – and radically reshape the terms of this awfully narrow and unproductive stoush. *Down Under Mystery Tour* itself stands to make an important contribution in such an enlivened and deepened conversation – but its own limits are clear.

Australian universities have a long way to go in educating people with disabilities, ensuring they can proceed to undertake advanced research, and then clearing the obstacles, and changing the norms of academic life, to make it possible for disabled professors to become a widespread feature of every part of academia. This imperative holds especially in disability studies, and in the many fields and disciplines, such as media, film, and cultural studies, where there are few visible and recognized researchers and practitioners with disability. As these governing circumstances, and disabling structures and relationships of research, are transformed, there will be many more disabled and non-disabled voices to be raised and heeded, when there comes another debate about disability. Hopefully disability studies itself, especially its critical variations, can prosper as a field in coming years, so that its many practitioners can be heard and sought out for their commentary, translations, and making of connections between universities, as a locale for research regarding disability, and wider society.

Films such as that initiated by Michael Noonan have a vital part to play in transforming the cultural politics of disability. Such texts remind us that our culture is indeed deeply shaped by ideas about our bodies, identities, and differences that disability signifies. Ultimately disability is central to culture in ways we are only just beginning to understand. The straw target of postmodernism taking hold in universities, and causing a decline in our values is so far off the mark here as to barely merit notice. The real scandal is that universities, and indeed culture and public life, might embrace new ideas about disability. Or more dangerous still, they could even encourage such things in ways that will elude the control of those who cleave to a traditional, paternal view.

Acknowledgements

This paper had its beginnings in conversations with the late Christopher Newell about the 'Laughing at/with the Disabled' controversy, that found their way into a paper given at the 2007 Cultural Studies of Australasia Conference in Adelaide. I am grateful to participants in that session for comments, and to two anonymous reviewers of this paper for their helpful suggestions. I also wish to thank Michael Noonan and John Hart for the opportunity to participate in a forum on *Down Under Mystery Tour*, and to Malcolm Bebb, Darren Magee, and James Bradley for the opportunity to discuss their experiences and perspectives on the film.

Note

1. My thanks to an anonymous reviewer of this paper for this important point.

References

Atkinson, P. (2009). Ethics and ethnography. *21st Century Society: Journal of the Academy of Social Sciences, 4*(1), 17–30.

Australian Bureau of Statistics. (2004). *Disability, ageing and carers, Australia: Summary of findings, 2003.* ABS cat. no. 4430.0. Canberra: Author.

Australian Institute of Health and Welfare. (2009). *Australia's welfare 2009.* Canberra: Author.

Campbell, F. (2009). *Contours of ableism: Territories, objects, disability and desire.* London: Palgrave Macmillan.

Christensen, C., & Rizvi, F. (Eds.). (1996). *Disability and the dilemmas of education and justice.* Buckingham, UK: Open University Press.

Deane, K., & National People with Disabilities and Carer Council. (2009). *Shut out: The experience of people with disabilities and their families in Australia. National disability strategy consultation report.* Canberra: National People with Disabilities and Carer Council, Department of Families, Housing, Community Services and Indigenous Affairs.

Department of Education, Employment and Workplace Relations. (2009). *2008 students: Selected higher education statistics, appendix 2: Equity groups.* Canberra: Author. Retrieved April 10, 2010, from http://www.dest.gov.au/sectors/higher_education/publications_resources/profiles/Students/2008_full_year.htm

Dingwall, R. (2008). The ethical case against ethical regulation in humanities and social science research. *21st Century Society: Journal of the Academy of the Social Sciences, 3*(1), 1–12.

Dowse, L. (2001). Contesting practices, challenging codes: Self advocacy, disability politics and the social model. *Disability & Society, 16*(1), 123–114.

Dowse, L. (2002). Who is asking the questions? A new politics of research with people with intellectual disability. *Intellectual Disability Australasia, 23*(1), 12–19.

Dowse, L. (2009). Some people are never going to be able to do that: Challenges for people with intellectual disability in the 21st century. *Disability & Society, 24*, 571–584.

Ellis, K. (2008). *Disabling diversity: The social construction of disability in 1990s Australian national cinema.* Saarbrücken: VDM-Verlag.

Ferrier, L., & Muller, V. (2008). Disabling able. *M/C Journal, 11*(3). Retrieved April 10, 2010, from http://journal.media-culture.org.au/index.php/mcjournal/article/viewArticle/58

Fraser, A. (2007, June 16). Dissenting dons out in the cold. *The Australian,* p. 21.

Fulcher, G. (1989). *Disabling policies? A comparative approach to education, policy, and disability.* London: Falmer Press.

Goggin, G. (2003). Media studies' disability. *Media International Australia, 108*, 157–168.

Goggin, G. (2009). Disability, media and the politics of vulnerability. *Asia-Pacific Media Educator, 19*, 1–19.

Goggin, G., & Newell, C. (2005). *Disability in Australia: Exposing an Australian apartheid.* Sydney: UNSW Press.

Haseman, B. (2007, April 18). Funny business [Letter to the editor]. *The Australian,* p. 26.

Healy, G. (2007, November 5). Disability row academics take money and walk. *The Australian,* p. 4.

Healy, G. (2009, January 21). Damages claim over disabled film. *The Australian,* p. 29.

Hickey-Moody, A. (2009). *Unimaginable bodies: Intellectual disability, performance and becomings.* Rotterdam, The Netherlands: Sense Publishers.

Hodge, B. (2007, April 18). Letter to the editor. *The Australian.*

Hookham, J., & MacLennan, G. (2007, April 11). Philistines of relativism. *The Australian,* p. 33.

Jakubowicz, A. (2003). Wheeling free? Disability studies meets media studies and the Australian media. *Australian Journal of Communication, 30*(3), 101–122.

Kim. (2007, April 13). Laughing at the disabled. *Larvatus Prodeo.* Retrieved April 10, 2010, from http://larvatusprodeo.net/2007/04/13/laughing-at-the-disabled/

Lane, B. (2007, May 28). Campus's disabled film row pops up on net. *The Australian*, p. 7.

Lane, B. (2008, September 17). New row over disabled film. *The Australian*, p. 26.

Livingstone, T. (2007a, June 12). QUT pair protest culture of 'fear'. *Courier-Mail*, p. 5.

Livingstone, T. (2007b, August 31). Film full of fuss goes online. *Courier-Mail*, p. 28.

Livingstone, T. (2007c, August 31). Harmless subject matter caught up in university politics. *Courier-Mail*, p. 28.

Livingstone, T. (2007d, November 2). Stoush costs uni $1m – QUT academic brawl ended by settlement. *Courier-Mail*, p. 25.

Meekosha, H. (2004). Drifting down the Gulf Stream: Navigating the cultures of disability studies. *Disability and Society, 19*, 721–733.

Meekosha, H., & Dowse, L. (2007). Integrating critical disability studies into social work education and practice: An Australian perspective. *Practice, 19*(3), 59–72.

Meekosha, H., & Shuttleworth, R. (2009). What's so 'critical' about critical disability studies? *Australian Journal of Human Rights, 15*(1), 47–75.

Newell, C., & Offord, B. (Eds.). (2008). *Activating human rights in education: Exploration, innovation and transformation.* Canberra: Australian College of Educators.

Newell, C., & Parmenter, T.R. (Eds.). (2005). *Disability in education: Context, curriculum and culture.* Canberra: Australian College of Educators.

O'Keefe, B. (2007a, June 6). QUT lecturer breakdown after misconduct hearing. *Courier-Mail*, p. 31.

O'Keefe, B. (2007b, June 27). Support for QUT lecturers. *Courier-Mail*, p. 31.

Queensland Advocacy Incorporated. (2007). *Annual report, 2006–2007.* Brisbane: Author.

Ryan, J. (2007). Learning disabilities in Australian universities: Hidden, ignored, and unwelcome. *Journal of Learning Disabilities, 40*, 436–442.

Shakespeare, T. (2006). *Disability rights and wrongs.* London: Routledge.

Siebers, T.A. (2008). *Disability theory.* Ann Arbor: University of Michigan Press.

Snyder, S., & Mitchell, D.T. (2006). *Cultural locations of disability.* Chicago: University of Chicago Press.

Social Relations of Disability Research Network. (1999). *Disability studies in Australian universities: A preliminary audit of subjects and programs which include the social dimensions of disability.* Sydney: School of Social Work, University of New South Wales.

Strong, A. (2007). *The disability community speaks out against QUT* [Video]. Retrieved April 10, 2010, from http://www.youtube.com/watch?v = xql7w3xPC8Q

I-cyborg: disability, affect and public pedagogy

Elizabeth Christie[a] and Geraldine Bloustien[b]

[a]University of Sydney, Sydney, Australia; [b]Hawke Research Institute, University of South Australia, Adelaide, Australia

In 2008 Elizabeth underwent a cochlear implant. The necessary but traumatic operation was approached in her usual creative way. To begin, Elizabeth researched the medical process and the ways other individuals had experienced the procedure and its aftermath. Then she set about documenting her personal response through *Facebook*, providing often confronting images of her transformation (as she put it) into a cyborg. This paper is a conversation between the two authors of this article, reflecting on and analysing Elizabeth's experience within the wider context of bodily enhancement and cosmetic surgery and exploring the role of the social networking site *Facebook* as a kind of public pedagogy that functions through affect. The two authors reflect first on Elizabeth's experience and her motives for such a public performance. Second, they explore some of the wider, underlying questions of negotiated subjectivity impacted by our ever-growing intimate and symbiotic relationship to new technologies. They argue that human beings evolving into 'cyborgs', as a result of new technological applications together with greater media convergence and digital technologies of social networking, offers an exciting potential for affective cultural interventions, new understandings of what it means to be human.

Introduction to a cyborg

Why *Facebook*? Just my feeble attempt to document my recovery process. Also, I can see what it looks like – I can't with a mirror because my head doesn't rotate 360 degrees. (Elizabeth Christie, in personal discussion with Geraldine Bloustien, June 2009)

In a sense our faces (and our bodies) don't belong to us but are rather part of wider mediascape. (Jones, 2008, p. 3)

The power of many form of media lies not so much in their ideological effects but in their ability to create affective resonances independent of content or meaning. (Shouse, 2005)

In early January 2009, Elizabeth underwent radical surgery to have a cochlear implant (CI).[1] The result would be that someone who has experienced severe deafness for almost all of her life would have to learn to negotiate with the world as a hearing person via a non-human artifact and intermediary. This paper is an attempt to document the process not just of the surgery but also to consider and analyse both the personal and the very public response to the surgery which Elizabeth invited via

Facebook. Less than a week after her surgery, Elizabeth posted pictures onto the social networking site of her shaved skull, complete with staples for the incision of the CI. In this paper, the two authors reflect first on Elizabeth's experience and her motives for such a public performance. Second, however, we explore some of the wider, underlying questions of negotiated subjectivity impacted by our ever-growing intimate and symbiotic relationship to new technologies. We argue that our evolving into 'cyborgs', as a result of new technological applications together with greater media convergence and digital technologies of social networking, offers an exciting potential for affective cultural interventions, new understandings of what it means to be human (Giroux, 2000; Shouse, 2005). But first, here is the context for this paper in Elizabeth's own words.

Background

> Though I was born with a hearing loss, it wasn't until I was almost three and a half that I was diagnosed with a moderate bilateral hearing loss that was most likely recessive in its origin (the birth of my younger brother who exhibited the same symptoms confirmed this suspicion). Shortly after, I received my first hearing aids, had speech therapy and went to mainstream public schools.
> Around the time I was in primary school, the cochlear implant (CI) was launched in Australia. At this time the criteria for receiving a CI were extremely stringent. Although my hearing had deteriorated over the years (at high school my loss was assessed as 'moderate to severe' and my last pre-implantation audiogram, at 33, shows a severe to profound loss), I did not recognise this and instead was keen to give many excuses for the increasing social symptoms (hardly ever going out, being overlooked for work and promotions, seeing other people with a fraction of my qualifications being taken more seriously than I was...). To reinforce the denial, I found I was particularly good at any solitary activity such as intensifying the work on my masters thesis, reading blogs and books, and endlessly re-watching *Gilmore Girls* and other captioned DVDs which gave me a sense that I was functioning just fine, thank you very much! But when my new super-powered hearing aids failed to meet my expectations, I started to investigate the alldeaf.com forums and, through hyperlinks, began to think about the CI.

Overcoming obstacles

Elizabeth's decision to get a CI was largely informed by the digital world. She had read numerous blogs, the most informative of which was http://contradica.blog-spot.com. The 'Chronicles of a Bionic Woman' found there, offered endless links to other implantees' blogs, valuable resources such as adaptive pitch tests and a video of 'Bionic Woman's' own activation, all of which would later prove to be very useful in terms of creating and modifying Elizabeth's expectations. The Internet offered pictures of the implant, which also quelled her fears about having something so alien attached to her head, and after rapid, but intensive research she decided to be 'implanted'.[2]

Taming the monster

The surgery of implantation of the electrodes into the cochlear and the chip and magnet into the skull runs some risks of temporary or permanent nerve damage affecting taste buds, or facial paralysis. However, for Elizabeth the surgery and recovery proved to be a very safe, quick and smooth process. What her body *did* resist, however, was the process of learning how to hear.

Activation and mapping is the process of 'switching on' and adjusting the levels of sound the electrodes receive for the ear/brain to hear. The process itself seems relatively simple. The cochlear implantee is plugged into a computer and the audiologist plays a series of beeps, which are only heard by the implantee. These beeps need to be identified and then adjusted for loudness. Yet there are significant challenges to this process. First, how does one who has never really heard loud sounds know if a sound is too loud or too soft? More importantly, how can sounds that have never been heard before even be recognised by the brain? Audiologists, doctors and surgeons refer to this as 'negative neural plasticity'. Neuroplasticity that is also referred to as brain plasticity, cortical plasticity or cortical re-mapping, is the process of change that neurons and the organisation of their networks undergo through bodily experience. Although the concept was first proposed in 1892 (see Cajal, 1991), the first neuroscientist credited with broadly disseminating the use of the term through medical publications and forums was Jerzy Konorski (Defelipe, 2006).

When a person is deaf, the brain lacks auditory input over the years, so it does not have the pathways to process or recognise sound. In order for the brain to reprocess sound it has to form new neural pathways which in turn rely on positive neuro stimulation. Cochlear implants or hearing aids are used to replace those lost sounds, with the result that the patient undergoes additional neural plasticity changes, as their brain gets used to hearing the sounds again. To Sandra Aamodt, editor in chief of *Nature Neuroscience*, cochlear implants are a quintessential example of neural plasticity. As she explained in her interview with Douglas Beck:

> People have some 25,000–30,000 nerve fibres on each auditory nerve. Yet we can replace that with 20–25 channels of auditory stimulation, and most recipients can use that absolutely minimal auditory information to make sense of sound in meaningful ways. (Beck, 2009)

Elizabeth's experience of these transitions was painful and demoralising. From reading blogs by previous implantees, she knew that for the activation she should have 'low expectations and then lower them', but she had also read numerous accounts of people suddenly being able to recognise the sound of people's voices (variously described as being like chipmunks, Darth Vader, people on helium):[3]

> I found that I was overwhelmed with the sounds of noise and was unable to recognise anything even resembling a human voice. For three weeks felt I was stuck in a world of tinnitus – only I could hear the roar of cacophony. In retrospect, the sounds I was hearing were everyday sounds, like wind, but because even in rooms of absolute silence the sounds were torturous, I didn't realise that these were the sounds of the outside world intruding. I thought was doomed to a lifetime of hearing the wrong things.

Elizabeth's age was against her – a child's brain is much more plastic and the neuro-pathways are easily formed. However, Elizabeth found that neural pathways, especially with determination, could still be changed! She started to spend hours listening to audiobooks (listening to and reading of the page at the same time), doing pitch tests and other sound tests available on the Internet. Quite unexpectedly, one evening as she was listening to the book, *The Curious Incident of a Dog at Night-time*, she realised that she could understand every word. After this point, she rapidly absorbed and recognised a range of sounds. Even though surgeons warned that it takes about a year to gain full benefit, within three months she found that even music started to sound 'natural' to her brain. The pleasure of music was particularly unexpected, as she had been warned that this was unlikely to be the case, due to the implant's emphasis on speech recognition.

I-cyborg – reassembled and re-embodied

The experience of implantation illustrates the way the body can be radically shaped by the digital. On the first and obvious level, is the impact of the CI itself and the ways transition from being deaf to 'hearing' (while still deaf) shapes (self) identity and personhood. To be a fully hearing being *immerses* one's corporality in the broader culture in a way that being sighted does not necessarily.[4] Using a CI changes the ways in which the individual engages with world, and how they experience their embodiment.

Medically speaking the CI is a prosthesis – it acts as 'an addition, a replacement, also an extension, an augmentation, and an enhancement' (Smith & Morra, 2006, p. 2). And while the use of the term 'prosthesis' now has replaced the term of 'cyborg' in academic discussion about implants and has 'become topological currency for describing a vague and shifting constellation of relationships among bodies, technologies, and subjectivities' (Sobchack, 2006, p. 19), cochlear implantees still frequently identify themselves as cyborgs or bionic. For example, on the blogs as they document and comment on their CI experiences, individuals constantly emphasise the sense of their human bodies being blurred with the machine. Their blog titles include:

- Just Another Cyborg
- CI Borg
- Electroded Droid Ear
- Bionic Ear Blog
- Bionic World, Life as a CI
- Chronicles of a Bionic Woman.

These, and other bloggers and forum posters, also talk about being 'activated', 'turned on', 'switched on'.

Such discourse speaks of a 'supplement', but it also emphasises the technology itself – the computer chip in the skull. The popularity of the use of 'cyborg' with the emphasis and excitement on the 'activation' by those with a CI, further highlights the significance of this. Some aspects of this fascination can be understood by referring to the adaption of other forms of prosthetic device. Indeed, in terms of process and adjustment, other 'appliances' such as false limbs, resemble the CI. It is interesting to note the parallels of Vivian Sobchack's 2006 experience of learning to walk with a prosthetic leg with the CI activation process. She described it as:

> A fairly lengthy and complex process that imbricated both intensive mechanical adjustment and physical practice... Although it took longer for me to develop a smoothly cadenced gait, I was functionally walking in a little over a month. (Sobchack, 2006, p. 17)

While the differences between the two types of adaption are minimal, the CI's process of mapping and forming new neuro-pathways seems to generate an additional degree of fascination with this process for the implantee.[5] One of the longer threads in the alldeaf.com forums is titled 'CI moments'. In this thread, set up by a poster, Neecy, the website becomes a place:

> where we all can post our CI moments – sometimes something neat will happen to us during our days/weeks but it's so small it doesn't warrant an entire new topic on its own... even something that simple can bring a smile to your face when you realize that 'I actually HEARD that!!!'[6]

This thread has posts proclaiming the joys of hearing the minute and seemingly mundane sounds of birds, a shop assistant, a phone conversation, or a train announcement. They are experiences that that the individuals never believed possible even once implanted. When prospective implantees write their wish-lists of sounds they want to hear, they are frequently very modest – some just want to hear speech or just background noise and are therefore delighted when the CI exceeds expectations. The experience of hearing for implantees is constantly surprising and evolving, but it is not an easy task. In addition to learning how to hear, implantees also have to learn how *not* to hear and how to filter out the background noise.

Political ramifications

So far we have considered the personal implications of the implant for Elizabeth. However, it is worth remembering that any relationship between humans and technology is complex and is far from being considered politically, socially or morally neutral.[7] Similarly, Elizabeth found that views concerning the acceptance of CIs were not universal and some perspectives were extremely negative. It seemed that while there is a widespread, commonplace acceptance of glasses, prosthetic limbs, etc., they are seen as *supplements* to body. For some, however, the CI is considered as unacceptable, even immoral, as it perceived to have the potential to destroy a community (Davis, 2007; Goggin, 2009, p. 495; Hauland, 2008).[8]

As with all prostheses and similar medical interventions, the CI also carries the implication that the distinction (in this case, Deafness) is a disability that needs to be 'fixed' rather an acceptable manifestation of difference, a language and cultural sub-group. By implication, the deafness is then a sign of negative distinction, something that is not 'normal' and should be altered to conform to the bodies of the majority. Graeme Clark, the inventor of the CI, addresses this problematic and ethical aspect in his Boyer lecture 'Restoring the Senses'.[9] Similarly, Lennard J. Davis, an American specialist in disability studies, highlights the way Deaf people often perceive themselves as a linguistic sub-group, rather than a disability (Davis, 1995).[10]

To be Deaf, is also to be culturally Deaf, meaning to belong to a community of deaf people with a shared language (Auslan, ASL or British Sign Language, for example). Culturally Deaf people tend to share a 'common community, a similar education in a Deaf setting, and a common cultural and social history – in short, the linguistic, cultural sub-group known as the Deaf' (Davis, 1995, p. 172) and as such, 'do not regard their absence of hearing as a disability, any more than a Spanish-speaking person would regard the inability to speak English as a disability' (Davis, 1995, p. xiv). Even the hearing-impaired who do not identify as Deaf need to articulate their position in relation to language as having a hearing loss shapes ways and methods of communication (such as lip-reading). Given that our auditory input shapes how we deal with the basis of human communication and consequently our culture, those with a hearing loss are likely to seek out a positive label encapsulating their experience and background, creating an alternative 'marker' rather than a negative one. Being Deaf, deaf, Hard of Hearing, or hearing-impaired, offers a handy explanation to the gaps in language and communication.[11] Similarly, the labeling of the self as a 'cyborg' or 'being bionic' points to two aspects of positive 'identity work' (see Wexler, 1992); both a recognition of the role the CI can play in shaping identity through hearing but also highlighting the role that the digital plays in helping the implantees to navigate their lives.

Surviving the extraterrestrial environments

Being a cyborg enables a markedly different way of functioning in the world. The term 'cyborg' was coined by Manfred Clynes and Nathan Kline (1960). They conceived of the cyborg as 'self-regulating man-machine systems' and used the terms to refer to 'the enhanced man' [sic] who could survive in extraterrestrial environments. They imagined that the cyborgian man-machine hybrid would be needed in the next technohumanist challenge – 'space flight' (Haraway, 2003).

The CI experience similarly allowed Elizabeth to 'survive extraterrestrial environments'. Before her implant, as her hearing lessened, the world became more distant and alien to her. Over the years, she found she had to tackle more and more obstacles to function 'normally' and she had to develop a bag of tricks to navigate this complicated terrain.

For example, as Michael Chorost, a CI recipient, points out, 'social norms are not taught, they are overheard, but one thing even the most skilled deaf people cannot do is overhear' (Chorost, 2005, p. 23). However, deaf people can observe and Elizabeth was particularly good at this.

Masquerading as deaf/normal

Watching how people did things and mimicking their language meant that Elizabeth had the appearance of being part of a 'hearing' community. For instance, she had the appearance of being a competent dancer, but she says she cannot dance. She needs others on the dance floor to copy their movements, as by herself, she does not know how to move nor what rhythm is appropriate, nor when to start or stop. She managed this dilemma by being extremely vigilant and aware of her movements in order to give a convincing act of enjoyment, freedom and normalcy. While these feelings might be true for those who can hear the music – being deaf meant for her that the emphasis was always on the act.

For many with a disability, the need for a disguise is twofold. The example of dancing illustrates the masquerade of appearing normal. As Tobin Siebers points out:

> When in the minority and powerless, Jews pass as Christians, blacks as whites, gay, lesbian, and transgendered people pass as heterosexual. Similarly, people with disabilities find ingenious ways to conceal their impairment and pass as able-bodied. (2004, p. 2)

For years Elizabeth pretended to understand and hear people and she was often correct in her deductions and interpretations. When she failed, she risked exposure. While this was sometimes embarrassing, her reaction was to exaggerate and play up the 'deaf card' even more. In other words, she simply replaced one masquerade with another.

The act of the double masquerade is one that Siebers discusses where the disabled 'also engage in a little discussed practice, structurally akin to passing but not identical to it, in which they disguise one kind of disability with another or display their disability by exaggerating it' (2004, p. 4). Depending on the audience, situation or mood, Elizabeth would often play up her deafness to get out of trouble, manipulate the situation, or to get a laugh. One advantage for disabled people is that even if the masquerade is detected, it is rare that they are confronted with the consequences of this. Examples of the delight deaf people experience in masquerade can be found in the 'smiley' and 'winky' icons in the alldeaf.com threads about exaggerating or 'playing up' deafness.

Performing the invisible

This reliance on the masquerade of being deaf contributed to Elizabeth's alienation towards those aspects of her self that constituted her disability; she never really considered herself deaf – or at least *so* deaf[12] to warrant special treatment and so receiving any consideration or dispensation for it, made her feel fraudulent. Consequently, she would often place herself in a situation where she was doubly disadvantaged. On the one hand, and paradoxically, the usefulness of masquerading as a hearing person sometimes had the effect of highlighting the severity of the disability, demonstrating to all that its effects were real. On the other hand, equally paradoxically, 'playing the deaf card' also allowed her to acknowledge that the perceptions of others and the discrimination often attached to those perceptions, were also very real. Either way it was a no-win situation.

In as much as deafness required certain masquerades, the digital world allowed for a greater performance. Less than a week after her surgery, and although she says she tends to be a 'lazy' contributor to *Facebook*, Elizabeth posted pictures of her shaved skull complete with staples for the incision of the CI (Figures 1 and 2).

Retroactively, Elizabeth perceives that her motivations and stated justifications for such a gesture might be multiple: first, posting the images online served an immediate pragmatic purpose. As she had not announced that she was getting a CI, Elizabeth felt it would save time explaining herself. However, she found that the strategy 'backfired' in the respect that the photos provoked more interest, clarification and led to further discussion. Second, the photos were also an attempt

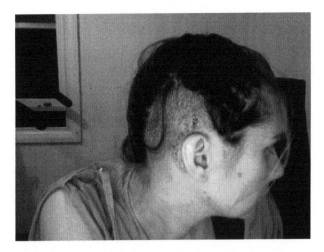

Figure 1. Elizabeth showing her shaved skull shortly after the operation. Photo: Elizabeth Christie.

to document the experience; Elizabeth found she was also curious about what others saw and what her body looked like *from the outside*. This was something that a mirror could not offer with any satisfaction. Third, the images were aimed to confront – the simultaneous 'grotesqueness' and minimal impact of the scar were posted in order to shock.

The reference to 'shock' or the 'grotesque' requires a closer examination for the issues raised here challenge the invisible nature of deafness as a disability. While the hearing aid, use of sign language, and the voice, might indicate that a person has a hearing impairment, overall deafness, unlike blindness or other physical disabilities 'is in some sense an invisible disability. Only when the Deaf person begins to engage in language does the disability become visible' (Davis, 1995, p. 77). Even the physical give-away signs noted above can be disguised, for there are many with a hearing loss

Figure 2. Elizabeth experimenting to 'see' her skull from another angle. Photo: Elizabeth Christie.

who do not know sign language, or their hearing aid or CI can often be hidden by hair. Even the surgical scar of incision from a CI is rarely noticeable for (as was in Elizabeth's case), the scar can completely fade months after the operation.

So it seems that at the very moment when Eizabeth's disability could *really* be invisible, she chose to highlight the process publically.[13] There are a number of ways this can be understood. First, the act of performing her deafness for shock value recalls Judith Butler's argument that ironic performance, for example, people in 'drag' can operate as a performative mechanism for destabilising cultural norms. While there has been an increasing popularity of using Butler's works on sex and gender in Disability studies (Samuels, 2002, p. 58) and although 'a number of writers transpose Butler's theories whole-heartedly into a disability studies' framework...analogising disability to gender/sex' (Samuels, 2002, p. 62), the act of posting pictures on *Facebook* draws attention to the performative (especially since she had not at that stage posted up any other picture). (For more discussion concerning representation of disability in new media, see also Goggin & Newell, 2003; Hauland, 2008.)

As the process of healing continued, Elizabeth recorded and posted images of her progress, illustrating her journey with images of the diminishing scars and the restoration of her hair (Figures 3 and 4).

Even more recently, for the first time, profile photos of 'the new Elizabeth' have been posted on her site, as Figure 5 illustrates.

However, another related way to consider the power of this type of what some may see as '*transgressive* performance' is to focus on the role of social networking sites, such as *Facebook* itself, and what new technologies can offer as new sites of public pedagogy. We noted above that Elizabeth's documenting and posting images of her surgery on *Facebook* was deliberately to document and shock, observing and portraying herself 'as other'. In so doing, albeit perhaps unintentionally, Elizabeth was also illustrating the ways in which visual images in particular contexts can also educate others through affect; leading potentially to new insights and empathy.

Figure 3. Elizabeth checking the progress of her hair regrowth one month after the operation. Photo: Elizabeth Christie.

Figure 4. Elizabeth wearing the cochlear implant processor. Photo: Elizabeth Christie.

Affect and public pedagogy

Over the last 10 years, Henry Giroux (2000, 2004) has been developing an expanded notion of public pedagogy. That is, he draws our attention to the ways that popular culture can become tools of cultural criticism offering pathways to particular modes of learning. For if, as Bauman has argued 'it is the private that colonizes public space, squeezing out and chasing away everything that cannot be fully, without residue, translated into the vocabulary of private interests and pursuits' (2001, p. 107), there are many sites of personal expression of popular culture which have also become opportunities for political intervention; public space reinterpreted as opportunities for public pedagogy:

> Profound transformations have taken place in the public space, producing new sites of pedagogy marked by a distinctive confluence of new digital and media technologies, growing concentrations of corporate power and unparalleled meaning producing capacities. Unlike traditional forms of pedagogy, knowledge and desire are inextricably connected to modes of pedagogical address mediated through unprecedented electronic technologies that include high-speed computers, new types of digitized film and CD-ROMS. The result is a public pedagogy that plays a decisive role in producing a diverse public sphere that gives new meaning to education as a political force. (Giroux, 2004, p. 75)

As a number of scholars have pointed out (Albrecht-Crane & Slack, 2003; Hickey-Moody, 2007, 2009) an oft undervalued and under-recognised vehicle of new pedagogies is affect, defined here not as a personal feeling but as prepersonal, instinctual (Shouse, 2005) or as 'certain milieus of sense, feeling, and expectation' (Hickey-Moody, 2007, p. 1) which become attached to the ways in which we experience the world and our everyday encounters with others. Affect then becomes the process through which alternative ways of perceiving and engaging with the other can be brought into being, physiologically engaging the viewers' or spectators' senses (Goggin, 2008). Such media include cinema, photography, music, dance and new media technologies including the Internet. They are powerful and effective vehicles, especially when, for example, challenging medical discourses of disability, because

Figure 5. Elizabeth in Italy 10 months after her successful cochlear activation. Photo: Elizabeth Christie.

they have the potential to 'reimagine . . . disabled bodies' (Hickey-Moody, 2007, p. 1) in the respect that:

> they can be used to fold a viewer into the embodied subjectivity of a disabled person and create new relationship between disabled and non disabled people. New affects are made this way. (Hickey-Moody, personal communication, 2010)[14]

Elizabeth's placing of the confronting images on *Facebook* also served as a form of intervention, challenging perceptions of disability in that they required an alternative mode of engagement and listening by others (see Goggin, 2009, p. 495).

See me for who I am

It is not unusual to see *Facebook* (and other Internet and social networking sites) as sites of social activism, where the various communities draw attention to themselves and 'celebrate' their difference, which destabilises itself from the expected norm. For CI recipients, *Facebook* groups include:

- The CI Community
- Cochlear Awareness Network
- Cochlear Implants Gang
- Bionic Ears

While the majority of the groups are informational or promotional devices for the three cochlear manufactures (Cochlear, American Bionics, Med-El), there are groups whose glee with being bionic is barely disguised ('My cochlear implant changed my life!'; 'Cochlear Implant is the best thing EVER!'; 'We've got a Cochlear Implant and love it!'; 'CI Rising Stars').

While Elizabeth is not usually comfortable in posting a picture of her face on *Facebook*, she had no problem in giving audiences views of what could be considered her most unattractive feature – the stapled scar of the operation on her skull. This act, above all others, now serves to be an ongoing reminder of her deafness to her inner circle of her friends, the radicalness of the procedure and, ultimately, of her transition to being a 'cyborg'.

Movement in discourse

Elizabeth's story expresses the potential for public spaces, including (online) social networks, to become sites of public pedagogy. As Giroux states, 'As a performative practice, pedagogy is at work in all of those public spaces where culture works to secure identities' (2000, p. 354). Elizabeth's use of public space to do this is, of course, not new. In his discussion of disability and the ethics of listening, Hamilton cites, among several other examples, the case of Neil Marcus, poet and actor, who used his severe neurological disorder as a platform at a university workshop for his confrontation of other people's responses to his marginal identity. Using the physical space as this platform, Marcus changed into a T-shirt that stated:

> Disability is not 'a brave struggle' or 'courage in the face of adversity'. DISABILITY IS AN ART. It is an ingenious way to live. (Hamilton, 2008, cited in Goggin, 2009, p. 490)

The public space of the Internet extends the possibilities for agency. Elizabeth created more than a space; she created a process, the movement from the personal to the pedagogical. The social networking 'public' was forced to confront the complexity of hearing impairment and the radical 'solution', the CI and even more importantly, Elizabeth's personal and emotional response to this procedure. In Elizabeth's provocative photographs, with their wry written narrative as a metaphoric slap-in-the-face, the public space became a site of rupture where 'friends' mirrored Elizabeth's process and were able to create their own narratives. Like Elizabeth, her friends could no longer 'switch off'. Deafness, as presented here, through the use of the public space, ruptured the narrative of sympathy that traditionally reinforces its status as invisible, and offered a space for exploration of the ethical dilemmas that surround the representation of disability. As Giroux has argued:

> As public discourse, representations can be understood for the ways in which they shape and bear witness to the ethical dilemmas that animate broader debates within the dominant culture. (2000, p. 355)

I-(more) human

In summary, Elizabeth believes that her transition into a cyborg, as part of her deep engagement and indeed, integration, with new media technologies, has had the paradoxical effect of making her feel more human. Elizabeth states:

> Just as Lithium can make the bipolar patients just like themselves only a little less so, the Silicon chip allows those with a hearing loss to be 'themselves', only much more so.

While the insertion of a computer chip and electrodes (an alien body) into her cochlear, has clearly altered her biological body, she feels that the blurring of machine and human is now indistinguishable (for her).

At the same time, this experience has improved both her body and 'mind' self image to a point where she feels, in a sense, 'super human'. The implant has significantly improved her hearing; the implications of what this meant was not grasped until several months after activation. With that improvement, her physical self and mindset have radically altered over the last few months. Due to the intertwining nature of the mind/body relation, she feels that the following categories overlap and should be read like a möbius strip:

> Physical:
> I'm in better shape than ever. After years of perceiving the gym and other places of exercise as intimidating and unwelcoming, I have sought out a membership to do yoga classes in order to restore my balance: the implant inevitably negatively affects one's sense of equilibrium and balance so it is important to try and rectify this. Now I find I can mix socially more easily with people instead of hiding behind an invisible self-constructed wall. I have become enthusiastic about fitness, attending spinning classes and aerobics.

> Social confidence:
> One unexpected implication of hearing meant that I have formed new friendships (I used to dread having to talk to strangers), and it has lessened the feelings of paranoia. When you can't hear what people are saying, there is a tendency to rely on the imagination, which can go for the worst scenario.

> Identity:
> I find that people seem far more receptive to what I am saying. Possibly it is because they only have to repeat things once since I will probably get it the second time round. This means I'm no longer hostile when learning to deal with new voices.

> It was only when I underwent the implant that I felt I went from masquerading deafness to being deaf. I have less hesitation in asking someone to repeat their comments, whereas in the past I knew there was no hope of understanding whether they repeated or not. In fact I often lacked the energy to try to make myself understood or to understand others. So I would pretend to either understand or play up my deafness in order to provide an excuse.

While she can hear now, Elizabeth still feels and identifies as being deaf. The practices and tricks of 'surviving extraterrestrial environments' remain. This in combination with her new-found hearing, has created a new being who is hyper-aware of the surrounds and senses. She has developed keen observational skills, is a fast reader and has an uncanny sense of smell. For her, these heightened senses emphasise her cyborgness, but at the same time make her more aware of her body. The CI changed her. Becoming part-computer made her – to borrow from Michael Chorost's subtitle of his book 'Rebuilt' – 'more human'. More than this, Elizabeth's public performance of becoming-cyborg created an affective space through which a public pedagogy of the cochlear implant occurred. *Facebook* mediated the changes in Elizabeth's sonic subjectivity and, in so doing, invited her online friends to re-think their assumptions about what it is to hear.

Notes

1. To simplify the account and discussion for the reader, Elizabeth and Gerry have decided to write about the surgery and experience of Elizabeth's cochlear implant in the third person for this article. This enables the two authors to interrogate the broader issues together.

2. Elizabeth talks of the process of her surgery as 'being implanted'; the implied loss of agency in this sentence – a surgical process that requires action from another being done to one's body – is significant for its complexity. Meredith Jones, who has written extensively on 'makeover culture' and cosmetic surgery (see Jones, 2008; Jones & Sofoulis, 2002) provides valuable insights about the negotiated processes of subjectivity that are equally applicable to CIs and similar procedures. Elizabeth's procedure and her response can also be understood as part of contemporary 'makeover culture', 'the process of becoming something better' (Jones, 2008, p. 1) with all of its inherent ambivalence and concerns about bodily and identity transformations.

3. The sounds that a cochlear implantee hears are not 'biological' sounds but computer generated which the brain has to learn to identify. The website www.earinstitute.org/ research/aip/audiodemos.htm offers a simulation for people who are NOT deaf or hearing impaired to demonstrate what speech and music would sound like through a cochlear implant. These simulations generated using the noise-band vocoder are a close approximation to what an implantee would hear (Shannon, Zeng, Kamath, Wygonski, & Ekelid, 1995).

4. Aristotle argued that the senses should be considered as a hierarchy with 'sight' as the highest of the senses, followed in order by hearing, smell, taste, and touch (Jutte, 2005, p. 61). This sense hierarchy has not been uncontested for others have argued that this hierarchy is universal but a social construct influenced by philosophy, human evolution, and technological progress (see Jutte, 2005, p. 61).

5. Perhaps this is because the device is placed inside the body and takes over *brain* function.

6. Retrieved June 18, 2009, from www.alldeaf.com/blogs/neecy/

7. One useful tool to think through some of these implications in terms of the relationship between human and non-human is Actor Network Theory (ANT), an innovative sociological approach developed by Science and Technology Studies scholars Michel Callon and Bruno Latour, together with the British sociologist John Law, and others (see Latour, 1993, 1994; also Haney, 2006). Their approach aimed to map the relations between humans, technology and material objects as they argued that all cultural processes are created by the interactions of the material and the 'semiotic' – interactions which are not fixed but evolve and change over time. Meredith Jones found such insights 'a particularly important idea when considering implants' (2008, p. 59).

8. Elizabeth's experience of the negative views on CIs was echoed in our related research into disability in 3D Virtual environments such as Second Life (SL). There we learnt that there were very strongly polarised opinions expressed in blogs and online forums about whether residents in SL who identified with a physical disability should represent themselves as such in the virtual world. (See Wood, 2008; Hickey-Moody & Wood, 2008, 2009; Bloustien & Wood, 2009.)

9. Graeme Clark's 'Lecture 5: Brain Plasticity Gives Hope to Children' in the Boyer Lecture series – Restoring the Senses (http://www.abc.net.au/rn/boyerlectures/stories/2007/ 2084251.htm).

10. In popular culture, this issue has been tackled effectively in the 1986 film and play *Children of a Lesser God* (director Haines, 1986). In this film the protagonist, Sarah Norman, a deaf teacher battles in her relationship with a hearing man who tries to make her use speech rather than her sign language.

11. The use of the term 'Deaf' as well as lower-case 'deaf' is deliberate. Within the Deaf community those who are hearing-impaired argue that the use of the lower-case deaf is someone who does not identify as being part of the Deaf community.

12. Elizabeth: Just to clarify, when referring to myself I use the lower-case word 'deaf' to distinguish from being culturally Deaf. Culturally Deaf would mean that I have taken on a Deaf identity. Aside from some time in pre-school, I went to mainstream schools (not one for the Deaf) and I don't use – much less know – sign language. So just to clear up any

confusion: Deaf with a capital = culturally Deaf and lower-case deaf just refers to a significant hearing loss.

13. It seems as though one of the aims of new technology and the design of the prosthesis is to make them as close as possible to looking 'authentic' or 'natural' – in other words hiding the appearance of the disability.

14. The potential of new engagement, empathy and immersion with the other through the physiological affective stimuli of visual and digital media has long been noted by other scholars, most notably by Taussig (1993) and Shaviro (1993). However, the extension into public pedagogy is still relatively new, as in Albrecht-Crane and Daryl Slack (2003), Sontag (2004a, 2004b), Giroux (2004), and Hickey-Moody (2007, 2009).

References

Albrecht-Crane, C., & Daryl Slack, J. (2003). Towards a pedagogy of affect. In Daryl J. Slack (Ed.), *Animations (of Deleuze and Guattari)* (pp. 191–216). New York: Peter Lang.

Bauman, Z. (2001). *The individualized society.* London: Polity Press.

Beck, D.L. (2009) *Neural plasticity, cochlear implants, vision, and more: Interview with Sandra Aamodt, American Academy of Audiology.* Retrieved May 20, 2009, from www.audiology. org/news/interviews/Pages/20090316.aspx

Bloustien, G., & Wood, D. (2009, June). *'Can I borrow your face for a minute?' Issues of aesthetics and bodily transformations in Second Life.* Paper presented at CFP – Cosmetic Cultures: Beauty, Globalisation, Politics, Practices, Leeds, UK. (Also in press in *Body and Society*)

Cajal, R.Y.S. (1991). *Cajal's degeneration and regeneration of the nervous system: History of neuroscience, No 5.* (R.M. May, Trans.). New York: Oxford University Press. (Original work published between 1917 and 1935)

Chorost, M. (2005). *Rebuilt: How becoming part computer made me more human.* New York: Houghton Mifflin.

Clynes, M.E., & Kline, N.S. (1960). Cyborgs and space. *Astronautics*, September, pp. 27–31. (Original work published in *Drugs, space and cybernetics, Proceedings of the Psychophysiological Aspects of Space Flight Symposium, Air Force School of Aviation Medicine, San Antonio, TX, May, 1960.* New York: Columbia University Press, 1960)

Davis, L.J. (1995). *Enforcing normalcy: Disability, deafness and the body.* London: Verso.

Davis, L.J. (2007). Deafness and the riddle of identity. *Chronicle of Higher Education, 53*(19), B6.

Defelipe, J. (2006). Brain plasticity and mental processes: Cajal again. *Nature Reviews Neuroscience, 7* (October), 811–817.

Giroux, H.A. (2000). Public pedagogy as cultural politics: Stuart Hall and the 'crisis' of culture. *Cultural Studies, 14*, 341–360.

Giroux, H.A. (2004). Cultural studies and the politics and public pedagogy: Making the political more pedagogical. *Parallax, 10*(2), 73–89.

Goggin, G. (2008). Innovation and disability. *M/C: Media and Culture, 11*. Retrieved February 18, 2010, from http://journal.media-culture.org.au/index.php/mcjournal/article/view/56

Goggin, G. (2009). Disability and the ethics of listening. *Continuum, 23*, 489–502.

Goggin, G., & Newell, C. (2003). *Digital disability: The social construction of disability in new media.* Lanham, MD: Rowman & Littlefield.

Hamilton, S. (2008, October 21). Disability is an art [Media release]. Retrieved February 18, 2010, from htttp://www.unsw.edu.au/news/pad/articles/2008/oct/Disability_workshop.html

Haney, W.S. (2006). *Cyberculture, cyborgs and science fiction: Consciousness and the posthuman.* Amsterdam: New York Editions, Rodopi.

Haraway, D. (2003). Cyborgs to companion species: Reconfiguring kinship in technoscience. In D. Ihde & E. Selinger (Eds.), *Chasing technoscience: Matrix for materiality* (pp. 58–82). Bloomington: Indiana University Press.

Hauland, H. (2008). Sound and belonging: What is a community. In H.-D. Bauman (Ed.), *Open your eyes: Deaf studies talking* (pp. 111–126). Minneapolis: University of Minnesota Press.

Hickey-Moody, A. (2007). Re-imagining intellectual disability: Sensation and outside of thought. In A.C. Hickey-Moody & P. Malins (Eds.), *Deleuzian encounters: Studies in contemporary social issues* (pp. 79–98). London: Palgrave Macmillan.

Hickey-Moody, A. (2009). *Unimaginable bodies: Intellectual disability, performance and becomings*. Rotterdam, The Netherlands: Sense Publishers.

Hickey-Moody, A., & Wood, D. (2008). *Imagining otherwise: Deleuze, disability and second life. Proceedings of Australian & New Zealand Communication Association Annual Conference, 2008, Massey, New Zealand*. Retrieved May 20, 2009, from www.massey.ac.nz/massey/.../HickeyMoody_Wood_ANZCA08.pdf

Hickey-Moody, A., & Wood, D. (2009, December). *Ethnography and the ethics of affect in virtual worlds*. Paper presented at The Australian Anthropological Society Annual Conference 2009: The Ethics and Politics of Engagement, Macquarie University, Australia.

Jones, M. (2008). *Skintight: An anatomy of cosmetic surgery*. Oxford: Berg.

Jones, M., & Sofoulis, Z. (2002). Orlan and Stelarc in the Middle Ages. In J. Zylinska (Ed.), *The cyborg experiments: The extensions of the body in the media age* (pp. 56–72). London: Continuum.

Jutte, R. (2005). *A history of the senses: From antiquity to cyberspace*. Cambridge, MA: Polity Press.

Latour, B. (1993). *We have never been modern* (C. Porter, Trans.). Cambridge, MA: Harvard University Press.

Latour, B. (1994). On technical mediation – philosophy, sociology, genealogy. *Common knowledge, 3*(2), 29–64.

Samuels, E. (2002). Critical divides: Judith Butler's body theory and the question of disability. *NWSA Journal, 14*(3), 58–76.

Shannon, R.V., Zeng, F., Kamath, V., Wygonski, J., & Ekelid, M. (1995). Speech recognition with primary temporal cues. *Science, 270*(5234), 303–304.

Shaviro, S. (1993). *The cinematic body*. Minneapolis: University of Minnesota Press.

Shouse, E. (2005). Feeling, emotion, affect. *M/C Journal, 8*(6). Retrieved February 21, 2010, from http://journal.media-culture.org.au/0512/03-shouse.php

Siebers, T. (2004). Disability as masquerade. *Literature and Medicine, 23*(1), 1–22.

Smith, M., & Morra, J. (2006). *The prosthetic impulse: From a posthuman present to a biocultural future*. Cambridge, MA: MIT Press.

Sobchack, V. (2006). A leg to stand on: Prosthetics, metaphor, and materiality. In M. Smith & J. Morra (Eds.), *The prosthetic impulse: From a posthuman present to a biocultural future* (pp. 17–42). Cambridge, MA: The MIT Press.

Sontag, S. (2004a, May 23). Regarding the torture of others. *The New York Times*. Retrieved February 21, 2010, from http://www.nytimes.com/2004/05/23/magazine/23PRISONS.html

Sontag, S. (2004b). *Regarding the pain of others*. New York: Picador.

Taussig, M. (1993). *Mimesis and alterity: A particular history of the senses*. London: Routledge.

Wexler, P. (1992). After postmodernism: A new age social theory in education. In R.A. Smith & P. Wexler (Eds.), *After postmodernism: Education, politics and identity* (pp. 56–82). London: The Falmer Press.

Wood, D. (2008, October). *Accessibility in 3D virtual worlds*. Paper presented at the Alliance Library Second Life Health Information Round Table.

Corporeal and sonic diagrams for cinematic ethics in Rolf De Heer's *Dance Me to My Song*

Anna Hickey-Moody

Gender and Cultural Studies, Main Quad, University of Sydney, Sydney NSW, Australia

Rolf De Heer's 1997 Australian feature film *Dance Me to My Song* was devised with the late Heather Rose, a person with Cerebral Palsy. The film also features a central performance by Heather (as the character of Julia) and is clearly about 'her world'. The ethic of engagement exemplified by this film resonates with what Gerard Goggin has termed an 'ethics of listening' that entails 'listening-as-if-disability-mattered'. This article takes up Deleuze's concepts of the diagram in order to argue that *Dance Me to My Song* is a valuable, although at times problematic, cinematic framing of disability. Deleuze's two concepts of the diagram offer a useful frame through which to consider the film, because respectively they map the potentiality of social relations and act as a means of erasing cliché. The film is a raw, visceral text, rich in diegetic sound intended to 'fold' the experiences of the protagonist into the subjectivity of the spectator/ aurator. This folding blurs and re-aligns relationships between disabled and non-disabled bodies and can be seen as a step towards erasing clichés attached to the disabled body. The disabled/able boundary is further blurred through ambiguous representation of Julia's carer, Madeline, as potentially disabled. The characters in the film perform a diagrammatic function of shaping possible relations between bodies and erasing cliché. Building on the platform provided by *Dance Me to My Song*, I contend that when cinema engages with the disabled body and soundscapes associated with the disabled body through an 'ethics of listening', new sonic and filmic bodies can be – and are – created.

Introduction: social and artistic diagrams

Breathing, listening, feeling are the stuff of which our life is made. *Dance Me to My Song* (De Heer, 1997) prompts us to breathe with the protagonist, Julia, to feel and be embodied again (with) the screen. The narrative in *Dance Me to My Song* tells the story of Julia, a woman with Cerebral Palsy who lives independently with the support of a carer, named Madeline (Joey Kennedy). The relationship between the two women is constituted through power struggles, competition for Eddie's (John Brumpton) affections and their psychological and physical needs for sexual intimacy. Rolf De Heer devised the film with the late Heather Rose, who performs the character of Julia, and the film is clearly about 'her world'. The ethic of engagement exemplified by this film resonates with what Goggin (2009, p. 499) has termed 'the ethics of listening' that entails 'listening-as-if-disability-mattered'. At the time of its release in 1997, this ethic of cinematic engagement offered a welcome change for spectators who had become accustomed to the more exploitative techniques of 'representing' disability featured in mainstream releases such as *Rain Man* (Lavinson, 1989), *What's Eating Gilbert Grape?* (Hallstrom, 1993) and *Forrest Gump* (Zemeckis, 1994).

The cinematic engagement with disability presented in *Dance Me to My Song* can be read through Deleuze's (1981/2005, p. 69) notion of art as a diagram – a 'stopping or resting point' from which new sensory structures emerge. In what follows I offer an extended précis of the film, in order to set up the terms for my analysis as the paper progresses. What I offer in the précis is a mapping of the film as a diagram of a social field, or, rather, I want to suggest that the film can be read as a diagram for social relations/sociability that are disability inclusive. Specifically, I suggest that on screen Heather Rose's body can be read as a diagram, a 'possibility of fact' (Deleuze, 1981/2005, p. 77) for a new texture of cinematic engagement with disability.

The proposition that *Dance Me to My Song* opens up, or maps, new social relations between bodies brings together two different ways in which Deleuze talks about the diagram. In his work on Foucault, Deleuze talks about the diagram in terms of mapping social relationships to reveal the archive, or 'expose relations between forces or... particular strategies' (1986/2006, p. 36)[1] while creating new possible maps for social relations. In his book on Francis Bacon, Deleuze considers art as a diagram that is expressive of possible facts or new experiences which he explains by stating that 'the operation of the diagram... is to be "suggestive"... to introduce possibilities of fact' (1981/2005, p. 71). The artistic diagram as a resting point generates an event (which Deleuze calls a 'catastrophe' (1981/2005, p. 77) that must be *passed through* in order to create a new textual form (the form which Deleuze calls *the Figure* (1981/2005, pp. 23, 47). The respective features of Deleuze's two concepts of the diagram are very different and I want to be clear that I am synthesizing these two concepts. Drawing on *Foucault*, I examine the social relationships in the film in terms of the history of the social construction of disability they reveal and the possibilities for new relationships between bodies that they create. Drawing on *Francis Bacon*, I focus on the affects produced by each of the characters in terms of the qualitative capacity for action generated by the respective bodies. In bringing together the two concepts of the diagram introduced above, I argue that through technologies of film sound and cinematography, *Dance Me to My Song* creates an original 'cartography which is coextensive with the whole social field' (Deleuze, 1986/2006, p. 30) through which to know our own bodies and relations between bodies via the body-figure of the film text.

In order to attain such power of suggestion, *Dance Me to My Song* first dismantles the clichés about disability that already populate the film text. That is, before a film is made, we can imagine it exists within a genre of already-made films about disability, and these existing films make clichés about disability that pre-empt the possible content of the film. In his work on *Francis Bacon*, Deleuze describes *clichés* as anonymous and floating images:

> which circulate in the external world, but which also penetrate each of us and constitute our internal world, so that everyone possesses only psychic clichés by which we think and feel, are thought and felt, being ourselves one cliché among others in the world that surrounds us. (Smith, 2003)

To this, I would add that cliché is also a transcendent mode of thought that generates what Deleuze calls 'sad passions' (1968/1990, pp. 262, 270, 283). For example, depictions of people with severe disabilities as being 'retarded' or 'mentally disabled', filmic representations of people with disabilities as 'special' people, historical images of 'freak' bodies, celebrated disabled athletes, all such public knowledges and figures, alongside the private beliefs surrounding them, fold together as mediascapes and lived cultures join in cultural imaginaries to produce depictions of disability. These depictions also become clichés. *Dance Me to My Song* both dismantles and re-inscribes existing filmic clichés about disability to offer a sonic and filmic figure of the [disabled] body.

Dance Me to My Song constructs its spectators primarily as listeners, or what I have elsewhere called aurators (Hickey-Moody & Iocco, 2004). This sonic focus is achieved via binaural sound, which is the product of recording microphones that are attached to actors' heads during filming. These microphones pick up left and right sound tracks, in a manner similar to most human ears. Through this technique, seemingly insignificant noises (such as swallowing and breathing) are brought to the forefront of the listener's awareness. When listening to the sound track wearing headphones, Julia's breathing reverberates through the listener's body, as it would do through her own small frame. This diegetic sound is intended to 'fold' the experiences of the protagonist into the subjectivity of the spectator/aurator and operates to blur and re-align relationships between disabled and non-disabled bodies. Through this relationship *Dance Me to My Song* creates new sonic and celluloid diagrams which are pedagogies of the disabled body that constitute a step towards erasing clichés attached to the disabled body.

A key problematic of both this paper and the film itself is the production of Julia's aural and celluloid body through a mapping of differential relations of friendship, care, femininity, sensuality, sexuality and the ingestion of food and its expulsion. Julia and her search for intimacy deconstructs dominant filmic representations of disability in many ways and I focus on these articulations of disability on screen that dismantle existing clichés. I also consider some ways in which, across the film text, the disabled body is expressed as a site of ambivalence (Kumari-Campbell, 2009, p. 25), primarily to the disabled character herself but secondly, to the viewer. My point in doing this is to gesture towards some of the ways in which *Dance Me to My Song* offers a sympathetic engagement with the daily labour and complexity of Julia's life. Rather than Julia's body being presented as a site of monstrous difference, Julia's experience of her own body is presented to the viewer, and part of this daily experience is that Julia experiences ambivalence (Kumari-Campbell, 2009, pp. 25, 47, 129, 131, 138, 158, 159) about her corporeality, but other times it is a source of pleasure. When Julia can't effect direct change, or act upon herself and others, Julia experiences internal ambivalence (Kumari-Campbell, 2009, p. 158) about her self and her relations with the world.

Madeline, Julia's carer is psychologically disabled (Starrs, 2008), although somewhat ambiguously represented as such, and her character blurs distinctions between able/disabled characters in the film. I will suggest there are problematic aspects of the ways in which Madeline is presented as disabled, however, the overarching ambiguity around her disability is useful to the extent that it deconstructs any binary between disabled and non-disabled bodies.

In many ways, *Dance Me to My Song* works to problematize easy distinctions between abled and disabled bodies. Through the use of non-diegetic sound and an intimate engagement with Julia's body on screen, the film offers a new celluloid modulation of disability.

Dance Me to My Song: the text

The film begins by introducing some differences in Madeline's and Julia's lives. These differences are important because Madeline's psychiatric disability is evidenced through her worldview and actions, which consistently erode her capacity to act. Julia's actions produce her subjectivity as a mixture of physically needing others so much that she is limited in her capacity to act on herself, but Julia also has more capacity to engage with the complexities of the world than Madeline. We see this discrepancy in the women's capacities as soon as the film begins: Julia has to wait every morning for Madeline to arrive before she can go to the toilet, because she needs to be assisted into her chair. Madeline is a stereotypically 'hysterical woman': depressed, self-obsessed and desperate for sexual attention from men. She resents having to work and, rather than rising and heading to work to assist Julia with her toilet, Madeline dresses slowly, staring at her breasts in the mirror. This first scene contains themes that foreshadow key events in the film such as Madeline's narcissism and her disdain for Julia. Needing to feel 'better' than other people, feeling insecure and hopeless, Madeline consistently puts Julia down while talking about her own need for a man. Madeline tries to find a man, without much success. However, her attempts extend to great length – she disables Julia's wheelchair and puts sunglasses on Julia's face while she makes out with a new boyfriend on Julia's couch and then has sex with him in Julia's bed. Julia wants to watch. Julia hasn't had sex and is curious to see what it looks like. Madeline later teases Julia for watching, saying her man had ridiculed Julia in her chair and Madeline is happy that her sexual partner found her more attractive than Julia. They fight and Madeline leaves the house – screaming at Julia 'you'd be dead without me'. Madeline can only love Julia to the extent that Julia makes her feel needed, or 'better than' Julia.

Reluctant to call for help and scared of being returned to institutional care, Julia waits on the front veranda, hoping for a helpful stranger to pass after Madeline leaves her alone. In so doing, she finds herself a man – Eddie. Julia accosts Eddie in the street, interrupting his path repeatedly until he realizes she 'wants something'. Julia badgers Eddie – she wants a glass of water, she needs her voice machine on her chair, 'please plug the phone in the study'. Eddie needs to go but is also amazed at Julia's tenacity. Julia doesn't quite reach Eddie's chest in her chair and her tiny frame looks almost childlike in comparison to his tall, muscular body. Through her voice machine, Julia asks Eddie repeatedly to 'come back, come back, come back'. Eddie leaves and we are not sure if he is coming back. Julia's friend Rix comes over and they get drunk and hoon around the suburb – Rix sitting on Julia's commode on wheels, attached to Julia's chair (Figure 1). Madeline comes back and tries to ban the return of Rix, stating that 'I don't want you having that dyke in here, Julia, she makes a bloody mess, and she'll give you all sorts of germs' (Rix is a Maori lesbian). Julia responds: 'She's not a dyke. She's gay.' Madeline finishes the exchange with: 'There's no fucking difference, come on, into the bathroom'.

Figure 1. Julia drives Rix.

Eddie comes back. With flowers. He is helpful and attentive. Madeline is jealous. Her boyfriend has been put in gaol for breaking his good behaviour bond and she feels hopeless without her man. While shovelling food into Julia's mouth (at a speed that seems like it is about to choke her), Madeline comes up with a plan to seduce Eddie. She wants Julia's handsome and caring friend for herself. Madeline proudly details the plan to Julia, who fights back by spraying her food all over Madeline. Madeline screams: 'Think about what it feels like to be sprayed with somebody else's shit.' Julia is left in her chair, immobilized, and covered in 'vitimized' food. Eddie comes to visit, but without her voice machine and with her chair immobilized, Julia can't answer the door. Eddie breaks in and finds out that Julia has been abandoned. She needs Eddie's help to go to the toilet. Afterwards, Eddie finds a condom given to Julia by Family Planning[2] in the bathroom. They joke about Julia having the condom and Eddie takes them out for an ice cream. But it's the wrong kind of pleasure – Julia doesn't want ice cream, she wants sex. In front of the Delicatessen owner, while the owner is serving up two 'double tornado' ice creams, Julia asks through her voice machine 'Fuck me? Fuck me?' Eddie downplays her request, assuming she is not serious.

Madeline comes back. She's got herself a new man – 'found him at the shopping centre'. She's off for a date with her new man and Julia rings Eddie, asking him to come over while Madeline is out. Eddie does come over and, at Julia's request; he dances with her to her favourite song. Things with Madeline's new man don't turn out quite as planned. He's not the gentleman Madeline hoped for. He rapes her. She returns to sleep at Julia' house, and clinging to Julia, cries 'you are the only person in the world who loves me, Julia'. Having seemingly given up on her own love life, Madeline pries into Julia's – she rings Eddie with Julia's voice machine, and pretending to be Julia, sets up another date for the pair. But Julia doesn't want to be set up with Eddie while Madeline is around. Madeline forces Julia into a candle-lit bath with Eddie, but Julia protests. Madeline quickly takes Julia's place in the bath with Eddie. Initially shocked, he then acquiesces to her seduction. Julia has to lie in bed and listen to them have sex, until Rix and her partner drop in to visit and take Julia out. But the distraction is only temporary. Madeline has 'fallen in love' with Eddie and tells Julia she could 'spend the rest of her life with him'. Julia responds by making a play for Eddie. It seems she was keen to sleep with him, just not while Madeline was in the house. The seduction takes place, while Madeline's car stalls in the middle of a street, leaving her late for work and leaving Eddie and Julia safely alone. For a while.

Madeline, who until this point had harboured hopes of a future with Eddie, enters Julia's house while the lovers lie naked on the bed. Madeline screams: 'Jesus – you bastard. You low life shit. You fuck cripples now, do you?' Madeline throws Eddie out of the house but Julia is furious. Madeline has ruined her precious moment and Julia can't contain her anger: she tries to run Madeline down with her electric wheelchair; she hits and bites Madeline. Seeing Julia and Eddie together and suffering Julia's anger also sends Madeline into a fury – Madeline threatens to kill Julia and means it. She leaves Julia in her immobilized chair all day; returning late in the evening with an eerie, make-believe 'it will be ok' attitude. Madeline puts Julia into bed, but the non-diegetic sound warns us things are not safe for Julia. Madeline decides to sleep on the sofa rather than return home, as she usually does. Julia is desperate to get rid of Madeline and as soon as she leaves the next morning, Julia rings Eddie to try to talk. His phone has been disconnected. Julia blames Madeline and when Madeline returns that evening Julia attacks her ferociously as soon as she opens the door. Madeline is taken by surprise and narrowly escapes being hit, front on, by Julia's chair. Keen to hold on to her job, but more so, desperately needing to feel needed, Madeline tries to smooth things over and make the situation with Julia work.

On her way to the shops one day, Madeline casually mentions to Julia that Eddie had sent Julia a letter from Italy and Madeline had torn it up and thrown it away. Madeline didn't think Julia needed to read what it had to say. As far as Julia is concerned, this is the last straw. She phones her homecare provider and asks them to stop Madeline's visits. She would rather return to institutional care than live under Madeline's control. A temporary worker is sent in while Julia's future care is organized, but once she leaves Julia tucked in bed we again hear the clumsy, low notes of warning telling us Madeline is on her way back to the house. She knows where the spare key is kept and she is furious. Madeline demands to know why Julia fired her. Julia offers a rather reductive take on the relationship, stating: 'I stole your boyfriend'. This is partially true, but is also an oversimplification that pushes Madeline's buttons. Julia wants to fight back. She repeats the statement, inciting Madeline's anger. Rix and her partner arrive with a carton of beer just in time to stop Madeline strangling Julia. Rix punches Madeline, who then crawls out of the house accompanied by Rix's polite request: 'please don't come back'. Julia wins. Her homecare provider organizes a series of interviews with new carers and, just before the first interviewee arrives, Eddie comes back, laconically asking 'have there been any phone calls for me?' Eddie and Julia dance around together, while the film cuts to Madeline kicking her old Toyota Corolla, which has broken down. Again.

Re-reading the text: unpacking *Dance Me to My Song*

The visceral realism depicting Julia's resistance is important for ethical and cinematic reasons. In ethical terms, the ways in which Julia's experience of embodiment is portrayed alerts us to the everyday labour associated with Julia's lived experiences and produces an awareness of context. This awareness of context is a point Deleuze makes in relation to the ethics of affect. Taking up Spinoza's philosophy, he argues:

> The great theories of the Ethics . . . cannot be treated apart from the three practical theses concerning consciousness, values and the sad passions. (Deleuze, 1970/1988, p. 28)

These 'three practical theses concerning consciousness, values and the sad passions' (Deleuze, 1970/1988, p. 28) constitute building blocks for Spinoza's philosophy. His first thesis, concerning consciousness, is that our consciousness is an illusion. Spinoza argues that, rather than being the origin of our thoughts and actions, we *are* the affects that our thoughts and actions have on us. We act, and through acting, produce ourselves. Julia produces herself as an expanded, productive body through relationship with Eddie, but as a limited, aggressive, controlling body through her competitive relationship with Madeline.

The portrayal of Julia and Madeline's relationship in *Dance Me to My Song* is one part of the film that cannot be read as a diagram for a cinematic ethics. The relationship clearly positions Julia as the better person, and I am left feeling like Julia could have at times shown more empathy and concern for Madeline because Julia generally seems more capable of demonstrating respect for others than Madeline. Although Madeline is not physically disabled, she appears to have a psychiatric illness or personality disorder and is much less able to have any kind of relationship with people than Julia. The fact that Julia only seems to see Madeline as help or as a threat surprises me, because Julia's reading of the other people in her life is more nuanced than her approach to Madeline. Julia erases clichés associated with the disabled body in many areas of her life and this film, but not in her relationship with Madeline.

Madeline uncovers an archive of pathological thought about female sexuality and psychiatric illness. While on the surface she problematizes a simple disabled/abled binary, her actions also limit possibilities for relation between differently disabled bodies. Madeline as a character brings together clichéd ideas about stratified social identities (such as the single woman, the poorly educated, the carer). She also embodies clichés of the hysterical woman, whose womb or sexual desire drives her, and makes her heartless. Deleuze argues that cliché embodies transcendent, or totally abstracted, thought. As cliché, transcendent thought is folded into subjectivity, decreasing a body's ability to act through limiting engagements with materialities. The character of Madeline limits how we might know carers, although De Heer is clearly making a point about the power imbalance between carers and their clients through the relationship dynamic. The relationship is nightmarish. In the film, these clichés of female sexuality and the power of the carer become a performance of a historical social condition of a woman in need, rather than an active way of dealing with a situation: Madeline can't care emotionally for Julia. Rather, she hurts Julia because she needs attention from men. De Heer's prior judgment, founded on the clichés from which the character of Madeline is composed, discounts the potentiality of Madeline and Julia's relationship.

Deleuze argues that transcendent thought encourages the experience of, what Spinoza calls, the 'sad passions' (Deleuze, 1970/1988, 1990). These 'sad passions' are affects that diminish a body's capacity to act. Essentializing beliefs about people with disabilities not only limit the capacities of people with disabilities to act upon others but also foreclose ways in which they may be acted upon by others. An everyday example of a sad affect in *Dance Me to My Song* can be found in the relationship between Julia and Madeline, who is, as I have noted, very abusive and who is described by Bruno Starrs (2008) as having a psychological disability. Starrs retells the narrative of the film in a fashion that foregrounds Madeline's predilection for producing sad affects, recounting that: 'Madeline has an emotional disability rather than a physical disability: several scenes in the film show her reduced to helpless tears' (Starrs, 2008, p. 4). This evidence of Madeline reducing her own capacity to act is expressive of the ways in which she also reduces the capacities of those around her. Starrs explains: 'The callous Madeline ... soon realizes Julia's strength is in her voice machine and she withholds access to the device as punishment: if she takes it away then Julia is less demanding' (Starrs, 2008, p. 4).

Such petulance can be considered a performance of Spinoza's 'sad passion' (Spinoza, 1996, 2001), an act prompted by the feeling that one's actions will have no positive impact, so one may as well act for self-serving purposes. Madeline creates sad passions through demonstrating a very clichéd way of understanding disability, which Julia's sexuality fundamentally disturbs. *Dance Me to My Song* then somewhat displaces these transcendent, clichéd ideas of disability through exploring ways in which Julia acts upon herself and others and by interrogating the ways in which other people in Julia's life grapple, or fail to grapple, with their own transcendent beliefs relating to disability.

Julia's relationship with Eddie is a more positive ethical diagram for social intimacies between disabled and non-disabled bodies. The relationship is romantic, perhaps unrealistically so, as it isn't that often one accosts a stranger on the street who turns out to be a best friend and romantic, sexual match. But the communication between Eddie and Julia is a valuable contrast to the alarming lack of communication between Madeline and Julia. Eddie offers a fabulous instance of ethical engagement. For example, to believe that a person is incompetent – like Madeline believes of Julia, denies Julia the chance to act freely. In contrast to Madeline's beliefs that abstract her opinion from lived events, Eddie's performance of ethics is an engagement with practicalities. *More than this, ethics is Eddie's engagement with practicalities that performs an awareness of context.* It is this awareness of context and acting in response to such awareness that makes Eddie's acts ethical. 'Ethics' is a way of acting and thinking that constitutes paying attention to practical details in relation to their political, historical and social context. Eddie respects Julia, listens to her feelings, needs and offers her emotional and physical care in a manner that is rarely patronizing. In the instance where Eddie does patronize Julia, in the ice-cream shop, she brings it up with him afterwards. He promises not to do it again. Their relationship has its very real, liveable moments as well as its more absurdly romantic aspects.

The fact that the film features a naked, sexually-themed scene between a woman with Cerebral Palsy and a man without a disability does not necessarily make the text useful in terms of thinking through disability (Figure 2). However, the focus on, and production of, Julia's body is important – this is not romanticized and it is fore-grounded throughout the text. The first time Julia meets Eddie she needs him to help her have a drink of water. The second time she meets Eddie she needs him to help her go to the toilet. When Julia and Madeline fight, it usually involves food, and Julia

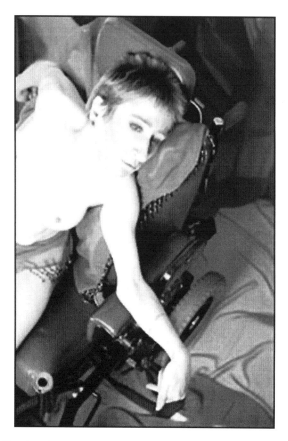

Figure 2. Julia half naked in her chair.

making a mess with food. Madeline ridicules Julia's body out of cruelty and Julia cracks jokes about her body in jest. Julia wants to dance and to be naked. Her body is composed of times of not working, and she wants sensuality: joyous sensations. Julia goes mad when Madeline temporarily ruins her intimacy. It was offering her respite from her body as a site of ambivalence (Kumari-Campbell, 2009, p. 158). Julia brings together a range of discourses of disability and remakes a new configuration of affects produced by, and attached to, the disabled body.

Breath with me, feel through me: sonic and celluloid diagrams

Dance Me to My Song creates new sonic and celluloid diagrams, which are pedagogies of the disabled body. The sound of Julia's breath and her swallowing shape the experience of listening (Goggin, 2009) to the film. The non-diegetic sound is really quite terrible – for the most part, it sounds like a cheap acoustic re-make of *Jaws* with a tango tune thrown in for the dance scenes. But the diegetic sound is original and very powerful. Julia's breath is heavy and her swallows are thick. The foregrounding of pedestrian noises that is noticeable in De Heer's films provides alternatives to assertions such as Michel Chion's suggestion in *The Voice in Cinema*

(1999), that spoken dialogue in the cinema soundtrack is the most privileged site of aural significance (Iocco & Hickey-Moody, 2005, p. 125). Voice is important for De Heer, but as a form of expression, not a just a vehicle for language. *Dance Me to My Song* contains more action and movement than dialogue. A range of sounds such as gurgling, swallowing, screaming and snorting express Julia's emotions, along with the mechanical modulation of her voice machine.

A critical aspect of what Deleuze, after Spinoza, calls 'joyful', or positive, encounters, is that they must fold back into their broader context in ways that enrich this context. This 'folding back in' is an example of the performative nature of ethics: *ethics is a productive movement*. Ethics is a movement in which one body acts on another, or is folded into another, enhancing the capacities to act of both parties in the encounter, while also strengthening broader contexts which extend beyond the specific encounter in question: contexts upon which the encounter implicitly depends. So my employment of the term 'ethical' is a performance of this reading of ethics as the affect of increasing one's power to act. *Dance Me to My Song* features some fabulous moments in which Julia feels sexy and loved — in these moments Julia increases Eddie's (her partner's) capacity to experience affection and Eddie's affection folds back into the context of Julia's life by enriching her experiences of physical affection and intimacy. The film also demonstrates tenacity as the positive affection mobilized through the challenges Julia faces. Moments of intimacy and physicality construct a diagram for an ethic of assembling the liveable, realistic, and inherently 'human' disabled body on screen.

Indeed, *Dance Me to My Song* as a cinematic framing of disability can be read as a public pedagogy in the respect that it teaches the spectator/aurator about the everyday experience of living with Cerebral Palsy through the ethic of engagement that drives the film's production. The engagement with Heather Rose's corporeality which features in *Dance Me to My Song* is a form of public pedagogy[3] that can be seen as a critical intervention in a public pedagogy of disability in which the female body of a woman living with Cerebral Palsy is taken up as the lens through which the film is constructed. Heather Rose's body – and her experiences of embodiment – are core modes of visual and sonic expression in the film. While this foregrounds the everyday experience of living with Cerebral Palsy, the employment of Heather's body as a key expressive device does not objectify disability, or construct Heather as 'monstrous' in ways that are common in earlier films about disability, such as Todd Browning's (1932) *Freaks*, Gustaf Molander's (1938) *A Woman's Face*, David Lynch's (1980) *The Elephant Man* or Joseph Marzano's (1977) *The Wheelchair*.

In terms of affect, *Dance Me to My Song* can be seen as a critical intervention in cultural imaginings of disability, and the production of clichés about disability, because Heather Rose's body and her experiences of embodiment are remade into sounds, images and affects that generate new relationships between the viewer and partial objects of disability.

Conclusions

Dance Me to My Song arranges and opens up the murmur of the archive of the female disabled body, female sexuality and mental illness, through canvassing the relations of power between a disabled body and a non-physically disabled body, and through interrogating two women's psychological and physical needs for sexual intimacy. More than this, though, *Dance Me to My Song* expresses sensations that are new to film media: as an art diagram it is expressive of 'possible facts' pertaining to sexing and sexualizing the visceral nature of Cerebral Palsy, and generating intimate encounters with the disabled body.

Julia, Madeline and Eddie's relationships map new possibility for relations with/across/about disability. They 'make...history by unmaking preceding realities and significations, constituting hundreds of points of emergence or creativity, unexpected conjunctions...[and] improbable continuums' (Deleuze, 1986/2006, p. 35). The sonic and celluloid body produced by the film offers new cinematic affects of disability to an existing archive of cinematic representations of disability (Ellis, 2008).

Building on the platform provided by *Dance Me to My Song*, cinema as a medium needs to engage more regularly with the disabled body as a cinematic frame in ways which acknowledge the viscerally intense, complex and laborious nature of the lives of people with disabilities. However, film as a medium must be careful not to present the disabled form as completely alien. In cinematic terms, the ways in which Julia's corporeality permeates the celluloid forms a core aspect of the film's gritty aesthetic and affective intensity. This becoming-body of the screen draws the spectator's attention to the joyful affects produced by affection and intimacy and the tenacity mobilized through the challenges of Julia's daily life.

These moments of ethical movement act as what Deleuze calls a diagram for mapping relations between bodies. *Dance Me to My Song* offers this relational diagram through an artistic diagram: through the cinematic and aural framing of a world in which we breathe with the disabled body. The pedagogical moment through which the film challenges its spectator and aurator to be worthy of these affects (to become in relation to them), constitutes a public pedagogy of disability through which both the body on screen and the body of the beholder/listener can be re-assembled in relation to the lived experience of disability. One might say, then, that the project of developing a cinematic ethics that is responsive to the disabled body is a question of inventing new diagrams for bodies.

The moments in *Dance Me to My Song* in which the aurator breathes with Julia, in which Julia's body consumes the screen and the subjectivity of the viewer, or Julia feels sexy and loved, are diagrams for a cinematic ethic of the live-able, realistic, and inherently 'human' disabled body on screen. It is in hearing Julia and feeling Julia that the spectator/aurator feels their own body differently and the celluloid becomes modulated as flesh.

Acknowledgements

Thanks very much to my blind peer reviewers and to Vertigo Productions for allowing reproduction of both images included in the text. Thanks also to Bridget Garnham for editorial assistance and Christian McCrea, Glen Fuller and Cassandra Loeser for their responses to earlier versions of this paper.

Notes

1. Specifically, Deleuze states: 'every diagram is intersocial and constantly evolving. It never functions in order to represent a persisting world but produces a new kind of reality, a new model of truth' (1986/2006, p. 35).

2. As the name suggests, Family Planning is a sexual health organization based in South Australia.
3. In considering *Dance Me to My Song* as a public pedagogy, I draw on the work of Henri Giroux (1999), who argues that pedagogy can't be confined to sites of schooling. Rather, pedagogy needs to be understood as applying to everyday political sites in 'which identities are shaped, desires mobilized, and experiences take on form and meaning' (Giroux, 2004a, p. 79). For Giroux, culture, including film, is pedagogical. People learn about themselves and understand relations to others through their position in lived cultures. An explicit consideration of how culture influences identity production and relations of power is, for Giroux, one of the intended outcomes of considering culture and cultural products as pedagogical. This is an important task because such knowledge of the role of culture is intrinsic to acquiring agency and 'imagining ... social change' (2004a, p. 79). For example, in his essay, 'Education after Abu Ghraib', Giroux (2004b) draws attention to how the nature of photographs and the technologies that produce them enable particular meanings; how these meanings connect with broader discourses and relations of power; how these sites allow or disallow resistance and challenge.

References

Browning, T. (1932). *Freaks* [Film]. USA: MGM Productions.

Chion, M. (1999). *The voice in cinema*. New York: Columbia University Press.

De Heer, R. (1997). *Dance Me to My Song* [Film]. Australia: Vertigo Productions.

Deleuze, G. (1988). *Spinoza: Practical philosophy* (R. Hurley, Trans.). San Francisco: City Light Books. (Original work published 1970)

Deleuze, G. (1990). *Expressionism in philosophy: Spinoza* (M. Joughin, Trans.). New York: Zone Books. (Original work published 1968)

Deleuze, G. (2005). *Francis Bacon: The logic of sensation* (D.W. Smith, Trans.). London: Continuum. (Original work published 1981)

Deleuze, G. (2006). *Foucault* (S. Hand, Trans.). London: Continuum. (Original work published 1986)

Ellis, K. (2008). *Disabling diversity: The social construction of disability in 1990s Australian national cinema*. Saarbrücken, Germany: VDM Verlag.

Giroux, H. (1999). Cultural studies as public pedagogy making the pedagogical more political. In *Encyclopaedia of philosophy of education*. Retrieved February 15, 2005, from www.vusst.hr/encyclopaedia/main.htm

Giroux, H. (2004a). Cultural studies and the politics of public pedagogy: Making the political more pedagogical. *Parallax, 10*(2), 73–89.

Giroux, H. (2004b). Education after Abu Ghraib: Revisiting Adorno's politics of education. *Cultural Studies, 1*, 779–815.

Goggin, G. (2009). Disability and the ethics of listening. *Continuum, 23*, 489–502.

Hallstrom, L. (1993). *What's eating Gilbert Grape?* [Film]. Austin, TX: J and M Entertainment.

Hickey-Moody, A., & Iocco, M. (2004). Sonic affect(s): Binaural technologies and the construction of auratorship in Rolf De Heer's *Bad Boy Bubby*. *Metro Magazine: Media & Education Magazine, 140*, 78–81.

Iocco, M., & Hickey-Moody, A. (2005). Christ kid, you're a weirdo: Aural construction of subjectivity in *Bad Boy Bubby*. In R. Coyle (Ed.), *Reel tracks: Australian feature film music and cultural identities* (pp. 122–136). London: J. Libbey.

Kumari-Campbell, F. (2009). *Contours of abelism*. London: Palgrave Macmillan.

Lavinson, B. (1989). *Rain man* [Film]. USA: Guber-Peters.

Lynch, D. (1980). *The elephant man* [Film]. London: Brooks Films.

Marzano, J. (1977). *The wheelchair* [Film]. Long Island, USA: JM Pictures.

Molander, G. (1938). *A woman's face* [Film]. Sweden: Svensk Filmindustry.

Smith, D. (2003). *Deleuze on Bacon: Three conceptual trajectories in The Logic of Sensation*. Retrieved December 9, 2009, from http://www.upress.umn.edu/excerpts/Deleuze.html

Spinoza, B. (1996). *Theologico-political treatise: A political discourse*. Retrieved July 17, 2002, from http://csf.colorado.edu/forums/longwaves/98/oct98/1203.html

Spinoza, B. (2001). *Ethics.* Ware, Hertfordshire, UK: Wadsworth.

Starrs, B. (2008). Enabling the auteurial voice in *Dance Me to My Song. M/C Journal, 11*(3). Retrieved December 9, 2009, from http://journal.media-culture.org.au/index.php/mcjournal/article/viewArticle/49

Zemeckis, R. (1994). *Forrest Gump* [Film]. USA: Paramount Pictures.

Stirring up the sediment: the corporeal pedagogies of disabilities

Jessica Robyn Cadwallader

Department of Gender and Cultural Studies, University of Sydney, Sydney, NSW, Australia

The centrality of Cartesian dualism to practices of university pedagogy obscures the role that bodily being-in-the-world plays in learning and teaching. This article uses Merleau-Ponty's account of embodiment to explore the pedagogical capacity of disability, specifically in relation to two university courses. I argue that the disabled other offers such radical difference that it intervenes, as Lévinas puts it, anachronistically, in the synchronicity of sedimentary styles of being-in-the-world. I consider the role that syncretic sociability – intercorporeality – plays in producing an incarnatory context within the classroom which challenges the 'common sense'ness of the ableism which so thoroughly shapes institutions, customs, power, sociality, and dominant styles of being-in-the-world.

Introduction

Many of the processes of learning have been theorised through an analysis of the role played by the body. Piaget's focus on the body understood that one of the key ways in which we develop from childhood is through learning our bodies: learning how they interact with the world, with other bodies, learning how they feel, and learning how to turn how they feel into knowledge. Yet this focus on children's bodies can risk implying that adult education is primarily or even fundamentally *cognitive*, a misconception that is only increased when we specify a university context, with lectures, tutorials and assessments which seem focused not on bodily being, but solely on the mind's capacity to grasp new knowledge and new methods (evidenced, perhaps, by the usually rather uncomfortable chairs found in contemporary classrooms).

However, as post-structuralist, feminist, and other critical frameworks have been brought to bear on the pedagogical assumption that Descartes was right when he declared that each of us is, primarily, a thinking being, the role of the body has been found to be far more significant to processes of learning and teaching than might once have been supposed. This article participates in this conversation, already occurring between such education theorists as Peters (2004), Giroux and McLaren (1991), Zavarzadeh and Morton (1991), and O'Loughlin (2006), by exploring Merleau-Ponty's (1964) theorisation of the intercorporeal formation of bodily comportments in order to consider the role that dominant styles of being-in-the-world play in maintaining 'common sense' (Ahmed, 2000, p. 29), as well as demonstrating that such bodily styles may be reshaped. I consider the reworking of bodily being instantiated by the corporeal engagement with the disabled other, and then extend this analysis to explore the way that pedagogical contexts, even if they may appear to 'only' involve 'conceptual' engagement with disability, can participate in this process.

This exploration of embodiment is informed by my experiences of university pedagogy, and the role of bodily being in teaching and learning, specifically in relation to teaching 'disability' in units of study which are not specified as 'disability studies' units. Over the last five years, I have been involved in teaching two units, one focused on queer theory, and the other on technologies of bodily alteration (primarily medical); both courses were created and convened by Associate Professor Nikki Sullivan at Macquarie University. Each course has a week focused on disability, and in both courses, disability often functions as the lynchpin upon which the rest of the course turns. This, I will argue, is because disability troubles a range of 'common sense' assumptions, and in so doing troubles students' habituated styles of being-in-the-world. It is this troubling, I suggest, that can be a powerful pedagogical tool, and one that works through understanding students as *embodied* subjects, rather than simply minds tucked away within bodies. In both of these courses, a key element of ensuring a 'troubling' context is to work to create a classroom context which approaches disability through the lens suggested by Lennard Davis (1995):

> To understand the disabled body, one must return to the concept of the norm, the normal body. So much of writing about disability has focused on the disabled person as the object of study, just as the study of race has focused on the person of color. But as with recent scholarship on race, which has turned its attention to whiteness, I would like to focus not so much on the construction of disability as on the construction of normalcy. I do this because the 'problem' is not the person with disabilities; the problem is the way that normalcy is constructed to create the 'problem' of the disabled person. (pp. 23–24)

The creation of such a classroom context does not occur only through discussion or rational, logical argument. Indeed, whilst such may contribute to the learning process, it is, I will argue, the intercorporeal reworking of perception that helps to 'activate' the often-suppressed pedagogical capacities of disability: that is, it is through an intercorporeal sharing of minoritarian perceptual practices that students re-member encounters with disability in ways that trouble the 'common sense' of their perceptual practices. These experiences so alter their perception of disability as to see it as no longer a problem, but as part of an institutional, discursive and corporeal system, the 'disability/ability system' (Garland-Thomson, 2002, p. 2) within which they themselves are implicated, and which ensures that disability can only ever matter and materialise as a problem.[1]

Syncretic sociability and the sedimentation of bodily being-in-the-world

Merleau-Ponty's work counters the gendered mind/body dichotomy which grounds liberal humanist conceptions of the subject and sociality. The mind/body split permits the configuration of the ideal subject as a (radically individual) mind inserted into the body, which is then inserted into the world, amongst other people. It has been and remains the dominant way of conceiving of subjectivity, and has thus shaped institutions, such as education, to engage primarily with a Cartesian subject.

Merleau-Ponty instead describes the subject as an embodied being always already thoroughly intertwined with the world and thus also with others; in fact, it is only as a result of this intertwining that the child – and although he is speaking developmentally, he also clarifies that this applies equally to the processes of adult subjectivity – can even develop a sense of him or herself.

He explains it as follows: initially, the child develops a sense, albeit basic, of his or her body's organisation as a totality, 'a perception of my body's position in relation to the vertical, the horizontal, and certain other axes of important co-ordinates of its environment' (Merleau-Ponty, 1964, p. 117). This is a 'corporeal' or 'postural' schema (p. 117), a basic organisation of perceptual experience developed prior to six months of age which links introceptive and extroceptive elements of bodily experience, enabling the immature child to orient himself or herself in a basic way in his or her environment.

In the child's encounter with the other, 'a perspective on the other is opened to me from the moment I define him [sic] and myself as "conducts" at work in the world, as ways of "grasping" the natural and cultural world surrounding us' (Merleau-Ponty, 1964, p. 117).[2] This process is not reflective, then: it is not that the child maps together the shape of the other's smile with his or her own feeling of his or her own lips, and then wills the smile; rather:

in perceiving the other, my body and his [sic] are coupled . . . this conduct which I am able only to see, I live somehow from a distance. I make it mine; I recover [reprendre] it or comprehend it . . . [a] transfer of my intentions to the other's body and of his intention to my own. (Merleau-Ponty, 1964, p. 118)

It is this intercorporeal intertwining of the subject and other that Merleau-Ponty (1964) identifies as 'syncretic sociability' (p. 120): '[T]here is thus a system (my visual body, my introceptive body, the other), which establishes itself in the child, never so completely as in the animal but imperfectly, with gaps' (p. 135). These elements, it is important to recall, do not experientially pre-exist their interrelation, but are the names – self, and world, and other – given to the threads that are later spun from the woolly experience of child-and-world-and-others.

This non-synthetic unity ensures that the other cannot be reduced or even fully encompassed by the syncretic relation with the subject: it is a 'non-dualistic divergence . . . that permits neither fusion nor absolute distance' (Reynolds, 2005). Syncretic sociability unifies self and other just as parts of an arm are unified: in the sustenance of difference:

[a] certain tactile experience felt in the upper arm signifies a certain tactile experience in the forearm and shoulder, along with a certain visual aspect of the same arm, not because the various tactile perceptions among themselves, or the tactile and visual ones, are all involved in one intelligible arm, not as the different facets of a cube are related to the idea of a cube, but because the arm seen and the arm touched, like the different segments of the arm, together perform one and the same action. (Merleau-Ponty, 2002, p. 175)

The impregnation of the subject's style of being-in-the-world with the corporeal styles of the other is a result of their being intertwined, rather than replicated through a reductive synthesis whereby two are made into one. It is precisely because it is not reductive that the other grants the subject his or her unique way of being-in-the-world. The difference of the other develops the subject in and through that subject's adoption and adaptation of the other's bodily styles. However, the other must be different, and radically so, because this process of adoption and adaption would not be possible if I coincided with the other. My experience of the other differs fundamentally from my experience of myself, even as these experiences are intertwined. Even in the pre-communicative state which Merleau-Ponty describes, it is not that the subject and other are synthesised or 'made one'; rather, this pre-communicative state produces the postural impregnation which grounds the realisation of the other's circumscribing of the subject in what Lévinas might describe as the ethical call, and the response of/in subjectivity.

As Merleau-Ponty (1964) puts it, it is only 'after [the establishment of syncretic sociability] that the objectification of the body intervenes to establish a sort of wall between me and the other: a partition' (p. 120). This objectification is two-sided:

> Both by the objectification of one's own body (say, through the mirror phase) and the constitution of the other in his [*sic*] difference, there occurs a segregation, a distinction of individuals – a process which, moreover, as we shall see, is never completely finished. (Merleau-Ponty, 1964, p. 119)

The difference between the two, and the comprehension that the subject is an object for the other, means that the subject, now delimited to his or her embodiment rather than ranging across the bodies of all the others he or she encounters, is brought into being.

Although Merleau-Ponty articulates this formation of embodiment in the context of juvenile development, it is important to understand that the syncretic relation is the grounding of the sociality which ensures that embodied subjectivity remains in process, and thus it is this syncretic sociability which so thoroughly shapes classroom pedagogies, in often unacknowledged ways. It is in the midst of this intercorporeal syncretic relation that the subject's corporeal comportment – a corporeal style of being-in-the-world which is specific to the subject and produced in and through his or her interrelatedness to those around him or her – is formed and reformed. A subject's style of being-in-the-world, or comportment, is the subject and all that he or she does: his or her perceptions, self-hood, introceptive sense, patterns of thought, ability to speak, sense of the erotic, gestures, ways of walking, and so on. As Diprose articulates it, it is in the intercorporeal relation that 'agency, perception, affectivity and, combining all of these, identity, are born' (2002, p. 69) and continue to be enabled, altered and developed throughout the subject's life. It is clear, then, that the educational process involves the intercorporeal re-formation of the subject's styles of being-in-the-world.

Yet, as any teacher knows, this process is not a simple process; students often demonstrate some form of resistance to what they are learning, for many different reasons. Although a subject's corporeal style always changes, it is not mercurially fluid. Some stability – and indeed, the possibility of a sense of self persisting through time – is engendered in and through the 'sediments left behind by some previous constitution' (Merleau-Ponty, 2002, p. 249): remnants of particular modes of engagement with the world, both in the subject's comportment and (through syncretic sociability) in the comportments of those around him or her. As a result, the subject's being-in-the-world is habituated; it becomes, as Merleau-Ponty puts it, 'sedimented' (2002, p. 150). The repetition of particular modes of engagement with the world adds layer upon layer to the palimpsest of my particular style of being-in-the-world. It is this that allows the development of a sense of self, persisting through time, and that thus allows the subject to be, as subject with a past, present and future. In producing some level of corporeal consistency in how I engage with the world, I can learn: I can perfect actions or techniques or perceptions precisely because they function, corporeally, as repetitions, sedimenting into my bodily grasp of the world. Thus, part of the appeal of Merleau-Ponty's work lies in the fact that it maintains the ambiguity of embodiment, with which teachers, knowingly or not, inevitably engage: as both that which enables me to do things, even new things, and as that which delimits on the basis of previous experience (where these two are, of course, thoroughly intertwined).

The modification of one's styles of being-in-the-world, however, do not happen in a vacuum. As we have already seen, it is in and through my relations with others – through syncretic sociability – that I come to have a particular comportment. Thus, on the one hand, the styles of being-in-the-world I am surrounded by reinforce my own (see Alcoff, 2001 for a discussion of this in relation to race and whiteness), forming what I will call 'common sense', discussed in the next section. On the other hand, these styles of being-in-the-world also ensure that my own comportments are never rendered fully static; and this will form the later discussion of the pedagogy of disability.

The first consequence is necessitated because the 'frequent confirmation' which Merleau-Ponty describes as part of the process of sedimentation lies not only in my own repetition of a particular mode of attunement to the world, but also the confirmation I receive through syncretic sociability, through my intercorporeal perception of the way that others are-in-the-world. Sedimentation is not restricted simply and utterly to my own history but to the interplay of my own experiences with the sedimentation of my particular cultural context. Even as the sedimentation of my comportment ensures that certain perceptions, experiences, and styles of thinking become 'the atmosphere of my present' (Merleau-Ponty, 2002, p. 514) these are reinforced in and through my relations with others. What we might identify as the 'incarnatory context'[3] of an individual's embodiment – where, obviously, each embodied subject exists within a multiplicity of intersecting contexts – significantly shapes their experience. The familiarity and pleasantness of particular experiences, or their capacity to transgress the limitations my habituated style of being-in-the-world,[4] cannot be unbound from the approval and value, or the absence of such, which is given them in the incarnatory context within which I occur. That which is experienced as most familiar is likely to not only be experienced as such by others, but is usually reinforced discursively and institutionally as normal and natural by the context within which the subject occurs, and this contributes to the shape of my comportment.

The common sense of disability

Understanding the ways in which styles of being-in-the-world are both sedimentary and contextually produced allows us to understand what, precisely, is being engaged, corporeally, in the classroom. This is not merely the insight that all students and teachers are bodily beings, but the political and ethical consequences of this. There is a contextually-defined 'common sense', a shared sense of how the world works, premised on shared 'perceptual practices' (Alcoff, 1999, p. 30) and both our casual and formal engagement with power/knowledge (as Foucault formulates it). It is important to recollect how *intimate* such 'common sense' is: it is not simply 'knowledge', or simply 'content.' As Merleau-Ponty is at pains to point out, 'I am not in front of my body, I am in it, or rather *I am it*. Neither its variations nor their constant can, therefore, be expressly posited' (2002, p. 173, my emphasis). Thus what is at stake in a student's entry into the classroom is not simply the ideas they have, or their knowledge, or their styles of thought, but their being-in-the-world: their very being, and their very world.

In relation to disability, then, it is important to understand the function of common sense in the embodied ableism present in the classroom (and I would suggest that this is important not only in classes which 'address' dis/ability explicitly, but in all pedagogical contexts). The ableism of dominant, embodied common sense is, however, radically pre-conscious: '[p]erception is not a science of the world, it is not even an act, a deliberate taking up of a position; it is the background from which all acts stand out, and is presupposed by them' (Merleau-Ponty, 2002, pp. xi–xii). Indeed, he goes on to say that 'perception is, not presumed true, but defined as access to truth. Inside such a system, perception cannot then be the object of analysis itself' (as cited in Alcoff, 2001, p. 273). As Alcoff demonstrates in relation to race, it is important to understand the politics of perception: perceptual practices are common-sensical because 'although racial classification does operate on the basis of perceptual [perceive-able] difference, it is also the case that perception represents sedimented contextual knowledges' (2001, p. 272). In other words, it is these 'sedimented knowledges' that enable the recognition of particular kinds of difference as visible and as racially meaningful: 'the process by which human bodies are differentiated and categorised by type is a process preceded by racism, rather than one that causes and thus "explains" racism as a natural result' (Alcoff, 2001, p. 272). Her point applies to corporeal difference more generally, and thus dominant perceptions of disability as lack, as broken, as tragedy, as incapacity, as failure, as pitiful, as not entirely human, as proximate to death are revealed to be the result of dominant, common-sensical perceptual practices. Disability, in other words, as the 'dustbin for disavowal' (Hevey, 1991, as cited in Shakespeare, 1994, p. 298) is perceived from the beginning as 'a problem', as Davis pointed out.

And it is precisely because of the relationship of disavowal between ability and disability that challenging these perceptions is often extremely troubling for students. This is the case even, or perhaps especially, for those who assume they share a 'liberal' perspective with the course materials, lecturers and tutors (an intriguing assumption, given that liberalism is thoroughly critiqued in both the courses under discussion), and are thus prepared to agree that people with disabilities are to be pitied and cared for. In the queer theory course, this often manifests itself as a 'concern' about what is 'really going on' when disabled people seek to be sexual or reproductive. It can also be troubling for students with disabilities ('visible' or 'invisible'), who, even if they are differently positioned in relation to the institutionalised notions of normalcy and ability, nonetheless participate to varying degrees in the same incarnatory context which constitutes their own bodily being as a problem. It is not surprising that the challenge of Davis' claim is so troubling:

it queries 'structure[s] of contemporary perception...[which] help constitute the necessary background from which I know myself. [It queries that which] makes up a part of what appears to me as the natural setting of all my thoughts' (Alcoff, 2001, p. 273). As Drew Leder (1990) observes, the 'able' body is a body which is precisely *not present* to the subject him or herself: it disappears, as Heidegger observed of tools, in use (in Leder, 1990, pp. 83–84). To *make present* the body for students, then, by bringing into question their grasp of the world, challenges the idea that they have transparent, supposedly 'disembodied' access to the world through their habitual bodily style. Thus this challenge upsets students' habituated comportments; and to recollect, this challenge is intimate enough to query their *selves*.

Given the contemporary fascination with science and scientific truth, albeit in a radically popularised form, it is perhaps unsurprising that one of the first responses from students to Davis' challenge is a recourse to 'nature' as a disavowal of responsibility: '*I* didn't say their bodies were wrong,' one student claimed. 'Nature did!' Such claims are often followed by some over-simplified evolutionary biology, which is generally deployed to argue the bodies of our 'cavemen' ancestors are to be taken as the able-bodied standard (a standard, I regularly point out, that the vast majority of people, 'able-bodied' or not, fail to achieve, yet without the blame or derogation accorded people with disabilities). Yet there is something more interesting going on in the turn to science as the authorisation of the supposed naturally-given standard of bodily being: our habituated perceptions are marked as neutral, and as natural. That is, as Alcoff (2001) explains in relation to race:

> [o]ur experience of habitual perceptions is so attenuated as to skip the stage of conscious interpretation and intent. Indeed, interpretation is the wrong word here: we are simply perceiving...[I]t is commonly believed that for one to be racist one must be able to access in their consciousness some racist belief, and that if introspection fails to produce such a belief then one is simply not racist. A fear of African-Americans or a condescension towards Latinos is seen as a simple perception of the real, justified by the nature of things in themselves without need of an interpretive intermediary of historico-cultural schemas of meaning. (p. 276)

When we see something, we tend to assume that we just see it, as it is, and 'science', at least as it is popularly imagined, *authorises* this presumption that the subject has a transparent and passive relation to the world, which in turn conceals the function of perception. Thus the challenge to the ableist perceptual practices of students is thorough-going: it also calls into question their entire grasp of the world.

The anachronism of disability: stirring up the sediment

One of the problems, then, that teachers confront when trying to teach students critical approaches to their own perceptions is that the sedimentary nature of embodiment makes it almost impossible to see beyond or otherwise to how one has already seen. It is this that prompts the turn towards 'nature' and 'scientific' discourse, as a way of claiming a higher authority to reinforce their perceptions (one which, as I have already noted, at least in the case of science, would not necessarily authorise such claims). This is what Merleau-Ponty's approach to embodiment reveals as being difficult: once a thing had been experienced in one way, over and over, it is difficult to so rework the sedimented orientation toward that thing that it might be experienced otherwise. In fact, according to Merleau-Ponty's conception of the body as *essentially sedimentary*, it is almost impossible for such a reworking to happen. Sedimentation occurs, according to Merleau-Ponty, in and through the interaction between time – implicitly conceived of as a series of presents – and the body. The body functions as the 'effective law' which permits one moment to be connected to the other (Merleau-Ponty, 2002, p. 173): it, the body, 'give[s] to our life the form of generality' (Merleau-Ponty, 2002, p. 169). It is the body which is held to be in common between various (radically different) experiences, such that sedimentation can occur (and in/as the body). It is bodily being which allows for a consistency between two moments so that 'what is acquired is truly acquired only if it is taken up in a fresh momentum' (Merleau-Ponty, 2002, p. 150): in the experience of this 'taking up', as a taking up of what has already been, lies the formation of habit. This reveals that Merleau-Ponty suggests that bodily being continues as the same, or is at least thought of and experienced as such, throughout its temporal experience. It is this taking of 'the body' as a norm that permits the constitution of sedimentation and its delimitation of bodily styles according to what has already been.

Yet according to Merleau-Ponty's own schema, it then becomes difficult to explain how corporeal experience *does* shift and change. It becomes difficult to explain how one might engage with the world differently. As he observes:

> Here once more we must recognize a sort of sedimentation of our lives: an attitude towards the world, when it has received frequent confirmation, acquires a favoured status for us...having built our life upon an inferiority complex which has been operative for twenty years, it is not *probable* that we shall change...Generality and probability are not fictions, but phenomena; we must therefore find a phenomenological basis for statistical thought. It belongs necessarily to a being which is fixed, situated and surrounded by things in the world. 'It is improbable' that I should at this moment destroy an inferiority complex in which I have been content to live for twenty years. That means I have committed myself to inferiority, that I have made it my abode, and that this past, though not a fate, has at least a specific weight and is not a set of events over there, at a distance from me, but the atmosphere of my present. (Merleau-Ponty, 2002, p. 514)

The 'phenomenological basis for statistical thought,' as Merleau-Ponty puts it, is the body. The body is the 'effective law', as we saw above. Yet it is not the body alone which is required for this imagining of sedimentary embodiment. Rather, *time* must be imagined, to some extent, as synchronous, as one moment after another, after another, as a line upon which we travel, a line which we, sedimentarily, gather up into ourselves, bodily.[5] This also requires that the body be fundamentally *normative*, as Merleau-Ponty claims: that the body recognise, somehow, that there is a similarity between *this* experience at this moment and *that* experience at that moment sufficient to create a 'favoured status' for us.

Although I would query Merleau-Ponty's implication that probability and generality are pre-discursive (given the centrality of the norm in both), I do not think that this is straightforwardly incorrect, as a description of contemporary styles of embodiment. Rather, I want to suggest that the constitution of the body as this normative, sedimentary material occurs according to what Butler (1993) identifies as 'process[es]...of materialization' (p. 2); that the production of the body as a construction, where:

[c]onstruction is neither a single act nor a casual process initiated by a subject and culminating in a set of fixed effects. Construction not only takes place *in* time, but is itself a temporal process which operates through the reiteration of norms. (Butler, 1993, p. 10)

But the question still remains: with this construction of time, and the way that this (in)forms bodily being, how is it possible to experience something as truly new, as truly unique, as fundamentally *not defined* by my previous experiences? And for teaching, this is particularly important: how does one introduce material to students in ways that allow its newness, and its difference from other ways of thinking and being, to affect them? How does one break open the fundamentally conservative function of sedimentary bodily being? And how does one activate previous experiences, sedimented in accordance with dominant comportments, so thoroughly shaped by ableism?

Given that sedimentation conjoins time and the body, these questions are about time. And for Lévinas, perhaps the pre-eminent theorist of non-normative ethics, our relation to time is shaped by our relation to the other. Lévinasian ethics is not about the calculated application of principles to a situation. It is, rather, about my affective relation with the other, where the other is always understood as incomprehensibly different to me: as always alteritous. Alterity is so radically other that the other's call disrupts my self-interested being: in being beyond comprehension, or 'thematisation', as Lévinas calls it, the other intervenes in my self-confident grasp of the world, in my capacity to know it. But he understands this as affecting *temporality*: the 'call' of the other, a call to responsibility, for Lévinas (1998), is *anachronistic* (p. 88). The call disrupts the otherwise-synchronous temporality of the subject, a synchronicity, as we have already seen, which grounds the sedimentary formation of the embodied subject.

As Merleau-Ponty puts it: '[b]y taking up a present, I draw together and transform my past, altering its significance, freeing and detaching myself from it' (2002, p. 528). Merleau-Ponty here appears to claim that there is an 'I' that intentionally takes up this present, but on my reading, this is not intentional, specifically because this particular 'present' is not just another moment in the linear, impersonal unfolding of time. Rather, this moment is given by the other, a gift of another time, a jolt 'outside' the dense temporality of my embodied subjectivity, time to be altered, to make present a new 'I' whose sedimented history is remade by this moment out-of-time. This is the present that stirs up the sediment, disjointing time so that the material, embodied subject is other than what they were. The 'effective law' of the body is itself troubled, altered, made otherwise to what it already had been, because it is given a moment of another time. It is in the generosity of the other that I am free, because it is the other's gift of time, and my responsiveness (premised on my sedimentary bodily being), that allow the alteration of the corporeality whose sedimentation produces the laws and tolerances by which I live. The gift of the other does not merely give me a new dance to dance, or a new space into which to move, or new knowledge to learn and comprehend, but a different 'me', a style of being-in-the-world that can and does dance and see and live and move in these ways. Perhaps more significantly, this alteration alters sedimentation, and in loosening the strictures of existing sedimentation, it allows for the possibility of further responsiveness: of new possibilities, of new dances, movements and embodied selves to become.

It enacts, viscerally, the contingency of sedimentation and the possibility of 'stirring up' how and why previous experiences have been understood. In demonstrating that the norm – 'the body' I take as the 'effective law' of who I am – is contingent and fundamentally alterable, it troubles the materialisation of subjectivity as individual, liberal, humanist and essential.

In classrooms, of course, this kind of change is often abrupt and observable (the 'watching them get it' moment that so many teachers gesture towards as the reason teaching is rewarding); sometimes it is a gradual shift. Numerous critical disability scholars have argued that disability fundamentally queries ability, in ways that those marked as able-bodied tend to find troubling: for example, Tom Shakespeare argues 'it is not us; it is non-disabled people's embodiment which is the issue: disabled people remind non-disabled people of their own vulnerability' (1994, p. 297). Such descriptions are useful, but even the phrase 'remind' appears to make this a matter of cognition, of calculation. To shift this into another register, and hopefully activate the challenge of disability that Shakespeare is marking, I often recount an experience like this in the classes on disability:

> I'm sure that this has happened: you're walking down the street, or in the supermarket, or at the library, or something, and you encounter someone with a visible disability. You might even double-take. And suddenly, you're conscious of your own body. You're suddenly thinking, 'Now, now, don't stare. Don't react; it's just another body. Okay. But do I usually stare at people walking past? How long do I look at them for? Am I looking for too long a time? Too short? How do I not react? What do I normally do? How do I usually walk? Do I usually smile at people I'm walking past? Do I even notice the people I'm usually walking past? Am I walking strangely? Is this normal?

Whilst this description usually elicits laughter – as might any recounting of internal 'dialogue' out loud – it is also an attempt to evoke the experience of disability produced by dominant comportments, an experience which is often dismissed as so 'natural' as to not even warrant discussion.

I recount this story not to legitimate this experience, but to enable a recognition of this corporeal experience of dis-com-fitting, in order to demonstrate the investment that our very ordinary, everyday experiences of ourselves and the world are heavily shaped by the 'ability/disability system'. It regularly draws out stories of moments when students felt their own, easy, habitual style of being-in-the-world challenged by the simple presence of a body they recognised as different (in a variety of ways). This shared recollection enacts a re-membering which reshapes the significance of that memory. It testifies to both 'common sense' and its troubling, and in a context which reshapes its significance from being simply a 'natural' response to one capable of analysis. Such a consideration reveals two unstable binaries. First, the line between self and other is, as Merleau-Ponty pointed out, blurry and indistinct, sufficiently that my body is never entirely and simply mine, and under my control, but is produced in relation to others, and their difference. Second, the line between ability and disability is similarly blurred, precisely because the capacity to feel oneself to be normal, to be able, is premised on disavowing disability, designating another 'disabled'. Being confronted by disability, then, can be troubling to that disavowal, and re-membering such an experience in this shared context 'activates' the anachronism of that moment, allowing it to shift outside habitual ways of negotiating disability.

Sedimentary classrooms

The process of 'stirring up the sediment' is an intriguing one to watch occur over the space of a semester. Intriguingly, even those students who grasp the significance of their own experiences of difference, and develop critical self-reflexivity quite swiftly, often begin a new class struggling to achieve the new perceptual techniques they had been comfortable with at the end of last week's class. Often students enter classes having 'forgotten' the work done the week before. I would suggest that this 'forgetting', however, is less a failure to cognitively recollect, and more the result of returning to their everyday incarnatory contexts, within which dominant styles of being-in-the-world re-sediment 'common sense'. The return to class, then, enables a resedimentation of the critical self-reflexivity which 'activated' the troubling experience of disability, and enabled an awareness of dominant perceptual practices.

In addition, the class itself becomes a unique incarnatory context, as the discussion continues throughout the semester. As the discussion and the sharing of experiences and critique continues, more students are prepared to interrogate their own reactions to disability, and their classmates' positioning of disability as a problem. This is not simply the result of 'knowing more', but of a shift in their styles of being-in-the-world, given the responses towards them (and articulations of common sense) within this context. For example, one student looked quite anxious as she told the class:

> I can get, you know, that people with *physical* disabilities are sexual, and should be able to be sexual, and all of that. But it's when we get to *cognitive* disabilities that I really can't tell what I think. I mean, I saw a girl on the bus with this guy, and he had Down Syndrome. And it was *really* obvious that they were together, and it made me feel really funny to watch them.

Other students nodded at this, and someone commented on the risks of exploitation between two people who are so radically differently situated; but then one observed:

> Well, yeah, we *would* feel funny, wouldn't we? Because that's how this works: we decide that disabled people aren't sexual, and then we're all weirded out when they are, because they're supposed to be *not like us*, and if they are, well then ...

This comment testifies to a shift in perception – it is not simply that the student has learnt enough to calculate an answer, but that she has shifted (and it was, in her case, a shift) from simply seeing disabled people as a problem, to seeing the way 'we' see disabled people (and the way this situates 'us' as a result) as a problem – as *the* problem. This student's experience of such a shift is not delimited to her, and her body; but is bound up with the incarnatory context within which it occurs. Thus her challenge to the student 'weirded out' by observing a person with Down Syndrome being sexual is not merely a conceptual challenge, but an intercorporeal acknowledgement of their participation in common sense, as well as maintaining a resistant comportment to it. This comportment allows the first student the possibility of re-membering her encounter with the couple on the bus in a way that might enable that experience to change her sedimented comportments, to critically engage with her own common sense. The capacity of syncretic sociability to produce an increasingly critical incarnatory context thus enables the sedimentation of these critical perceptual practices for individual students.

Indeed, the space of the class itself attains a sedimentary significance for students. This is, perhaps, particularly evident in the queer theory classes, where many students who either 'out' themselves early in the semester as queer, or demonstrate varying levels of anti-homophobia, find negotiating with the idea of people with disabilities having desires, sexual feelings and sex quite troubling. This phenomenon is intriguing because they have often spent weeks challenging the more homophobic members of the class over their perspectives – for example, claims that 'they'd be alright except that they're so *in your face*' and so on – only to find themselves mouthing similar ideas in relation to disability. They are then challenged not only by others but by their sedimented sense of the context – by their own prior experiences of challenging others.

It is quite common, by the end of the semester, and especially in the 'Changing Bodies, Changing Selves' course, to have sections of the seminar in which students recount discussions with family or friends. Such discussions are often marking the difficulty of fully expressing, say, an *argument* about the social model of disability (though obviously the discipline of essays often requires more of their rational and logical capacities) especially in contexts thoroughly shaped by common-sensical spaces, which are now experienced as sources of affront and indignation. Such discussions testify to the alterations of their perceptual practices to mark upon, rather than treat a neutral, 'common sense'. Their willingness, or even eagerness, to discuss these encounters within the classroom demonstrates a desire to work out how to manage encounters between their own still-uncertain shifts in their style of bodily being and the dominant styles of being-in-the-world they encounter outside the classroom.

Conclusion

Processes of learning do not only involve what has been known, in the aftermath of Descartes, as 'the cogito'. Rather, learning is an embodied process. I have argued that disability, in troubling sedimented styles of being-in-the-world, enables a reworking of the sedimentary structures of habituated comportments. The 'activating' of experiences of disability and disabled others can be enhanced by the corporeal encounter with other, non-common-sensical styles of being-in-the-world, such as those embodied by lecturers, tutors, guest lecturers, films, and each other. The interaction between the material and the other bodies they encounter, both those which are apparently at least temporarily able-bodied, and those which are not, creates an incarnatory context that is disjointed from the 'common sense' supposed by dominant bodily styles. Syncretic sociability, then, in the classroom, plays a key role in rendering the textual, conceptual and other allegedly 'disembodied' knowledge corporeally accessible and significant. This alternative incarnatory context can also be confronting, because it is the 'common'ness of shared styles of being-in-the-world that reinforce our own grasp of the world. Yet it is this incarnatory context that can support and allow the alteration of students' and teachers' styles of being-in-the-world in ways that enable disability to be experienced as radically other, rather than the mere disavowed underside of ability, and thus as pedagogically important in reshaping comportments to form ethical ways of being-in-the-world.

Acknowledgements

I would like to thank the contributions of two anonymous reviewers and Dr Anna Hickey-Moody for her encouragement and collegiality. I would also like to thank Associate Professor Nikki Sullivan for her support and encouragement of my teaching practice on the two courses under discussion, and for offering a rare collegial space within which to discuss and develop a critical, self-reflexive pedagogical practice, which informs much of this paper.

Notes

1. I would like to emphasise, at this point, that this established position within critical disability studies does not reduce or dismiss the difficult experiences that are often, in the current cultural context, associated with disability. Rather, it understands this connection between disability and difficulty as contingent, rather than natural, and as a key dynamic in sustaining the privilege associated with being (temporarily) able-bodied. Such a position seeks to bring into focus *how* disability comes to be constituted as a problem, thus neither naturalising disability as problematic, nor denying those experiences of it *as* problematic.
2. I use [*sic*] to mark the use of the masculine pronoun as the generic. As, for example, Elizabeth Grosz (1994, p. 108) has noted, there are problems with Merleau-Ponty's presumption of the masculine body as the generic, which this use of the masculine pronoun represents. It is not within the purview of this paper to discuss in detail the unmarked gendering of Merleau-Ponty's account of embodiment. However, given that the argument here is about corporeal difference (of which sexual difference could be understood as one subset), it is important to mark the apparently unremarkable: the masculine, able body through which his account is offered. Numerous feminist theorists have reworked Merleau-Ponty's account with a focus on women's bodies. See for example Young (1990), Weiss (1998) and Grosz (1994). Other scholars have considered Merleau-Ponty's account in relation to disability: for example, see Edwards (1998), Turner (2001), Iwakuma (2006), Toombs (1995), and Hughes and Paterson (1997). These accounts help to draw attention to the inadequacies of Merleau-Ponty's presumption of an able-bodied, European male as the model for all forms of embodiment, and I seek to attest to both his exclusions and the work of other scholars in addressing such inadequacies. It is also worth noting on this point that the majority of Merleau-Ponty's account of embodiment in *Phenomenology of Perception* depends upon the contrast between 'ability' and 'disability' as it occurs by juxtaposing 'normal' bodily being-in-the-world with the aphasias, agnosias and other perceptual 'disabilities' of Schneider, Goldstein's patient and case study (see Merleau-Ponty, 2002, p. 90, n. 2 for these details).
3. The term 'incarnatory context' is my own, coined to elaborate both the local corporeal contexts – families, groups of friends, schools – and the much larger contexts such as nations, or even global concerns, which contribute to the shaping of specific styles of embodiment.
4. For a more detailed analysis of these 'bodily tolerances', see Cadwallader (forthcoming).
5. For more details on these 'lifelines', see Sara Ahmed's discussion (2006, pp. 153–156).

References

Ahmed, S. (2000). *Strange encounters: Embodied others in post-coloniality.* London: Routledge.

Ahmed, S. (2006). *Queer phenomenology: Orientations, objects, others.* Durham, NC: Duke University Press.

Alcoff, L.M. (1999). Philosophy and racial identity. In M. Bulmer & J. Solomos (Eds.), *Ethnic and racial studies today* (pp. 45–59). London: Routledge.

Alcoff, L.M. (2001). Toward a phenomenology of racial embodiment. In R. Bernasconi (Ed.), *Race* (pp. 268–283). Malden, MA: Blackwell.

Butler, J. (1993). *Bodies that matter: On the discursive limits of sex.* London: Routledge.

Cadwallader, J. (forthcoming). Why do we hurt: Merleau-Ponty and the politics of suffering.

Davis, L.J. (1995). *Enforcing normalcy: Disability, deafness, and the body.* London: Verso.

Diprose, R. (2002). *Corporeal generosity: On giving with Nietzsche, Merleau-Ponty, and Lévinas.* New York: State University of New York Press.

Edwards, S. (1998). The body as object versus the body as subject: The case of disability. *Medicine, Health Care and Philosophy, 1*(1), 47–56.

Garland-Thomson, R. (2002). Integrating disability, transforming feminist theory. *National Women's Studies Association Journal, 14*(3), 1–32.

Giroux, H.A., & McLaren, P.L. (1991). Radical pedagogy as cultural politics: Beyond the discourse of critique and anti-utopianism. In M. Zavarzadeh & D. Morton (Eds.), *Theory/pedagogy/politics: Texts for change* (pp. 152–186). Urbana: University of Illinois Press.

Grosz, E. (1994). *Volatile bodies: Toward a corporeal feminism.* Sydney: Allen & Unwin.

Hughes, B., & Paterson, K. (1997). The social model of disability and the disappearing body: Towards a sociology of impairment. *Disability and Society, 12*, 325–340.

Iwakuma, M. (2006). The body as embodiment: An investigation of the body by Merleau-Ponty. In M. Corker & T. Shakespeare (Eds.), *Disability/postmodernity: Embodying disability theory* (pp. 76–100). London: Continuum.

Leder, D. (1990). *The absent body.* Chicago: University Of Chicago Press.

Lévinas, E. (1998). *Otherwise than being: Or, beyond essence* (A. Lingis, Trans.), Pittsburgh, PA: Duquesne University Press.

Merleau-Ponty, M. (1964). *The primacy of perception: And other essays on phenomenological psychology, the philosophy of art, history and politics* (W. Cobb, Trans.). Evanston, IL: Northwestern University Press.

Merleau-Ponty, M. (2002). *Phenomenology of perception* (C. Smith, Trans.). London: Routledge.

O'Loughlin, M. (2006). *Embodiment and education: Exploring creatural existence.* Dordrecht, The Netherlands: Springer.

Peters, M. (2004). Education and the philosophy of the bodies of knowledge and knowledges of the body. In L. Bresler (Ed.), *Knowing bodies, moving minds: Towards embodied teaching and learning* (pp. 13–28). Dordrecht, The Netherlands: Kluwer Academic Publishers.

Reynolds, J. (2005). Maurice Merleau-Ponty. In *Internet encyclopedia of philosophy.* Retrieved February 21, 2010, from http://www.iep.utm.edu/merleau/

Shakespeare, T. (1994). Cultural representations of disabled people: Dustbins for disavowal? *Disability and Society, 9*, 283–299.

Toombs, S.K. (1995). The lived experience of disability. *Human Studies, 18*(1), 9–23.

Turner, B.S (2001). Disability and the sociology of the body. In G.L. Albrecht, K.D. Seelman & M. Bury (Eds.), *Handbook of disability studies* (pp. 252–266). London: Sage.

Weiss, G. (1998). *Body images: Embodiment as intercorporeality.* New York: Routledge.

Young, I.M. (1990). *Throwing like a girl and other essays in feminist philosophy and social theory.* Bloomington: Indiana University Press.

Zavarzadeh, M., & Morton, D. (1991). Theory pedagogy politics: The crisis of 'the subject' in the humanities. In M. Zavarzadeh & D. Morton (Eds.), *Theory/pedagogy/politics: Texts for change* (pp. 1–32). Urbana: University of Illinois Press.

Anxiety and niceness: drawing disability studies into the art and design curriculum through a live brief

Nicole Matthews

Department of Media, Music and Cultural Studies, Faculty of Arts, Macquarie University, NSW, Australia

This article considers the way that affect shaped the unfolding of a curriculum initative which aimed to expose undergraduate art and design students to the insights of critical disability studies. This initiative, funded by the Big Lottery and managed by disability charity Scope, asked students in art, design and multimedia programmes in four UK higher education institutions to engage with a live brief: to develop inclusive illustrated children's books and digital media. By focusing on the affective dimensions to this project and especially what Sianne Ngai refers to as the 'minor emotions' – not fear or passion or hatred, but, for example, anxiety – this article traces the way such feelings and associated 'taste concepts' influenced the engagements, disengagements and judgements of students, staff and the project's management.

Introduction

Brenda Jo Bruggemann, Rosemarie Garland-Thompson and Georgia Kleege have argued for the importance of bringing:

> disability as a topic, as an idea, as a category of analysis, as a historical community into the subject matter of every single field and discipline across the entire academy. (Garland-Thompson, Kleege, & Brueggemann, 2005, pp. 27–28)

However, it would appear from a quick review of recent writing within a range of disciplines that the voices of people with disabilities, ideas emerging from the disabled people's movement and a discussion of processes of disablement, have yet to take a central place in the undergraduate curriculum, outside of the discipline of disability studies itself (e.g. Davis, 2006; French & DePoy, 2002; Gabel & Danforth, 2002; Goggin, 2003; Linton, 1998; Scullion, 2000, Treby, Hewitt, & Shah, 2006; Ware, 2001). Simi Linton has argued that fractures within the academy have made it difficult to situate the insights of critical disability studies in the curriculum. In particular, she discusses the distinction between applied disciplines, where disability *has* been included in textbooks and classroom discussion, but in a deeply problematic way, and the liberal arts, where, in contrast 'disability imagery abounds in the materials considered and produced ... yet because it is not analyzed, it remains as background,

123

seemingly of little consequence' (Linton, 1998, p. 110). In applied disciplines such as social work, education and nursing, disabled people have in the past been constituted as 'problem' individuals, framed by medical models of disability, rather than as members of a minority group battling discrimination. In the arts and humanities, in contrast, disability and disabled people are rarely considered at all. While in the USA in particular, the humanities have proven a fruitful location for disability studies research and writing, in Michael Bérubé's account, liberal arts programmes still require a 'make-over' to incorporate considerations of disability centrally into liberal arts programmes (Bérubé, 2006).

What strategies might be adopted, then, to raise the profile of disability studies across the arts and humanities? Focusing on US higher education, Sherry Adrian (1997) discusses three possible approaches. First, foundational survey courses in disability studies programmes may be opened up to non-major students as an elective. Second, interdisciplinary courses may be developed to form part of the general education requirements of the undergraduate curriculum. Brenda Brueggemann has documented the successes and the challenges of example of the latter strategy for achieving such 'infiltration' and 'integration' of disability studies, via a compulsory freshman composition course offered by an English department (Brueggemann, 2002; see also Wilson & Lewiecki-Wilson, 2002). She argues that presenting ideas from disability studies as a core part of the curriculum to a wide range of disabled and non-disabled students:

> opened up an astonishing array of topics to research and write on ... [and gave] many
> students (no, not all of them) ... meaningful personal and passionate ways to connect to
> the material, social and individual world of disability. (Brueggemann, 2002, p. 334)

This article will focus, however, on Adrian's third approach to broadening the impact of disability studies in the undergraduate curriculum: incorporating core concepts from disability studies into particular disciplines. This approach is particularly useful in higher education systems, like those of the UK and Australia, where professional education often takes place at undergraduate level, rather than after initial generalist education. Australian and British students choose a specialism earlier in their academic careers than in that of their peers in the USA, and compulsory 'general education' components to undergraduate degrees are rare. Consequently, much emphasis in recent UK policy and practice developments has been put into embedding innovative teaching within subjects and disciplines. In this way, new ideas about teaching can be located within discipline-specific pedagogies and practices, such as studio-based teaching within art and design, working 'with the grain' of disciplinary 'tribes' (Becher & Trowler, 2001).

This article will offer an account of a curriculum intervention embedded in a discipline, art and design, offering rich pickings for humanities disability research (e.g. Davis, 1995, 1997; Davidson, 2004; Hevey, 1992) but in which critical disability studies is far from the centre of the existing curriculum. My interest is to explore the complex relationship between affect and equity in the way this intervention is played out. I will argue that affect as it unfolds in the classroom and the studio is a key consideration in students' and teachers' experience of a curriculum that seeks to draw on the key ideas of critical disability studies. By focusing on the affective dimensions to this project and especially what Siane Ngai (2005a) refers to as the 'minor emotions' – not fear or passion or hatred, but, for example, anxiety – this case study throws light on some of the reasons for the neglect of critical disability studies in the wider humanities curriculum.

Illustrating inclusive stories: a live brief in disability studies

During 2005–06 and 2006–07, art, design, illustration and multimedia students at four UK universities participated in a 'live brief': to illustrate, animate or make multimedia products based on inclusive children's stories. This curriculum intervention provides examples of a range of strategies that might be adopted to help bring the ideas of disability studies and the voices of disabled people and their allies into the curriculum. It also points towards some of the tensions and difficulties – particularly those revolving around affect – that can emerge in 'mainstreaming' disability studies in the undergraduate classroom.

In each institution, the live brief was embedded in courses that did not explicitly flag disability as a theme – for example, in units entitled 'Applied Image' or 'Illustration for Younger Audiences' or in final-year negotiated projects. In each case, an entire cohort was given an initial brief about a wider national project, entitled 'In the Picture', which encouraged the book world to include disabled people in children's books. Students were given a selection of children's stories written by local disabled people and families of disabled children to read, and undertook a short disability awareness training session. In all but two of the eight subjects that incorporated the brief, students were given a choice of either engaging further with it or undertaking other projects. Those who chose it received a substantial reader of critical disability studies articles including articles by Colin Barnes, Kathy Saunders, Richard Rieser, David Mitchell and Sharon Snyder. Participating students were also given an opportunity to participate in a range of follow-up activities including discussing their ideas with children's writers with experience of disability or workers in disability arts organisations, attending an integrated youth group to discuss children's books, and receiving feedback on draft work from the authors of their stories or other local disabled people. The reading and advice provided to students strongly reflected the social model of disability which was espoused by 'In the Picture' as its underpinning philosophy (see Matthews, 2009).

Most of these stories used in the project were generated by disabled people and families of disabled children in writing workshops run during 2005–06 in Merseyside, in the north of England, as part of the 'In the Picture' project, funded by the UK's Big Lottery scheme and run by Scope, one of the UK's largest disability charities. One further story was collectively written by a group of disabled children working in collaboration with a professional writer under the auspices of a local Deaf and disability arts organization, North West Disability Arts Forum. Many students produced suites of images, interactive on-line books and animations drawing on the 23 stories emerging from these workshops. Others used the brief as starting points for their own self-penned illustrated narratives, animations and games.

My account of the project here is based primarily on interviews with eight academic members of staff involved in the project and 27 of the 61 students who have to this point produced work in response to it. Other sources of data included participant observation, analysis of reflective documents and logs, as well as creative work, and a short qualitative questionnaire distributed to the students who attended initial briefings. Despite three years of closely following the emergence of the project and sharing some spaces and activities of some of the participants, my research, like most 'media ethnographies' (Nightingale, 1993), could not be described in an uncomplicated way as 'ethnographic'. My approach, however, shares some similarities with what Foley and Valenzuela describe as critical ethnography. Critical ethnographies, according to these writers, are politically engaged, seeking to generate outcomes which can shape policies and practices. Some critical ethnographers draw on collaborative research methods, and many seek to account for their findings in ways that are accessible not simply to other academic researchers but others – activists, practitioners and policy-makers – with an interest in the research project (Foley & Valenzuela, 2005, p. 220). This paper draws on just a few of these sources, primarily interviews and observations of the unfolding project. (For more detailed discussions of the stories and images emerging from the project, see Matthews, 2008, 2009.)

My account is both that of an insider – an academic in an adjacent discipline at one of the participating universities with a longstanding engagement with the national project – and as an outsider, both to the disciplines of art and design and the particular departments within which the curriculum development took place. In other respects, too, I had this dual insider/outsider status, having become involved initially in the project as the non-disabled parent of my disabled son (Ryan & Runswick-Cole, 2008).

The core concerns of the initiative, then, were around representation: diverse, inclusive forms of representation. The project aimed, in the words of its website, to 'promote inclusion of disabled children in early years picture books' – to put disabled children 'in the picture', defined (via the *Oxford English Dictionary*) as: 'the state of being fully informed or noticed'. It has been suggested that 'affects ... are not to do with signification or "meaning" as such' but instead have a life 'beneath' or paralleling signification (O'Sullivan, 2006, p. 43). However, in observing the unfolding processes of this 'live brief' it became clear that the affective explained a great deal about the engagements made or not made around the project. The domain of the affective had real significance in shaping which students chose to engage with the project and the kind of work they produced, and whether student work ultimately made it onto the project website and potentially into the public eye. As such, representation and the affective were closely entwined.

The terms affect, emotion and feeling have come to be increasingly central to discussion within cultural studies in recent years. As a number of writers have noted, these terms are used variously, to signal a range of disciplinary locations and theoretical investments (Ahmed, 2004; Gregg, 2006; Probyn, 2004). Despite the specificities of the ways these terms have been used, most contemporary accounts of both emotion and affect share an emphasis on the embodiment of affect and on its intersubjectivity. Those in a Deleuzian tradition further stress the non-conscious status of affective intensities. In this paper, however, I want to draw on Ngai's particular understanding of affect. Her account captures this intimacy between representation, politics and affect in ways which I think are useful for my purposes here. She uses the phrase 'taste concept' to consider emotions as they are evoked by art and other commodities with an aesthetic dimension (Ngai, 2005a, 2005b, p. 834). I will use the notion of a 'taste concept' here to start to make sense of some of the aesthetic but also implicitly political judgments and selections made by participants in this curriculum interventions – judgments about what projects are interesting or cool; what artwork is appropriate to a politically 'worthwhile' brief, and which images should be displayed on a website of best practice.

'Nothing about us without us': who talks about disability in the classroom?

A number of writers have pointed out the radical and transforming effect of the presence of disabled teachers in the classroom (Garland-Thomson et al., 2005; Linton, 1998). As Linton (1998) points out, the presence of disabled professors avoids the tendency, evident in the existing curriculum on disability, to objectify people with disabilities – 'them' – to be analysed or pathologised. In the light of institutional barriers and discrimination working against the inclusion of disabled people within higher education (e.g. Wilton, 2006), she argues that a key responsibility of non-disabled teachers is to lobby for the employment of more disabled academics.

That said, a very real question for teachers in a higher education system which does not include enough disabled teachers is whether non-disabled (or not currently disabled) teachers can and should seek to incorporate the insights of disability studies within the curriculum, and if they do, what the consequences might be. None of the teaching staff involved in the case study discussed here, for example, identified as a person with a disability. Moreover, this curriculum intervention was part of a wider project run by Scope, a large impairment-focused disability charity that had been subject to much critique from British disability activists in the past (Benjamin, 2004; Carvel, 2004; Shakespeare, 2005). Not only have such charities been seen as highjacking the liberatory language of the disability movement for their own purposes, but the types of imagery they produce in their own advertising has been subject to stinging criticism (e.g. Hevey, 1992; Meekosha & Jakubowicz, 1996; Oliver, 2004). In the words of Linda Ware, in such circumstances 'dare we do disability studies?' (Ware, 2001).

While the voices of people with disabilities in the classroom can be radicalizing, Kleege notes a flaw in the view that the simple physical presence of a disabled teacher provides a guarantee that students will shift their perspectives on disability:

> I do resent any inference that the mere fact of my disability augments my teaching qualifications or that there is a pedagogical value in exposing my disability to nondisabled students. This practice smacks too much of the freak show and casts me in the role of goodwill ambassador sharing the quaint beliefs and customs of my alien world. (2002, p. 312)

Shirin Housee (2006) explores some of the consequences if teachers from marginalised groups are presented as solely responsible for teaching about the politics and power relation of 'their' group's marginalisation. She notes, for example:

> if white folks do not teach race/racism issues, then whiteness remains associated with mainstream sociology, and blackness with 'race' and racism ... If black people alone teach 'race'/racism issues this could mean that this is all we can teach. (Housee, 2006, p. 79)

Similarly, curriculum interventions such as the one considered here provide opportunities for disabled students to draw on their own experiences. One second-year student involved in this project disclosed her dyslexia to her tutors for the first time in the process of creating an animation based on a story written by a dyslexic author. However, other disabled students expressed interest in and support for the project privately to academic staff, but chose not to engage with the brief in detail. Disabled students are a valuable resource in integrating critical disability studies into the curriculum (see Snyder, 2004), and bringing such projects into generalist programmes may provide a first opportunity for disabled students to encounter critical disability studies. However, Kleege's comments on the perils of obliging staff to act as exemplars for non-disabled students rings true for students too.

I would argue that it is the responsibility of currently non-disabled teachers to provide space in the curriculum for their students to consider and interrogate, for example, conventions of representing disabled people (see also Wilson & Lewiecki-Wilson, 2002). Disability is a key category in the organization of a wide range of conceptions in western philosophy and visual culture. As such, non-disabled students and teachers can interrogate their experiences of privilege within 'ableism', drawing on insights from disabled writers and theorists, artists and colleagues (see Kumari Campbell, 2008). However, the consequences of attempting to draw disability studies into the curriculum without the authorising voice of a teacher with personal experiences of disablement raises significant questions around affect and aesthetics.

Absences and anxieties

A feeling of lacking expertise around the subject of disability and representation emerged repeatedly in interviews with the art and design staff and students who became involved in the project:

> If I'm really honest, I think that all of us started the project so keen to be right – to be correct. There was this overwhelming sense of 'I don't want to do it wrong' ... because you have that kind of anxiety I think for the students, and really initially with myself, you think it's almost safer to avoid it. (Staff member)

> I was talking to a guy who'd been in the meeting and he said he didn't wanna do it because he thought he'd do it in the wrong way – he might represent it wrong, maybe he'd add humour to it but it'd be taken the wrong way or something and he didn't wanna do that – that's why he kind of stepped back. (Student)

> I think I was a bit anxious about doing it, and portraying them in the right way and things like that – just had a few anxieties. (Student)

Linda Ware notes similar responses in high school teachers. She cites the comments of one teacher, known as an inclusive practitioner by his colleagues: 'I felt that I lacked the authority to talk about disability; that was someone else's job' (Ware, 2001). Ware links such beliefs to the medical model of disability and a culture of 'expertism' around disability (see also Marshall, Ralph, & Palmer, 2002; McLean, 2005, p. 72; Troyna & Vincent, 1996). This anxiety about speaking out of turn or inappropriately on a subject about which you are insufficiently expert was a key affective dimension of the responses to the 'live brief' – not only from staff and students, but also project management (and indeed myself) and perhaps rightly so.

Within critical disability studies there has been frequent consideration of the range of emotions that underpin the ways non-disabled people imagine and relate to disabled people or conceptions of 'disability'. Meekosha and Jakubowicz (1996) in their commentary on the impact of charity advertising, for example, comment: 'the industry works at creating consumers of disability as spectacle, and as they experience the emotions of pity, fear, horror, sympathy, gratitude (for their escape) they are urged to give to charity' (p. 89). This same repertoire of emotions – fear, denial, horror – is identified within much critical disability studies as prompting the emergence of role of tropes of disability in art, literature and the media (e.g. Davis, 1997; Longmore, 1997; Mitchell & Snyder, 2006).

However, I would once again like to take my cue from Ngai in her focus of what she calls 'minor' emotions, rather than the more dramatic terrain of shame, fear or hate explored in much other work on emotion (e.g. Ahmed, 2004; Zembylas, 2006). In particular, anxiety seems to be key to the affective responses to this project. In framing her book, *Ugly Feelings*, Ngai emphasises the way in which the kinds of minor, negative feelings she discusses – paranoia, irritation, anxiety – 'obstruct agency' (2005a, p. 14). Writers on disability and education have similarly stressed the way anxiety can block social change. Julie Allan, for example, comments in her discussion of a classroom project concerning the ethics of inclusion:

> the ambivalence and uncertainties that the mainstream students had (for example, in situations where they felt anxious about or sorry for certain students) were disabling. (2005, p. 283)

I am cautious about the process of reading the anxieties that were not only audible in interviews, but palpable in the presence of student and teachers as participants in the project. Descriptions of affect as intensity, forces which can move people, seek to de-emphasize the individual as 'owner' of a feeling and rather stress the intersubjective formations of affect. This notion of 'affective contagion' (Gregg, 2006, p. 9) resonates with my observations in this project. However, accounts of affect also stress its unpredictability: 'You do not know beforehand what a body or a mind can do, in a given encounter, a given arrangement, a given combination' (Deleuze, cited in Probyn, 2004, p. 37; see also Albrecht-Crane & Slack, 2007, p. 99). I would add the point, also made by Gregg in her consideration of affective voices within texts, that it is a real and interesting question who is moved by affective intensities and how they are moved.

These qualities of affect present challenges for attempts to draw out the presence of feeling using qualitative research methods. Affect may not be overtly mentioned in interviews, as Ariel Ducey notes in her account of the affective dimensions to adult education of health workers (2007, p. 193). Or feelings may be evoked in a stumbling or circuitious way as in this comment by a student about their perceptions of disability before engagement with the project: 'I definitely didn't know much about anything, or ... and maybe I had a slight negative feeling, not in a really horrible way, but, I don't know...'. As a participant observer, one may have a strong sense of affective intensity, but that sense may speak as much to one's own emotional responses as the feelings or intensities of others. My own anxieties as a non-disabled researcher in a field which one might characterize currently as strongly shaped by identity politics (Oliver, 1999; Shakespeare, 2006) was amplified by my awareness of the heavy criticism directed towards charities by disability activists. Undoubtedly, such feelings shaped my own perceptions of what I observed during the unfolding of the project.

That said, Ngai's account of the underpinning metaphors used to talk about anxiety in film, literature and philosophy are suggestive, given the recurrence of the language of anxiety in interviews I conducted with students and staff involved in the project. Ngai cites Kierkegaard's influential account of the origins of anxiety – as having no object, or having 'nothing' as its object. Ngai and her sources see anxiety as a form of projection – both in a temporal and a spatial sense. Anxiety is projected into the future, or into an absence. In the context of this curriculum intervention, I would argue that the absence of a definitive authorized voice, such as a teacher or advisor with personal experience of disablement, to guide or approve of the productions of art and design students was a key source of anxiety.

If affect can be contagious, part of the sense of anxiety present among students and staff may have been 'caught' from those from Scope managing the overall project. 'In the Picture' was part of Scope's attempt to reposition itself as a campaigning organization with a focus on disabled people's human rights. As the project's website notes, 'In the Picture' was 'part of its Time to Get Equal which is working to change the way disabled people are perceived and treated'.[1] Given the critiques which had been offered of the organization in the past, the stakes for the organization and those within it in appearing to get the social model of disability 'right' were high. Indeed, one of the key resources for writers and illustrators appearing on the project website acknowledges and perhaps valorizes such anxieties in its title 'Am I getting it right?'

The strategy adopted by the project was to use 10 principles drawn from the social model of disability to underpin its collection of images and guidance to the book world. This approach drew from activists like Richard Rieser a concern to refrain from re-circulating the problematic imagery of the children's literature of the past (Rieser, 2006; Rieser & Mason, 1992). This approach contrasts with the critiques of a positive imagery approach offered by writers like Tom Shakespeare, David Mitchell and Sharon Snyder. In the 1990s, Shakespeare suggested that:

> a new Disability Correctness is undermining the possibility of film-makers dealing with impairment at all ... [T]here is a dangerous willingness to take offense at supposed violations of equality principles. (1999, p. 165)

Students engaging with the brief were exposed a range of perspectives with both Mitchell and Snyder's arguments for the value of transgressive representations and Rieser's early work included in their pack of reading. Nonetheless, the emphasis placed by the project management and within some of these readings on tight, normative frameworks may have made some students feel that this brief was an inappropriate place for aesthetic transgression and play.

Making nice

What were the consequences of these anxieties? The combination of the anxieties of students and of the project management emerged, I would argue, in a sequence of selections: the way in which students self-selected into participating in the project, and then the way some of the work they produced was selected to appear on the project's website of exemplary images. Such decisions about which stories were to be included on the website were made by a small group comprising parents of disabled children and disabled artists from the local steering group for the 'Stories' strand of the project. These choices were guided by written advice of an editor, a well-known disabled author. Commissioning and selections of images for the 'image bank' were made by the project manager, again, with the advice of the steering group of the broader project group. Clear patterns emerged in the types of images and stories selected for inclusion which, I would suggest, speak both to the anxieties of those making selections and the aesthetico-political sensibilities that underpinned these choices.

One way of describing the 'approved' images could be through Mitchell and Snyder's (2001) taxonomy of the way representations of disabled people have been critically framed. The approach taken to selection of images on the website might be described as 'social realism'. Mitchell and Snyder, however, point out that:

> the call for more realistic depictions of disability provided another side of the negative imagery coin because to critique inadequate, dehumanising, or false representations is to simultaneously call for more acceptable representations. (2001, p. 200)

In contrast to much illustrated fiction for young children, very few of the images commissioned or selected from student work for the 'image bank' of good practice were anthropomorphized animals or toys, or imaginary creatures. The images selected included only one anthropomorphic illustration, an exception was offered by an established illustrator, rather than commissioned by the project. For example, one student's work, which was considered by the art and design staff to be one of the best responses to the brief, depicted an inclusive school. Rather than drawing children in a realistic style, she depicted both disabled and non-disabled children in the form of brightly coloured monster figures ('kids like monsters', she remarked). Its departure from realism and perhaps the historical reference use of the language of monstrosity to refer to impairment (Barnes, 1992; Hevey, 1992; Norden, 1994) may have played an unspoken role in the decision not to include images from this work in the archive of exemplary images, along with the story's rather heavy borrowing from the plotline of *Charlie and the Chocolate Factory*.

However, another way of understanding the responses of students and project manager to the anxieties provoked by the live brief would be through something more like Ngai's notion of a 'taste concept'. This notion, Ngai notes, describes a quality that might on the one hand seem to inhere in an artistic or indeed an everyday object. Yet, on the other hand, it might be viewed as emerging from a particular act of interpretation. Here affect and representation, object and interpreter are inseparably linked. Stumblingly articulated in the interviews was a widely shared conception of what the combination of children's books and representations of disability signified. The language of colour and tone was often used to point towards this aesthetic. As one student put it:

> The cool kids in our class weren't into that ... 'no we don't want to do that, that's really sad'. They had a view it was a bit immature and a bit kiddie, kind of thing ... there are a

lot of guys in my class who are, like, dudes, who are like quite cool and quite gritty and they like to do like their really odd animations that are all kind of dark and sinister.

In contrast, one of the illustrators who not only enthusiastically took to the project but whose work was also highly valued by the project manager, noted about her own style:

> my kind of illustration is definitely very sweet kind of thing, it doesn't really have much darkness to it. I definitely lean towards, err, yeah, not looking at the world through rosy glasses, but making it just a nice ... I like nice things.

This impulse to 'niceness' was reflected in interviews with a number of student illustrators in which they noted that the brief had attracted them because of their interest in socially valuable or non-commercial projects. If 'In the Picture' operated within (or perhaps tried to create) a space between charity and rights discourses, 'niceness' (or perhaps what Mat Fraser (2008) has referred to as 'PC's awful politeness') appears to be the aesthetic of this intermediary zone. The historical association of the discourse of the sentimental with children, and disabled children in particular (Longmore, 1997), perhaps overdetermined the use of this aesthetic within the project, despite the increasingly diverse and experimental approaches to picturebooks taken by writers and illustrators since the 1970s (Lewis, 2001; Pinsent, 1997; Saunders, 2000).

In contrast, some of the student illustrators whose work was not selected for the website described their own work in these ways:

> ...lively colourful drawings ...

> ...the particular drawing style is simple, it's bold, it's fun...

Librarians responding to the completed student work used the same language of colour to categorise and describe children's books. They contrasted contemporary styles of illustration – 'fun and bright', 'stronger ... sharper images', 'more in your face' – and more conventional 'wishy washy gentle images', noting that children's books including disabled characters 'look very old fashioned as well. It's not just that they sound very old fashioned, but they look like they've been on the shelves for years and years'; 'If it's amateurish or the illustration isn't as good or the colours aren't as bright, or lots of stuff like that, they'll look like second tier stock'.

Gentle, water-coloured, nice imagery, on this colour spectrum, is old fashioned, the opposite of dark and gritty and also of cool. Such shared 'taste concepts' seemed to swirl through the decision making and art making of a range of participants in the project. The consequences of the project's ultimate valuing of 'niceness' are evident, but at the same time hard to describe. Ngai's detailed account of the non-identical, but perhaps related, notion of cuteness perhaps gives us some starting points. Cuteness is, she argues, 'names an aesthetic encounter with an exaggerated difference in power' (Ngai, 2005b, p. 282), a mode of representation which accentuates 'helplessness and vulnerability' (Ngai, 2005b, p. 819). Ngai's account suggests that, despite the anxiety-driven attempts to remain safely on the terrain of realist 'niceness', such representational strategies chosen by student illustrators, or preferred by the steering committee selecting exemplary images, point towards the very conflicts and inequalities to which they studiously attempt to avoid referring.

Affect and outcomes

I do not want to underestimate the significance of curriculum interventions like the one I am describing. For all its limitations, it was a transformative encounter with the questions of equity and inclusiveness in representation for students who may go (and in at least one case, already have gone) on to become professional illustrators. According to their own accounts, most of the students involved had never addressed questions of disability in their studies, and some had barely considered questions of equality, power and representation at all. In interviews, students frequently framed their work on the project within broader struggles for equality, making unsolicited comparisons between the now accepted need to represent ethnic diversity within children's book illustrations and the imperative to include disabled characters. For multimedia students in particular, engagement with the brief also prompted consideration of questions of accessibility.

Some students commented that involvement in the project had already shaped the kind of work they had subsequently produced during their degrees. Such shifts in practice exemplify the transformative possibilities of critical disability studies when drawn into the broader curriculum. After her involvement in the live brief, one student went on to include disabled children within sketches for a healthy eating campaign. Another, reimagining a published children's book as an assessment for another unit, introduced a number of disabled characters into some of the book's many crowd scenes. A third, working on illustrated nursery rhymes after her engagement with 'In the Picture', reports rethinking an initial plan to represent Georgie Porgie, the boy who kissed the girls and made them cry, as someone with a facial disfigurement. She commented:

> I just completely steered away from that in the end because I thought, it just didn't seem appropriate, really. In the end I ended up doing it as a much older guy flirting with a younger girl.

In the short term, this kind of live brief can allow teaching programmes without in-house expertise in disability studies to incorporate such ideas in their curriculum, drawing on the advice and input of disabled professionals and arts workers and disabled people more generally. The experience of this project suggests that once programmes have invested in resources and developed teaching materials, one-off initiatives linked to short-term funding may become embedded in the curriculum, creating a demand for permanent teaching staff with a specialism in disability studies. Disability charities can be one well-resourced and connected source of live brief projects. However, connections with disability arts organizations and disabled writers may prove to generate more fruitful partnerships. Arts organizations may be more open to the inevitable ambiguities of creative work and recognise the need to create territories in which students can productively reimagine their work without excessive anxiety about 'getting it wrong'.

Albrecht-Crane and Slack (2007) argue that one of the merits of an emphasis on affect in the classroom is the way in which it directs our attention away from 'pre-established identity affiliations' (p. 105) in our thinking about what happens in learning and teaching. Certainly, refocusing on affect underscores the complexity, unpredictability and intersubjectivity of what happens in classrooms, studio spaces, libraries and all the other spaces where learning encounters occur. However, I hope my detour into the emergence of both anxiety and niceness in this 'live brief' has emphasized which bodies are in the classroom and the kinds of experience they can draw on, shapes the kinds of affective intensities present there.

Mitchell and Snyder (2001) comment that 'representation inevitably spawns discontent' (p. 212) and note that 'it is the heart of our own politics that cannot be strictly channelled into straightforward catalogues of "acceptable" and "unacceptable" representations' (p. 213). However, in championing what they call transfigurative resignifications – those representative strategies quite the opposite of the 'nice', rather both cool and dark – Mitchell and Snyder see a central place for disabled artists 'alarm[ing] the dominant culture with a seeming canniness over the terms of their own subjugation' (p. 209). While Mitchell and Snyder seek to move away from a normative approach, giving scope for the transformative possibilities of irony and pastiche, identities, and the question of who speaks, do really matter here.

In the context of the project I have been discussing here, I would argue that the absence of disabled people in the project management team and in the classroom in this curriculum provoked anxieties that were an obstruction to agency and prompted a retreat to the terrain of aesthetic 'niceness'. In some senses, 'In the Picture' sought to invoke transformations and becomings, inviting new relationships between artists, writers, editors and disabled people. However, a pedagogy that might enable these becomings depends on the particular kind of intersubjective spaces that can make such transformations happen.

Acknowledgements

The research on which this paper is based was deeply shaped by conversations with Surya Shaffi, and her insights have been much missed during its writing. Thanks also to Amy Vitali for assistance with editing an earlier version of the paper, and to John Scannell, Russell Smith and those attending a related talk at UNSW's Disability Studies and Disability Research Centre; and especially to those who generously gave their time to be interviewed for the research.

Note

1. See www.childreninthepicture.org.uk

References

Adrian, S.E. (1997). Disability, society, and ethical issues: A first-year experience for university students. *Intervention in School & Clinic, 32*(3), 178–184.

Ahmed, S. (2004). *The cultural politics of emotion.* Edinburgh: Edinburgh University Press.

Albrecht-Crane, C., & Slack, J.D. (2007). Towards a pedagogy of affect. In A. Hickey-Moody & P. Malins (Eds.), *Deleuzian encounters: Studies in contemporary social issues* (pp. 99–110). Basingstoke, UK: Palgrave Macmillan.

Allan, J. (2005). Inclusion as an ethical project. In S. Tremain (Ed.), *Foucault and the government of disability* (pp. 281–297). Ann Arbor: University of Michigan Press.

Barnes, C. (1992). *Disabling imagery and the media: An exploration of the principles for media representations of disabled people* (Report No. 1). Halifax, UK: The British Council of Organisations of Disabled People and Ryburn Publishing.

Becher, T., & Trowler, P. (2001). *Academic tribes and territories: Intellectual enquiry and the culture of the disciplines* (2nd ed.). Buckingham, UK: The Society for Research into Higher Education and Open University Press.

Benjamin, A. (2004, April). Going undercover. *The Guardian*, Society Section, p. 8.

Bérubé, M. (2006). *College makeover: Disability studies.* Retrieved September 20, 2006, from http://www.slate.com/id/2130329/

Brueggemann, B. (2002). An enabling pedagogy. In S. Snyder, B.J. Brueggeman & R. Garland-Thompson (Eds.), *Disability studies: Enabling the humanities* (pp. 317–326). New York: Modern Language Association of America.

Carvel, J. (2004, October 6). Demonstrators rattle Scope. *The Guardian*, Society Section, p. 4.

Davidson, M. (2004). Concerto for the left hand: Disability (in the) arts. In M. Davidson et al. *Conference on disability studies and the university* (pp. 615–619). Atlanta, GA: Emory University, MLA.

Davis, L.J. (1995). *Enforcing normalcy: Disability, deafness, and the body.* London: Verso.

Davis, L.J. (1997). Nude Venuses, Medusa's body, and phantom limbs: Disability and visuality. In D.T. Mitchell & S.L. Snyder (Eds.), *The body and physical difference: Discourses of disability* (pp. 51–70). Ann Arbor: University of Michigan Press.

Davis, L.J. (2006). Life, death, and biocultural literacy. *Chronicle of Higher Education, 52*(18), B9–10.

Ducey, A. (2007). More than a job: Meaning, affect, and training health care workers. In P.T. Clough & with J. Halley (Eds.), *The affective turn: Theorising the social* (pp. 187–208). Durham, NC: Duke University Press.

Foley, D., & Valenzuela, A. (2005). Critical ethnography: The politics of collaboration. In N. Denzin & Y. Lincoln (Eds.), *A handbook of qualitative research* (3rd ed.) (pp. 217–234). Thousand Oaks: CA:Sage.

Fraser, M. (2008, February 15). Go ahead – take a good look. *The Guardian*, Film and Music Section, p. 6.

French, G.S., & DePoy, E. (2002). Theoretical approaches to disability content in social work education. *Journal of Social Work Education, 38*(1), 153–165.

Gabel, S., & Danforth, S. (2002). Disability studies in education. *Disability, Culture and Education, 1*(1), 1–3.

Garland-Thomson, R., Kleege, G., & Brueggemann, B.J. (2005). What her body taught (or, Teaching about and with a disability): A conversation. *Feminist Studies, 31*(1), 13–33.

Goggin, G. (2003). Media studies' disability. *Media International Australia, 108*, 157–168.

Gregg, M. (2006). *Cultural studies' affective voices.* Basingstoke, UK: Macmillan Palgrave.

Hevey, D. (1992). *The creatures time forgo: Photography and disability.* London: Routledge.

Housee, S. (2006). It's not coz I'm black or brown or female, but coz I know the stuff of 'race' and racism. In S. Jacobs (Ed.), *Pedagogies of teaching 'race' and ethnicity in higher education: British and European experiences* (pp. 73–94). Birmingham: C-SAP.

Kleege, G. (2002). Disabled students come out: Questions without answers. In S. Snyder, B.J. Brueggeman & R. Garland-Thompson (Eds.), *Disability studies: Enabling the humanities* (pp. 308–316). New York: Modern Language Association of America.

Kumari Campbell, F. (2008). Refusing able(ness): A preliminary conversation about ableism. *m/c: Journal of Media and Culture, 11*(3), n.p.

Lewis, D. (2001). *Reading contemporary picturebooks: Picturing text.* London: Routledge.

Linton, S. (1998). *Claiming disability: Knowledge and identity.* New York: New York University Press.

Longmore, P. (1997). Conspicuous contribution and American cultural dilemma: Telethon rituals of cleansing and renewal. In D.T. Mitchell & S.L. Snyder (Eds.), *The body and physical difference: Discourses of disability* (pp. 134–158). Ann Arbor: The University of Michigan Press.

Marshall, J., Ralph, S., & Palmer, S. (2002). 'I wasn't trained to work with them': Mainstream teachers' attitudes to children with speech and learning difficulties. *International Journal of Inclusive Education, 6*(3), 199–215.

Matthews, N. (2008). Picturing difference: Discourses of disability in illustrated children's stories by parents of autistic children. *Popular Narrative Media*, *1*(1), 59–66.

Matthews, N. (2009). Contested representations of disabled children in picture-books: Visibility, the body and the social model of disability. *Children s Geographies*, *7*(1), 37–50.

McLean, M. (2005). Emancipatory understandings for allies. In P. O'Brien & M. Sullivan (Eds.), *Allies in emancipation: Shifting from providing in service to being of support* (pp. 65–78). Melbourne: Thompson.

Meekosha, H., & Jakubowicz, A. (1996). Disability, participation, representation and justice. In C. Christensen & F. Rizvi (Eds.), *Disability and the dilemmas of education and justice* (pp. 79–95). Buckingham, UK: Open University Press.

Mitchell, D., & Snyder, S. (2001). Representation and its discontents: The uneasy home of disability in literature and film. In G.L. Albrecht, K.D. Seelman & M. Bury (Eds.), *Handbook of disability studies* (pp. 195–218). Thousand Oaks: CA:Sage.

Mitchell, D., & Snyder, S. (2006). Narrative prosthesis and the materiality of metaphor. In L.J. Davis (Ed.), *The disability studies reader* (2nd ed.) (pp. 205–216). London: Routledge.

Ngai, S. (2005a). *Ugly feelings*. Cambridge, MA: Harvard University Press.

Ngai, S. (2005b). The cuteness of the avant-garde. *Critical Inquiry*, *31*, 811–847.

Nightingale, V. (1993). What's 'ethnographic' about ethnographic audience research? In J. Frow & M. Morris (Eds.), *Australian cultural studies* (pp. 149–161). Urbana: University of Illinois Press.

Norden, M.F. (1994). *The cinema of isolation: A history of physical disability in the movies*. New Brunswick, NJ: Rutgers University Press.

Oliver, M. (1999). Final accounts and the parasite people. In M. Corker & S. French (Eds.), *Disability discourse* (pp. 183–191). Buckingham, UK: Open University Press.

Oliver, M. (2004). If I had a hammer: The social model in action. In J. Swain, S. French, C. Barnes & C. Thomas (Eds.), *Disabling barriers – Enabling environments* (pp. 7–12). London: Sage.

O'Sullivan, S. (2006). *Art encounters Deleuze and Guattari*. London: Palgrave Macmillan.

Pinsent, P. (1997). *Children's literature and the politics of equality*. London: David Fulton Publishers.

Probyn, E. (2004). Teaching bodies: Affects in the classroom. *Body and Society*, *10*(4), 21–43.

Rieser, R. (2006, October). *Disability and children's books: A historical overview*. Paper presented at the 'In the Picture' conference, London.

Rieser, R., & Mason, M. (1992). *Disability equality in the classroom: A human rights issue*. A Disability Education Handbook. London: Inner London Education Authority.

Ryan, S., & Runswick-Cole, K. (2008). Repositioning mothers: Mothers, disabled children and disability studies. *Disability & Society*, *23*, 199–210.

Saunders, K. (2000). *Happy ever afters: A storybook guide to teaching children about disability*. London: Trenton Books.

Scullion, P. (2000). Disability as an equal opportunity issue within nurse education in the UK. *Nurse Education Today*, *20*, 199–206.

Shakespeare, T. (1999). Art and lies? Representations of disability on film. In M. Corker & S. French (Eds.), *Disability discourse* (pp. 164–172). Buckingham, UK: Open University Press.

Shakespeare, T. (2005, January 10). *Sweet charity?* Retrieved April 13, 2010, from http://www.bbc.co.uk/ouch/features/charity.shtml

Shakespeare, T. (2006). *Disability rights and wrongs*. London: Routledge.

Snyder, S. (2004). Geographies of uneven development: How does one make disability integral to higher education? In M. Davidson et al. *Conference on disability studies and the university* (pp. 533–541). Atlanta, GA: Emory University, MLA.

Treby, E., Hewitt, I., & Shah, A. (2006). Embedding 'disability and access' into the geography curriculum. *Teaching in Higher Education*, *11*, 413–425.

Troyna, B., & Vincent, C. (1996). The ideology of expertism: The framing of special education and racial equality policies in the local state. In C. Christensen & F. Rizvi (Eds.), *Disability and the dilemmas of education and justice* (pp. 131–144). Buckingham, UK: Open University Press.

Ware, L. (2001). Writing, identity, and the Other: Dare we do disability studies? *Journal of Teacher Education, 52*(2), 107–123.

Wilson, J.C., & Lewiecki-Wilson, C. (2002). Constructing a third space: Disability studies, the teaching of English, and institutional transformation. In S. Snyder, B.J. Brueggeman & R. Garland-Thompson (Eds.), *Disability studies: Enabling the humanities* (pp. 297–307). New York: Modern Language Association of America.

Wilton, R.D. (2006). Working at the margins: Disabled people and the growth of precarious employment. In D. Pothier & R. Devlin (Eds.), *Critical disability theory: Essays in philosophy, politics, policy, and law* (pp. 129–150). Vancouver: University of British Columbia Press.

Zembylas, M. (2006). Witnessing in the classroom: The ethics and politics of affect. *Educational Theory, 56*, 305–324.

A rhizomatics of hearing: becoming deaf in the workplace and other affective spaces of hearing

Vicki Crowley

School of Communication, Languages & International Studies, University of South Australia, Adelaide, SA, Australia

This paper stages a corporeal and affective trail through plateaus of 'Becoming deaf' in the workplace of academia. The paper aims to display the unfamiliarity of deafness in a profession whose ability to speak and hear the written word is all too commonsense. In this piece, Deleuze and Guattari's 'rhizome' acts as sensibility and motif as a body deafens. I make use of photography, poetry and poesis as multi-textual pedagogy for engaging with the disjuncture between advocacy and experience, and to draw attention to the dysphoria of theorising affect and the multidimensionality of experiential relations of affect. The paper argues that deafness/becoming deaf is always a form of hearing and the 'strange label' of disability is brought into question just as it increasingly opens presence, tension, texture, and interdependence.

Each next step is momentous, in its own little way:
it is the event of a caught fall.
. . .
There is event. There is anomaly.
There are jilted expectations.
(Brian Massumi, 2002, p. 218)

A rhizome has no beginning or end; it is always
in the middle, between things, interbeing, *intermezzo*.
(Gilles Deleuze and Felix Guattari, 1987, p. 25)

Plateau one: a place to begin

Unlike a structure, which is defined by a set of points and positions, the rhizome is made only of lines; lines of segmentarity and stratification as its dimensions, and the line of flight or deterritorialization as the maximum dimension after which the multiplicity undergoes metamorphosis, changes in nature. (Deleuze & Guattari, 1987, p. 21)

This paper begins with the concept of the rhizome as a research sensibility. In Deleuze and Guattari's *A Thousand Plateaus: Capitalism and Schizophrenia* (1987), a rhizome is a method of conceptual arrangement that is 'anti-genealogy' (p. 21) and uproots ideals of linearity, singularity and hierarchy. A rhizome is comprised of motion, of directions and dimensions bringing into play signs and non-signs. This paper performs a rhizomatic that consists of various textual forms or 'plateaus' where a plateau is 'any multiplicity connected to other multiplicities by superficial underground stems in such a way as to extend or form a rhizome' (Deleuze & Guattari, 1987, p. 22). As plateau and rhizome this paper is about experience and the extratextual; about encounters with disability and some of the disturbances and abjections that ooze from faltering narratives as disability becomes an encounter. It is about a floundering and a turn to alternative forms for becoming; to photography, to poetry and poetics, self-narration, play and affect. Perhaps it is that sometimes events and experience and our mundane encounters with the text beg the company of ordinary items to test textual capacity, to make material the rhizome (Deleuze & Guattari, 1987).

For the purposes of this paper, elements – disparate and partial – are placed together as a performance of dysphoria. The dysphoria is not the medical, clinical kind. I take up dysphoria as a form of critique.[1] Medicine profoundly misrecognises and refuses psychic and bodily capacity and persists in recourse to 'dysphoria' where dysphoria is opposite to euphoria and carries with it a diagnosis of clinical depression. This clinical imposition, this clinical state is an enforced fixity that insists on the primacy of some originary that must not be challenged or redefined. Disability operates in such a way. The originary of disability that must not be challenged or redefined is the 'able' body. In Deleuze and Guattari's terms this is a refusal of becoming and becomings; 'the never ceasing to become' (1987, p. 277). I stage dysphoria here as a form of vertigo – a conscious connectedness to the incorporeal psychic knowing that is 'line of flight' – the simultaneous apprehension of territorialisation, deterritorialisation and reterritorialisation. The dysphoria is the struggle to keep becoming and withstand the territorial tug that is affirmed everywhere through binaries and normalisation. It is dysphoria as 'a line of flight' comprised of unfolding forces, connections and mutations (Deleuze & Guattari, 1987).

The narrative begins with anecdotes of small events and artefacts. The narrative wends into amplified fragments of a kind that we as academics often link to our situated thinking, our situated selves, or that insert themselves into a problem we are thinking about. Thinking is a 'heard' and listened to process. It includes the voice that can be heard in our head, even when we may not be able to hear the utterances of those we listen and attune ourselves to. Thinking is words and sentences from outside and alongside that routinely press into our hard-working interior voice. It is these wordscapes that make hearing so much a part of writing and of scholarship. Our world, between and among us as academics, is for the most part, a world of good ears. When hearing breaks down the tenuousness of ordinary situatedness becomes acute and the security of any taken-for-granted foothold begins to give way. Within the freefall of dysphoria fragments of conversations, points of argument and sounds pile on top of each other like theories that do not connect properly. Yet, it feels like they should connect, or that I should somehow be able to make them connect.

Inside the dysphoria images stand out amongst the noise as clearly visible statements. In this paper I illustrate this dysphoria with a spill of images and text. I perform the affect of what happens when the ordinary parts of an academic life collide, in collision and collusion with their literal place (a book on a shelf, an open book on a desk, papers piled high), their figurative place (reception of peers, students) and to perhaps implore the 'more' of a text that it cannot but suggest. In what follows images are positioned as being more stable than words. The camera shutter snaps. An image appears. The freeze frame that says more or less, more and less can draw parallels between small and big things. In terms of the images presented here, there is, what Susan Sontag (1977, p. 3) would have us know as a grammar, 'a viewing ethics', 'a furnishing of evidence'. The impulse to create photographic images is a compositional effort to effect an ethics of seeing that accompanies the feeling and experience of partial hearing and hearing white noise – a dysphoria of white noise. In this instance the will to image making is merely a strategy to inch closer to what is yet to unravel or be unravelled – a becoming. My images record a relationship between vision and experience which has become privileged through attention to the place of hearing and sound in my academic life.

The privileging of the visual emerges out of a sounded attention to disability. My deafness and the deafness that this paper performs, however, is not 'Deaf'.[2] My deafness is outside the Deaf Community whose experience is articulated through a corporeality of a language I do not speak. The paper stands outside such communities. As Petra Kuppers writes:

> Many disabled people do not see themselves as part of a movement or a group of movements, as part of a minority formation, or even a civil rights group. And even those who do, who accede to group identity, struggle often with the contradiction that pertains to all group identifications: to be oneself, singular, and to be part of a group, alike. (2009, p. 221)

The paper, however, recognises the politics of disability that Leslie Roman writes of when she notes:

> The conventional routes for the professional institutional understanding of disability and impairment come from a long history of 'caring professions' and service management ideologies, as well as from eugenics, segregated and residential schooling, and a whole host of 'othering' practices and policies tethered to the power of medicalized authority and discourses. (2009, p. 3)

The new and creative endeavours of disability studies such as in the recent work of Hickey-Moody (2009), Kuppers (2009), Kuppers and Marcus (2008), Shildrick and Price (2005), Goggin (2008), Loeser (2003), Loeser and Crowley (2009), Newell (2007), Goggin and Newell (2005), Davis (1995), and McRuer (2006), can be seen for instance in the performing arts of Angryfish/Robin Surgeoner, No Strings Attached Theatre of Disability, Mind the Gap, MoMo Dance Theatre, CanDoCo and Restless Dance and have moved to counter medicalised and othering positions often with a view to directly impacting on school pedagogy as well as a broader cultural politic.

While in the outer margins of these creative endeavours, this paper is composed around and riven with a Deleuzian sense of affect and sensation and where transformation and force give form. As Deleuze writes:

> Force is closely related to sensation; for a sensation to exist, a force must be exerted on a body, on a point of the wave. But if force is the condition of sensation, it is nonetheless not the force that is sensed, since the sensation 'gives' something completely different from the forces that condition it. (1990, p. 48)

Affect here is taken as 'pre-individual bodily forces augmenting or diminishing a body's capacity to act' and 'in-formational' (Clough, 2008, p. 1). 'Affect', as Brian Massumi (2002, p. 35) writes, 'is autonomous to the degree to which it escapes confinement in a particular body whose vitality, or potential for interaction, it is'.

And, as Massumi goes on to argue, affect is multiple and affects are 'anchored in (functionally limited by) the actually existing, particular things that embody them' (2002, p. 35). I aim to generate specific affects of dysphoria through image and words, and this affect of dysphoria is a minor pedagogy of disability: a sensory exposition of my experience of deafness.

Plateau two: Images

A rhizome ceaselessly establishes connections between semiotic chains, organizations of power, a circumstance relative to the arts, sciences and social struggles. (Deleuze & Guattari, 1987, p. 7)

Imagine (Figures 1–3)

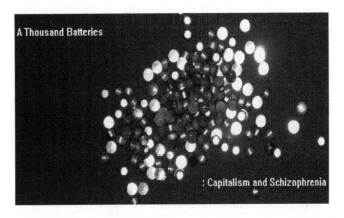

Figure 1. Front matter, a rhizomatics of hearing. Photograph: Vicki Crowley, 2007.

The materiality of batteries connects to the conceptual content of what is heard.

Figure 2. All in a day's hearing. Photograph: Vicki Crowley, 2007.

The rhizome extends, breaks and begins again. When a multiplicity of this kind changes dimension, it necessarily changes in nature as well, undergoes a metamorphosis. (Deleuze & Guattari, 1987, p. 21)

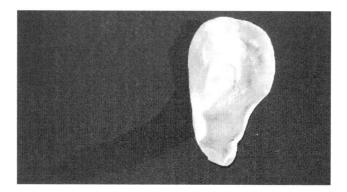

Figure 3. In the shadow of the phallus: lend me your ear amid the whisper of nothing. Photograph: Vicki Crowley, 2007.

Plateau three: Poetry

In a darkened room an atonal voice begins:

Immanence-stop-.&/ampersand-colon-: a good ear

Part 1

some
bodies
don't
hear,

do they?

Part 2

within

upon

of

hear

ear

earring
ears that ring
ringing ears

listen-up! (oops, catch the phrase . . . register, you say things differently here)
l-i-s-t-e-n
huh?
i beg your pardon?

sorry, i didn't quite catch that?
what did you say?
say that again?
ok, politely, can you please say that again?
i'm sorry, can you repeat that?
please?
ah-ha!

hm, mmm
hm, ha, hmh

what did they say?

oh god, what did they say?

pardon me?
what was that?

did I miss something?

what did I miss?

oops, sorry, did you say something to me?
I beg your pardon, i missed that?
come again?

could you please repeat that for me?

hang on, i wasn't listening properly?
sorry, can you say that again, i'll concentrate now.

okay, i'm listening

i'm listening now.

Plateau four: Interior meandering – empirical moments

[A]ny point of a rhizome can be connected to anything other, and must be. This is very different from the tree or root, which plots a point, fixes an order. (Deleuze & Guattari, 1987, p. 7)

To become deaf is to have once had ears that worked without question, like almost everybody else. No pause of time between the sound travelling from another to me. Instant. No routine question of the vulnerability of auditory acuity.

I scour the conference room (and the hallways that brought me here), the keynote speaker, the audience to the keynote, looking for hearing aids. This is an empirical study. I have been struck by the good hearing of academics. I wonder what that tells me about work, our work and the workplace of academics?

I watch closely as the only big name academic I know of with a significant hearing impairment navigates the academic world. He stands at the front of a room and speaks quietly, too quietly for me to listen to without straining but no-one else calls out, 'could you speak up please'. I wonder if he hears his voice loudly, if he too, from time to time, asks those whose company he is in if he is shouting – the irony of hearing oneself as shouting when, without assisted hearing, we would be asking others to speak loudly, to speak at a level that others might hear as shouting and at the risk of physical pain of shouting, ironically intensified as actual hearing diminishes. I am embarrassed to ask him to speak more loudly for many social fears – that I interrupt his important words, for fear that I interrupt the connections and listening orders that the others in the room have tuned themselves to, for fear of being seen as odd and annoying ('What's the problem? I can hear'). And then, when it comes to Q & A, he makes a little explanation about his hearing impairment and moves to stand before each individual questioner but does not repeat the question, as it is assumed everyone has heard. I watch him watching closely. He has assumed that academics have good hearing.

Through a combination of not hearing and my distractedness about hearing/not hearing I have missed a lot of the topic (just as certainly as I have missed much of the question), all this as I watch the performance of sound saving, sound managing. I also see the signs of a body tuning in, working hard to hear, having laboured hard to think and produce something that others will want to think and hear alongside. This body, this embodiment of a little 'abnormality' is only ever a badge of honour, an 'out' statement if one is Deaf. It is not a celebratory identity marker like queer, or emo, 'stealth' or, black – albeit that each of these is profoundly conflicted to the point of being potentially deadly. Deafness is popularly read as a nuisance, an irritation, an annoyance, a bother, a pain unevenly shared, unevenly labile. Deafness is shifted between the one who asks for a repetition or more volume and the one asked to provide it. But it is also so mundane, so much a non-event in the event of hearing. These residual rituals of hearing aid detection are more tedious than instructive and no amount of telling of this kind of story will do anything other than get acknowledgement from those who know what one is talking about. The moment is not told here for 'reform' or for 'equity'. It is rather to display an 'in-betweeness' and an assemblage of 'interstitiality' (Deleuze & Guattari, 1987). But do I want these forms of conversation? My response to my question is both an uninterested 'perhaps occasionally'. But my response is still more folded. It includes the shout of 'No!' but is followed quickly by the elsewhere and altered incorporeality that is its own becoming – a curiosity for what resides deeply inside these altered auditory relations.

Then my mother gives me the latest glossy brochure from her audiologist. *Soundscape, Your Hearing Health Bulletin* has a lead article that trawls through the repertoire of characteristics of hearing impairment, the actual depth of their meaning erased in the gloss of advertising speak. 'Hearing impairment forces a life of isolation on you, like being a prisoner in solitary confinement from your everyday world' (Connect Hearing, n.d., p. 1). How awful is this scenario? Its layer of 'truth' is a truth, a 'reality'. I swallow the pain of just how cruel and isolating deafness can be; its hideous legacies of idiocy and incarceration never far from the surface, enacted and hailed in erasure and in reminder. Jovial in its outlook, the lead article goes on to laud 'the new lease on life' afforded by the hearing aid. Prosthetic wearers and readers can feel gratified and congratulated on their choice of hearing 'instrument' and their choice of hearing care provider. Hearing impairment wavers as multi-layered nuisance factor and a psycho-social trauma.

Soundscape does not mention the sores that ill-fitting moulds cause or the rough treatment meted out by careless technicians as they impatiently shove a hearing aid into an ear when difficulty is experienced at managing these increasingly micro devices.[3] The mundane repetitions of hearing loss are easily overlooked. And a thousand batteries are gathered. For, though we are advised to dispose of them with care, there is no recycling place or repository to help us do that – no pharmacist or audiologist will help with this act. The batteries gather and spill into the work of everyday. I read a text and a battery goes flat. It is not that I cannot hear the words I read but the soundscape in which I read the words flattens. My soundscape becomes muffled and I can read with one ear to the digitised surroundings and one ear to a quieter, muted, ambience. But I have been distracted from the task at hand as I attend to the imbalance of senses and replace the battery. As the work of Cassandra Loeser (2003), Lennard Davis (1995) and others demonstrates – the labour of deafness is intense.

The classroom has been a place of terror for the request to repeat and to 'please speak loudly' moves from being not able to hear to no longer being spoken to. Witness the visible, physical turning away of the seated student: first the movement from the hip, the torso, the shoulder, the head and lastly the eyes recede and then they seek other faces and other mouths. The dysphoria here is ambient, atmospheric and cold. I become a body that holds no knowledge, no communicative capacity, a watching body to be spoken around or spoken to by others who might 'fill me in'. I am no longer human in the way I was only seconds before. I am filled in with summaries and gestures. I try to shake off my redundancy to fight the chill of being dismissed as simply old, or old and dumb. In here I know and hear the ghostly affect, the haunt of all deafness: 'dumb', unintelligent and speechless. I am rendered dumb – the capacity for speech actually diminished by the action of the turning away body, the ended exchange, the withdrawal of words. Of course in the classroom I have the power and capacity to manoeuvre around such moments and my repertoire of pre-emptive and evasive strategies has grown. But as a regular roll out I am told, 'Don't worry, it doesn't matter', – a kindness and perhaps a truism, but I cannot know either for sure for I have not heard. A synthesis of forces is in play. Reductive moves assemble and the internal dynamics and the intricacies of pedagogy as being hinged on sociality dances before me and dances with me to provide the need for greater atunement of physical body to physical body. I have learned to read a finer print than I have previously encountered. The dysphoria is curious and I move to become more curious. On the one hand, the label 'disability' becomes increasingly nonsensical and on the other, its 'fluid forces, flows, air, light, and matter' are such that 'a body or a word does not end at a precise point' (Deleuze & Guattari, 1987, p. 11). The dysphoria is a becoming. There is more and not less in play. A reterritorialisation takes place.

Plateau five: The strange carnalities of disability

> [A] rhizome is not amenable to any structural or generative model. It is a stranger to any idea of genetic axis or deep structure. (Deleuze & Guattari, 1987, p. 12)

As is so often the case, I find myself drawn to and amid what at first glance appears and feels to be a dysphoria – the space between advocacy (and its relationship with policy) and the 'sieve of chaos . . . just beyond our familiar thresholds' (Frichot, 2005, p. 64) that is 'experience' as De Landa would put it, the 'extensive spaces' that human beings, themselves, are (2005, p. 82). This again announces a paper that hovers and lurches, a tandem act, touching aesthetics, an aesthetic, lingering on gathered notes on 'experience' and its self-thwarted position as research tool, subject ascription – always abject, always attempting to mask its futility, a morose state, a melancholia. A question of affect and affection; affection as a fondness for attempt at suspending ephemera in flight – a specimen-like object, held in formaldehyde or some similar syrup in sealed container, held to the light, turned this way and that for a better look, a closer inspection, a gleaning of knowledge, a better knowing. How to understand disability?

This could be any paper on methodology but for now, it is a paper that began in moments of transition from routine ordinary body that can be worked on and with in varying degrees of intensity (labours, desires, satiations, absurdity, a breathing parody of mind body divisive indivisibility) and as body that science and medicine would label 'deaf'. An image comes to mind: it is of a washing line. The clothes have been unpegged, dropped into the basket, with one last item remaining on the line. It is one of those buff-coloured luggage tags that has a stiffened and shiny red circle strengthening the bit around the hole where the string goes, the label hangs from the peg, pegged to the line via its coarse string. The label reads 'Disabled'. The writing is not mine. I did not hang this item out to dry. But there is no mistake. It is a label for me. Its origins are my genes and for as long as the women in my family have been hanging out and gathering up clothes on lines, they, at some point in their lives, come to this label. They have gone deaf, become deaf – very deaf.

My great grandmother sat in her chair in her long dress with her cone-shaped horn, lifting it to her ear to try to catch the conversation, the question addressed to her, often just sitting, observing the routines of life around her. Observing smiles, laughter, chat, silences, pauses in conversation, animated bodies, mobile faces, expressions. Did she think she may have the thread of conversation? She possibly spent the last years of her life not daring to speak in case the thread was a complete figment of an imagination. An imagination once sharp, involved, on target – now random. My fate is not hers. I have technology and possibly new forms of operations (surgical interventions), sophisticated in their success (see Christie & Bloustien, 2010, in this issue), as diabolic as ever in their failure. But it was not this image that brings me to the point that is now this writing. It is having been a regular academic, going about my business and then typically, years after the event, getting hearing aids now referred to in polite speak as hearing instruments. I can appreciate a kinship between hearing instrument and musical instrument – this prosthetic variously designed, to make sounds, to enhance sound, albeit with someone else's action rather than my own instrumentation.

I come to other intensities, the kinds of questions that this label, this tag that hangs before me: when to wear it; how does one wear it? It is like any identity label – a hovering between an estrangement and the act of being labelled. But what happens when it becomes visible; how does its invisibility impinge on aspects of my work? What might thinking about those impinge-ings, those infringements mean for my big questions? My big questions, my driving and homing instinct: how to go about things, thinking, speaking in ways that create space, are open to becoming, how to go about the art and crafts of living in ways that are convivial while encouraging, urging analysis beyond the commonsense?

My hearing instruments, unlike my mother's and her grandmother's, are read by others as visually discrete, at times seen as 'even like ear jewellery'. They are not small, but they are dark coloured and although I do not attempt to 'hide them' or style my hair to 'hide my hearing aids', acquaintances often comment on 'not seeing' my hearing aids, 'not realising' that I am deaf. As discrete as my hearing aids may be to the hearing world, they are never unnoticed by people with disabilities of all kinds. Indeed the evidence of the prosthetic has from time to time been conduit to the possibility of an altered practice of pedagogy. In a small honours class it transpired that one way or another we all had a disability and each disability was profoundly different to each other. While for each of us *'my* disability' was never the actual focus of discussion in the classroom, our round table of how the week and research had progressed brought states of being into becoming student, becoming researcher, and becoming in a seminar. Medical appointments, glitches in adaptive technology, spikes in pain and mood management were criss-crossed milieu – the 'surroundings', 'medium' ('as in chemistry'), and 'middle' (Deleuze & Guattari, 1987, p. xvii); 'always the middle' (Deleuze & Guattari, 1987, p. 21). It seemed that each seminar would take shape and bend backwards, sideways and forward like the movement of a branch in the breeze from the information and approach that emerged. The labour of study and the management of body were indivisible and they were always present. Our pace, our attention became a change in nature. For an outsider-observer it might seem that we worked a slowness of wading through treacle – a stickiness, a tactility put to time – another sense dimension, inaudible affect.

How is all of this a lesson for pedagogy, a lesson that 'measures' in scholarly work?

Just as with photography or the body, we must work not just beyond the scripted word – but into the multiple significations that brought the script to be. I find myself reconsidering terms like disaster and catastrophe. Is this a kind of death or a form of engagement with death? Is this, does this coming to a label enact a frozen, chilled moment, a facing off of mortality, a forced relinquishment of privilege?

I read the poem at the symposium and I was later asked – 'was that a coming out?' I was shocked by this: how, even why, would the reading of some words be read as 'coming out'?[4] I was confused, but perhaps the questioner was right after all – all the while floods of shame, confusion, contortion. But again, I am brought to this question of our repertoires for disability. Is this 'coming out' frame itself a certain degree of shared inadequacy? Is it the paucity of capacity – capacity once rendered substantial now unhinged from its unquestioned confidence?

The catastrophe is not disability *per se*; it is not 'becoming deaf' or becoming deaf in the contradictory world of 'advocacy' or the workplace. The catastrophe is the discursive domain of disability – its capture by god, medical, social and other liberal narratives such that we are more tongue-tied than a tongue whose physicality constrains the formation of language and speaking. This is not to say that disability, becoming disabled is not catastrophic in the sense of crashed embodiment or non-normative physical and intellectual comportment. It is to say that being and becoming disabled is held in tension; there is the insolubility of 'disability' – the impossibility of the label to ever be without trace – its utterance reverberates like white noise – an inaudible audibility. It leaks. The affect of sound – more or less/ more and less than the normative – it is this work that strives for a life (life) in recognition of multiplicity of material need and an ethico-aesthetic that is a proliferation.

Plateau six: 'Experience' – an historical hailing and new bodily assemblage

[I]t [the rhizome] brings into play very different regimes of signs, and even nonsign states. (Deleuze & Guattari, 1987, p. 21)

'It is often the case', as Leslie Roman writes, 'that scholarship is punctuated or interrupted by life's unexpected turns' (2009, p. 2). It was not that one day I woke up and 40% of my hearing was gone, or that in the classroom I suddenly could not hear, nor that distorted or no sound made sense. My hearing loss is gradual[5] and was not problematic until it reached a point where classic tropes of hearing impairment occurred – blank looks as I said something that had just been said by someone else, the fourth time of asking a student to repeat what they said and the complete disdain and dismissiveness or abandonment of the conversation that comes with these occurrences – where indeed a certain affect (shared space) is lost and another (refused shared space) takes over. None of this suddenly brought about a relationship with disability.

The getting of hearing aids, however, is an act of classing a body. The classing of that body may be at the very edges of that classification of D/deaf and deafness but it is entry into, 'disability'. At the time of getting hearing aids my deafness was at a level where it is possible to continue as if life is unaltered – a body part weakens or abates, medicine, science and technology kick in.[6] However, the responses[7] of those around meant that Disability with a capital D appeared – a lurking apparition, haunting and haunting its histories of abjection and contemporary disability struggles, for instance, of adequate care and accommodation,[8] respite for carers and the immensity of expensive medications, and the repetitive labour of getting to and from doctors, specialists and pharmacies.

The kaleidoscope of affect, event and experiment at work in the gathered practices of this paper bring me closer to the disjuncture and dysphoria that is especially acute in the distance between the forms of argument I make when it comes to addressing 'experience' and when the question of 'experience' remains central to the subject and our practices of recognition and responsibility (Butler, 2005). Within the broad philosophical considerations lies a pedagogical collision between methodological practice, teaching research methodology and the 'evidence of experience' – especially those moments invoked almost two decades ago in the wake of feminist intervention into the relationship between the personal and the political.[9]

The label on my imaginary clothesline is attached to luggage, where luggage is always in transit, going this way or that, from somewhere to someplace else. It is 'a draft, a wind, a day, a time of day, a stream, a place, a battle, an illness' (Deleuze, 1995, p. 141) – it is, I hope, of the French *expérience*, both experience and experiment 'without aim, or end' (Deleuze & Guattari, 1983, p. 371), 'the separation and the mixing', 'the one and the multiple' (Deleuze & Guattari, 1987, p. 371). It is not without disability as a series of life-sapping tropes of the 'tragic, pitiful or whiney, monstrous, devious and heroically inspirational' (Roman, 2009, p. 1).

It is from the question of experience, this question of the political-personal, this question of the limits of poststructuralism, the question of 'the turn to affect' (Ahmed, 2004; Clough, 2008; Massumi, 1995), this amalgam of tropes that short-cut questions of intrinsic and extrinsic interferences. It is within these that I am troubled by my recourse to 'experience' and the solidification that might come from expressive forms; of compositional approaches, to being open to this bloc of sensation (Deleuze & Guattari, 1994), to resist the literal in the visual while all the while keeping wide open the eye that always sees more than the mouth can sound out at any one time. While this same visual has its literal before it, it is never alone. Any attempt to suspend rather than capture is already a departure and loss. So, what of this confusion, this chaos? It makes little difference to a state of hearing, my state of hearing – the mechanics of hearing aids, their labour and carbon footprint, the self-care where the ear waxes as the hearing wanes. But it does make a difference – for in here, this hearing, juridical, clinical, medical and historical – in this hearing that is mobile between its muted-ness and its state of being digitally enhanced – in the hearing is flight and the passage of possibility. Alongside my ordinary mundane work life and its sounded encounters with pedagogy, I can delight in the play of potential. I can look to that label 'Disability' and approach it in awe, to wonder at becoming-deaf/deaf becomings and ways of knowing that are a dismantling of the practical and rational.

Plateau seven: The pedagogy of affect

> A rhizome may be broken, shattered at a given spot, but it will start up again on one of its old lines, or on new lines. You can never get rid of ants because they form an animal rhizome that can rebound time and time again after most of it has been destroyed. (Deleuze & Guattari, 1987, p. 9)

The dissolution that gives way to all that is already there and made the more apparent by moments of affect, moments of sensation, moments of intensification, in here is a pedagogy of possibility – primary, secondary, tertiary – but more, much more. At some points this work makes contact with what Gerard Goggin refers to as 'a new general theory of listening-as-if-disability-mattered' (2009, p. 499) just as it touches the oppressive grit realities and actualities of non-normative bodies. But the hope of this work is to effect an assemblage that at the very least serves to remind me to proceed in my work with an eye and ear to the more; to 'landscapes and faces, visions and becomings' (Deleuze & Guattari, 1994, p. 177) and to that which might be there and that I cannot immediately sense. That too, we continue to consider 'experience' and our embodied relationship to it, to engage with our students, colleagues and readers as embodied affective beings, drawing on and reviewing experience, event, sensation, experiment, considering the over-coding of disability including the extent to which disability as word, as object, as constituting the subject exists, comes into being or has been 'the object of someone else's address, attention, desire, abuse' (Walden, 2009, p. 59) all the while being a laborious part of an ordinary life. Affect brings an expanded empirical field – it also enables us to work, live and play in a dispersed symbiosis cultivating practices for increased survivorship especially as it just may be as Massumi writes (2002, p. 43), 'For that seeping edge is where potential, actually, is found'.

It is through becoming deaf and deaf becoming that brings me to ask questions about disability, affect and education: Is there any fidelity between pedagogy and affect; can there be a tertiary-sector pedagogy that weaves together compositional parts able to let those weavings wear thin to the point of being threadbare, disassemble and resemble/reassemble? What can we do in our practice, beyond our instructional practices of directive reform, to account for new and better forms of coming-together, belonging-together, becoming-together?

The amalgam of images, poetry, prose, in this instance, came about through facing the limits of writing, where narrative falters, where loss appears (Butler, 2003) and where small acts give rise to pause or begin to insinuate the more that is in play and at stake. None of this seeks any attachment to universality nor claims to be much more than an idiosyncratic working through, a re-presentation of grappling to cleave misapprehension from misapprehension. And yet it is experience in communion with a store of work, labouring and cared for non-normative bodies, and, to ignore the impulse, the thinking and the affective, would be to continue the desubjectification that is the co-companion of much of our good work. It marks the intensities of the surface of academic life and the labours and affect across and in which it is produced and extracted.

In this paper I have risked the reproduction of actual private practice – the shift in gear, the planes and plateaus that have kept me company as I exteriorise interior machinations and experience that 'caught-fall' of Massumi (2002, p. 218). The shape that this paper has taken lends itself to multi-textual pedagogy. However, it is not a multi pedagogy that is the selection of non-print form, policy or community text as a singular site or singular form. Nor is it a form of singularity of a side by side kind of multi-forms or the seriality of multi-textual product or artefact (poetics, poetry, fiction, photography) that provides possibility. Rather, it is to offer the dysphoria, to produce in the reader some sense of that dysphoria, to move as if with me into fleeing, flowing, leaking, eluding. These are the sensations that occur as one transits in and out of each slanted plateau – moving from one to the other being hailed and propelled. It is to incite a micropolitics 'that brings everything into play, but on a different scale and in different forms' (Deleuze & Guattari, 1987, p. 199) in the hope something takes place in the volatility.

Guattari writes:

> Affect is a process of existential appropriation through the continual creation of heterogeneous durations of being…[G]iven this, we would certainly be better advised to cease treating it (affect) under the aegis of scientific paradigms and to deliberately turn ourselves toward ethical and aesthetic paradigms. (1996, p. 159)

What might a pedagogy of affect do? It might multiply the objects of inquiry – to insist that the objects of inquiry take place within the academic body, as body and as body becoming shapes the becoming we espouse in practices of social justice pedagogy. While this is not a plea for all academics to excoriate their own dysphorias, it does suggest that our interstitial becoming may entail practices of becoming that can ferment transformation alert to the 'caught fall' between and among forms of expression that hold recognition of the something and always more. Production, aesthetics, ethics, materiality. How to speak disability? It might help us to pose and to love difficult questions, without effacement, without erasure and to immerse ourselves amid the enduring mystery that is body, affect, becoming – becoming pedagogy, becoming disability.

Acknowledgements

Special thanks go to Amelia Walker for her inspiration and generous support in relation to poetry, to Cassandra Loeser, to Claire Woods, Michael Galvin and Jackie Cook for other forms of inspiration and generosity in hard times. Also to my writing group, to friend reviewers (including Anna Hickey-Moody, Bridget Garnham and Julia Horncastle), to blind reviewers for their invaluable insights and critique: thank you. A final huge thank you goes to my Honours research methods class of 2009 – a class that grabbed me by the throat and in which we all gained a form of composure as we lurched and learned about embodiment, affect and the prospect of shortened lives in research practice.

Notes

1. I also take it up as a practice informed by and as an act of solidarity with those who experience the medical capture – 'gender dysphoria'. In a most pernicious and striking manner the western medicine and the medical profession seem unwilling and unable to apprehend transgender outside of psychiatric illness and disorder. See for instance the work of Nestle, Howell, and Wilchins (2002), Judith Halberstam (2005), Susan Stryker (1998), and Currah, Juang, and Minter (2006).
2. The Deaf Community is a bilingual identity group comprised of people with hearing impairment who communicate through spoken and sign language. They see themselves as an 'oral' culture whose identity is grounded in sign more than in written forms. The Deaf Community's history of struggle for recognition (including combating eugenicist ideation) is documented by authors such as Susan Burch (2002) and Douglas Baynton (1996) in the USA, Trevor Johnston (2006) in Australia, and Mieke Van Herreweghe and Myriam Vermeerbergen (2004) in Europe.
3. The no longer agile or the arthritic hands of ageing people often struggle to manage the finely made and tuned instruments and their own frustration can be met with frustration and rough treatment by technicians.
4. My response is relayed here without any intention to assert or deny equivalence or to suggest that there is not an important conversation to be had, already existing and in progress. Having to announce myself as deaf does not parallel having to announce myself as lesbian, queer, etc. This clearly speaks to an all too common constrained relationship with disability and is a question for another paper and one that queer scholars in disability are pursuing.
5. I was not yet 40 when it was suggested to me that I needed to see a hearing specialist. It was not for another decade that I got hearing aids and was told that if I 'stayed at home and only went to the shops once a week then I could do without them'. The 'world of isolation' for the hearing impaired is well exemplified in this casual aside by the hearing specialist.
6. The ability of medicine, science and technology to 'kick-in' in the context of hearing is one where affluence really counts. Hearing technology is costly. Most prosthetic companies have a range of low-cost, medium-cost, and high-cost hearing aids. The quality of hearing and the ease of use between the three is vast. The pace of technological innovation and advancement means that hearing aids are well out-dated in five years. The current cost of two hearing aids at the high end is about $10,000–12,000. This is beyond the means of very, very many people and especially those who have multiple medical needs. The right to good hearing is nowhere a social norm.
7. These included people noticing the hearing aids and responding by shouting or mouthing words in more distinct ways, the discomfort of acquaintances and even some friends, along with a sometimes palpable 'omg' of 'oh no' or even immediate impatience and visible evident calculation of deafness equals intellectual impairment. All of these become accentuated when old age is added into the equation – there is nothing cool about deafness and older ageing.
8. As, for instance was displayed in 'Breaking Point' (2010).
9. I find myself returning to Joan Scott (1991), 'The evidence of experience', its next iteration as 'Experience' in *Feminists Theorize the Political* (1992) and to the recent return to her work in the special edition of *Cultural Studies <=> Critical Methodologies* (see Berry &

Warren, 2009; Moriera, 2009; Pollock, 2009; Warren & Berry, 2009) to inspect a site of my own dysphoria, an eruption of my own ambivalence.

References

Ahmed, S. (2004). *The cultural politics of emotion*. New York: Routledge.

Baynton, D. (1996). *Forbidden signs: American culture and the campaign against sign language*. Chicago: Chicago University Press.

Berry, K., & Warren, J.T. (2009). Cultural studies and the politics of representation: Experience? Subjectivity? Research? *Cultural studies: Critical Methodologies, 9*, 597–607.

'Breaking point'. (2010, February 15). *Four corners*, ABC Television. Reporter: Wendy Carlisle, Retrieved March 6, 2010, from http://www.abc.net.au/4corners/content/2010/s2817123.htm

Burch, S. (2002). *Signs of resistance: American deaf cultural History, 1900 to World War Two*. New York: New York University of Press.

Butler, J. (2003). Afterword. In D.L. Eng & D. Kazanjan (Eds.), *Loss, the politics of mourning* (pp. 467–474). Berkeley: University of California Press.

Butler, J. (2005). *Giving an account of oneself*. New York: Fordham University Press.

Christie, E., & Bloustien, G. (2010). I-cyborg: Disability, affect and public pedagogy. *Discourse: Studies in the Cultural Politics of Education, 31*(4), 483–498.

Clough, P.T. (2008). The affective turn: Political economy, biomedia and bodies. *Theory, Culture & Society, 25*(1), 1–22.

Connect Hearing. (n.d.). *Soundscape, Your Hearing Health Bulletin*. Issue 02.

Currah, P., Juang, R.M., & Minter, S.P. (Eds.). (2006). *Transgender rights*. Minneapolis: University of Minnesota Press.

Davis, L.J. (1995). *Enforcing normalcy: Disability, deafness, and the body*. London: Verso.

De Landa, M. (2005). Space: Extensive and intensive, actual and virtual. In I. Buchanan & G. Lambert (Eds.), *Deleuze and space* (pp. 80–88). Edinburgh: Edinburgh University Press.

Deleuze, G. (1990). *The logic of sense* (M. Lester & C. Stivale, Trans.). New York: Columbia University Press.

Deleuze, G. (1995). *Negotiations*. New York: Columbia University Press.

Deleuze, G., & Guattari, F. (1983). *Anti-Oedipus: Capitalism and schizophrenia* (R. Hurley, M. Seem, & H.R. Lane, Trans.). London: Athlone.

Deleuze, G., & Guattari, F. (1987). *A thousand plateaus: Capitalism and schizophrenia*. Minneapolis: University of Minnesota Press.

Deleuze, G., & Guattari, F. (1994). *What is philosophy?* New York: Columbia University Press.

Frichot, H. (2005). Stealing into Gilles Deleuze's Baroque House. In I. Buchanan & G. Lambert (Eds.), *Deleuze and space* (pp. 61–79). Edinburgh: Edinburgh University Press.

Goggin, G. (2008). Innovation and disability. *m/c: Media and Culture, 11*(3). Retrieved December 14, 2009, from http://journal.media-culture.org.au/index.php/mcjournal/article/view.Article/56

Goggin, G. (2009). Disability and the ethics of listening. *Continuum: Journal of Media & Cultural Studies, 21*, 489–502.

Goggin, G., & Newell, C. (2005). *Disability in Australia: Exposing a social apartheid*. Sydney: UNSW Press.

Guattari, F. (1996). Rotonellos and existential affects. In G. Genosko (Ed.), *The Guattari reader* (pp. 158–171). London: Blackwell.

Halberstam, J. (2005). *In a queer time and place. Transgender bodies, subcultural lives*. New York: New York University Press.

Hickey-Moody, A. (2009). *Unimaginable bodies: Intellectual disability, performance and becomings*. Amsterdam: Sense Publishers.

Johnston, T. (2006). W(h)ither the Deaf Community? Population, genetics, and the future of Australian sign language. *Sign Language Studies, 6*, 137–173.

Kuppers, P. (2009). Toward a rhizomatic model of disability: Poetry, performance, and touch. *Journal of Literary & Cultural Disability Studies, 3*, 221–240.

Kuppers, P., & Marcus, N. (2008). *Cripple poetics: A love story.* Ypsilanti, MI: Homofactus Press.

Loeser, C. (2003). The ecstasies of exchange: Reconfiguring hearing disabled masculine subjectivities in rave space. *Australian Journal of Communication, 30*(3), 69–82.

Loeser, C., & Crowley, V. (2009). A natural ear for music? Hearing (dis)abled masculinities. *Popular Music, 28,* 411–423.

Massumi, B. (1995). The autonomy of affect. *Cultural Critique, 31,* 83–109.

Massumi, B. (2002). *Parables for the virtual: Movement, affect, sensation.* Durham, NC: Duke University Press.

McRuer, R. (2006). *Crip theory: Cultural signs of queerness and disability.* New York: New York University Press.

Moreira, C. (2009). Unspeakable transgressions: Indigenous epitemologies, ethics, and decolonizing academy/inquiry. *Cultural Studies: Critical Methodologies, 9,* 647–660.

Nestle, J., Howell, C., & Wilchins, R. (Eds.). (2002). *GenderQueer: Voices from beyond the sexual binary.* Los Angeles: Alyson.

Newell, C. (2007). Narrating normalcy: Disability, medicine and ethics. *Journal of Developmental Disabilities, 13*(2), 65–68.

Pollock, D. (2009). Beyond experience. *Cultural Studies: Critical Methodologies, 9,* 636–646.

Roman, L. (2009). The unruly salon: Unfasten your seatbelts, take no prisoners, make no apologies!. *International Journal of Qualitative Studies in Education, 22*(1), 1–16.

Scott, J.W. (1991). The evidence of experience. *Critical Inquiry, 17,* 773–797.

Scott, J.W. (1992). Experience. In J. Butler & J.W. Scott (Eds.), *Feminists theorize the political* (pp. 22–40). New York: Routledge.

Shildrick, M., & Price, J. (2005). Deleuzian connections and queer corporealities: Shrinking global disability. *Rhizomes, 11,* Fall 2005/Spring 2006. Retrieved December 14, 2009. http://www.rhizomes.net/issue11/shildrickprice/index.html

Sontag, S. (1977). *On photography.* New York: Penguin.

Stryker, S. (1998). The transgender issue. *GLQ, 4,* 145–158.

Van Herreweghe, M., & Vermeerbergen, M. (Eds.). (2004). *To the lexicon and beyond: Sociolinguistics in European Deaf communities.* Washington, DC: Gallaudet University Press.

Walden, A. (2009). Butler on subjectivity and authorship: Reflection on doing philosophy in the first person. *The Pluralist, 4*(2), 55–62.

Warren, J.T., & Berry, K. (2009). Introduction: The evidence of experience, cultural studies, and personal(ized) scholarship. *Cultural Studies: Critical Methodologies, 9,* 595–596.

Index

Page numbers in **Bold** represent figures.

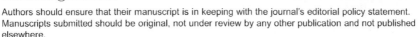